MORPHEMES
For Little Ones

Bringing the **Magic of Language** into K-3 Classrooms

DEB GLASER

Deborah R. Glaser, EdD, LLC
Boise, ID

www.morphememagic.com

Morphemes for Little Ones: Bringing the Magic of Language to K-3 Classrooms
Copyright 2023 Deborah R. Glaser

Design: Steve Mead Graphic Design

Library of Congress Cataloging-in-Publication Data
Names: Glaser, Deborah R., Author

Title: Morphemes for Little Ones: Bringing the Magic of Language to K-3 Classrooms
ISBN: 978-0-578-27827-8

TABLE OF CONTENTS

PREFACE

I began considering writing this K-3 book about language and morphology after several kindergarten and lower grade teachers asked me to please write a book about morphological awareness for them. My immediate response was, "Sure, I can do that!" However, I quickly became overwhelmed and set the idea aside, after all, I had just promised myself that I would retire, and realized I was going to have to first define what retirement meant for me.

As it turns out, retirement for me means continuing to write. Writing is a love of mine: developing teaching processes that transfer research to practice, translating research for teachers to help them build awareness of how students learn, while developing awareness of practices that are most beneficial, and those that are not.

I spent the first 20 years of my teaching career teaching children with dyslexia and other reading difficulties before moving into a non-profit dyslexia learning center. In this center, I taught students, prepared tutors, and began teaching teachers during the early years of the Reading Panel focus on the five components: phoneme awareness, phonics, fluency, vocabulary, and comprehension. After another 25 years of training and advising educational groups, and writing other books, I wrote *Morpheme Magic: Lessons to Build Morphological Awareness for Grades 4-12.*

My venture into the task of helping teachers build the self-confidence needed to teach morphology firmly established my addiction to words. My love of words, my curiosity about words, was so rich that I wanted every teacher to share this passion and sow the seeds of word-loving in their classrooms!

And it happened. The magic of words, the eagerness with which teachers have taken on morphology for their own learning, and then learning with their students, has been truly gratifying.

Words grow in increments as language develops. A first spoken word, "ball" becomes "balls" when a colorful display of beach balls is approached at the store. "Deer" becomes "deers". "Jump" changes to "jumped" when talking about playing a game of jumping from rock to rock with friends at the park. These are examples of a morphological complexity that young children produce without receiving explicit instruction about morphology. This early acquisition of spoken language is building a foundation upon which reading will be built.

Enter the lower grades, "We want a book to help us teach morphology too!" The requests became constant. This placed me in a tricky situation. We know that even in 2nd grade morphological awareness contributes to a myriad of literacy skills, but a question surfaces: How can we focus on morphology with a developmentally appropriate focus, and evidence-based practice for little ones? The research is clear that morphological awareness is important, even in the early grades, but we lack the proven processes to help us know how to provide this instruction.

My pondering around this question always brings me back to "awareness". Language develops incrementally over time. Children come to us with a knowledge of the language they have heard in their worlds. They intuit the morphological components of their language as expressed in their choice of words and their oral language. It is our task, then, to create learning environments where we purposefully create an awareness of the language our students speak.

What we do know about effective instruction has been built into the lessons in this book: Structured Literacy, explicit and systematic instruction, repetition, integrated language components, a growing focus on decoding, spelling, and vocabulary, and lots of oral language support. These elements of instruction do have support in the research and they are evident in every *Morphemes for Little Ones* lesson.

Morphemes for Little Ones is one tool teachers can confidently use to *Bring the Magic of Language into K-3 Classrooms*. This manual will guide teachers as they establish morphological awareness, the ability to identify, isolate, and manipulate morphemes in words during phonics lessons and throughout the day. Thank you for joining me in this magical journey.

Enjoy the magic!

Dr. Deb

INTRODUCTION

WELCOME TO THE MAGIC OF MORPHEMES!

Morphology is important. You know this because you are reading this. You care enough to have heard that morphology is one of the most neglected language components, you care because you are curious, because you don't want to miss out! I care because you are here and your students need you.

Morphology is indeed magical – words magically appear in our lives, and each word has its story, its hidden meaning for us to uncover and discover. It takes a lifetime of experience and study to fill our personal lexicons.

Morphology is elusive. By the mere act of choosing the words to write just now, I am breaking into the crust of morphology, reaching into my mental lexicon to find the words that will convey my thought. These words will convey the meaning I intend, each word a morpheme or combination of morphemes. But then, isn't morphology just like vocabulary? Sort of, but morphology goes much deeper than single words and their meanings.

Our students come to us with well-established morphological knowledge. Children possess an implicit understanding of language that enables them to form sentences changing verb tense as needed, knowing subconsciously what words are nouns, verbs, or adjectives. If they hear, "I saw a blue today," they will probably ask, after some quiet pondering, "A blue what?" This knowledge, that blue cannot be the object in a sentence, nests deeply in their subconscious understanding of the roles that words play, words and word parts, and their meanings. Language is a fascinating science.

One of our jobs, as reading teachers, is to create a conscious AWARENESS of that language, the morphological components of the language students produce during spoken language and now are learning to read and write. What does this mean? What does this work entail? The lessons in this book answer those questions and will help you do this important work.

THE LANGUAGE RICH CLASSROOM

Language is your constant companion in the work you do with students. From your first greeting in the morning to the concepts you teach, language is always there, the constant tool of your trade. Language is also our students' constant companion: speaking the language to convey wishes and observations, hearing and listening to language spoken and read to them, reading directions and books, and writing sentences, notes, and spelling words. You are your students' constant companion, an all-important presence in their lives, and your students are a constant companion from morning greeting to end of the day and even sometimes after the school day is over our students' stories continue to accompany us.

Think of your classroom as the perfect incubator in which to develop morphological awareness. Language rich classrooms are classrooms in which lots of language is happening – they are rich with conversation, discussion about topics and community, about stories, and learning. We find teachers guiding students to express their thinking aloud, to explore words and their meanings, and teaching students how to decode and read words and sentences, and write words and sentences.

The language rich classroom generates an awareness of spoken language through incidental and purposeful instruction about words and about spoken and written language. The awareness our students develop is necessary for learning a written language - reading, spelling, and writing.

When I ask teachers to tell me about a language rich classroom, their answers many times begin with describing a *print rich* environment: lots of books, labels around the room, anchor charts, etc. These are all good examples of classrooms that can *foster interest* in reading, but frequently missing in this discussion is the element of spoken language.

Language rich classrooms are full of language being modeled, spoken, and listened to. Carefully posed questions and speaking opportunities engage students and teachers in rich discussions where:

- New and varied vocabulary is presented and applied.
- Sentence composition is modeled and explored by students.
- Ideas are formalized into words and conveyed with more confidence over time.
- Learning is revealed through oral expression.
- Spoken language becomes the rehearsal and conduit for written language.

The lessons in **Morphemes for Little Ones**: **Building the Magic of Language in K-3 Classrooms,** are designed to help develop and grow language rich classrooms. It is through a combination of implicit exposure and explicit and systematic instruction of morphology that young students gradually become aware of the language they speak. Morphological awareness sets the stage for learning to read and write.

THE LANGUAGE BRAIN AND READING

Language is a remarkable gift for which humans are biologically wired. We are learning the language that surrounds our world from the moment of our birth forward. No explicit instruction is required, for most individuals, to learn to understand and produce language. Most researchers will say, "We have a language brain." Indeed, we do have a language brain. And it is that language brain that must adapt its purpose and processes in order for reading to occur.

Learning to speak is natural but learning to read is not. Reading is an invention. Early linguists discovered that words could be decomposed into their separate speech sounds and that each sound could be assigned its own symbol to represent it, a miracle actually. Understanding this written system, based on the alphabetic principle, requires an awareness of phonemes, graphemes (the letter or letters that spell those phonemes), and as it turns out, awareness of morphemes (the meaningful parts of words).

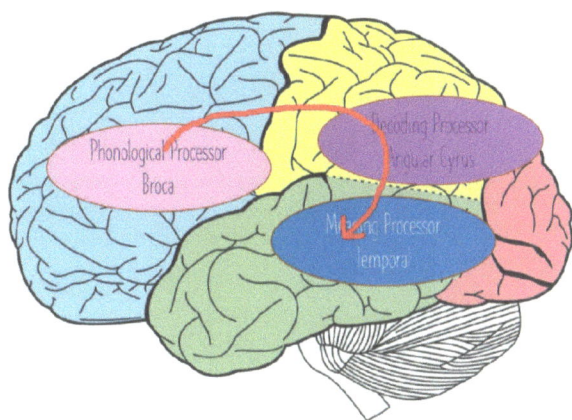

The Language Brain

Spoken phonemes are perceived, and decoded enabling access to meaning.

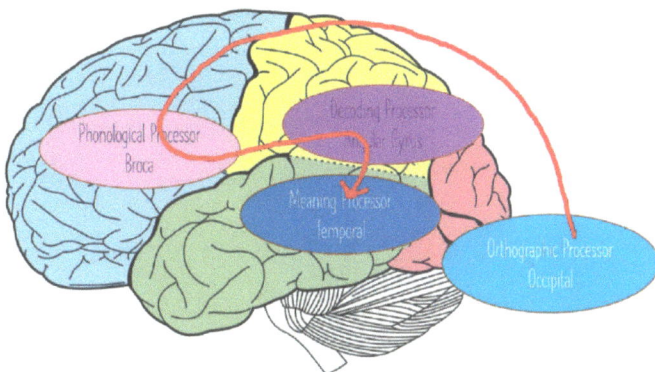

The Language-Reading Brain

Written graphemes are linked to phonemes, and decoded enabling access to meaning.

The language brain remains a language brain, even after it has adapted to decode and gain meaning from written language. This is important for educators to remember. Teaching morphological awareness successfully is going to incorporate the whole language brain: *phonology* (the speech sounds), *orthography* (graphemes and the phonemes they spell), *morphology* (meaningful forms in words), *syntax* (the part of speech and the roles words play in sentences), and an individual's innate sense of how language is used to verbally reason and problem solve with language.

When preparing to use this book of lessons, it is important to understand how the language components are intentionally embedded within the lesson structure. The language components work together to help students access meaning when reading:

1. **Orthography** - Students learn graphemes - letters and letter combinations. Graphemes, upon sight, kick the reading process into action.

2. **Phonology** – Whether producing language or listening, students depend on the sound(s) of words to connect them with meaning. When reading, students associate speech sounds with graphemes. Once graphemes are decoded, it is phonology that provides the access to word meaning. By the way, this process of decoding and accessing meaning happens simultaneously once word recognition is automatic.

3. **Morphology** – Students who have awareness of meaningful forms that make up words, recognize, decode, and access meaning more efficiently.

4. **Syntax** – Students use words within a well-defined sentence structure. A word's part of speech determines how the word will be used when grouped with other words.

When we teach decoding and encoding, we have the perfect opportunity to also teach awareness of morphemes. The language components phonology, orthography, and morphology, are reciprocal. They each support the other as this awareness of morphemes develops.

Application of these reciprocal language processes can be found in the *Morphemes for Little Ones* lessons. Students will identify the phonemes in the morphemes, decode as they connect the phoneme to the grapheme (if students are decoding), and then explore the meaning by hearing and using the words.

MORPHOLOGICAL PRODUCTION AND MORPHOLOGICAL AWARENESS

A wise friend once reflected, "A child's language is tied to her identity." This simple statement had a profound effect on my thinking about language and morphology instruction, especially with little ones.

We know that language is intimately tied to the development of reading and writing. There are students in our classrooms whose language varies from the language they are expected to read and write. It is common for students' home language to differ from the phonemes, syntax, and morphemes of the language spoken in classrooms and the words and books they will read. Honoring the language our students speak by avoiding judgment that considers one language variety superior to another, is a feature of the language rich classroom.

The young reader's familiar language, their spoken language, reveals their implicit knowledge about language. These willing young learners, come to us speaking the language they learn in their homes, eager to learn to read. The classroom becomes the environment where all children are exposed to the language they will read and spell.

Morphological knowledge is reflected in an *implicit* awareness of phonemes and morphemes spoken within an individual's familiar language structure. For learners speaking more than one language variety, developing as readers and writers requires learning the differences between their oral language and print (Washington & Seidenberg, 2021). **Morphemes for Little Ones** lessons are built upon this understanding to help teachers create an explicit awareness of phonemes and morphemes in both spoken and written language.

Young children's familiar language is going to come in handy when they begin to learn to read. The many systems of spoken language begin to reveal themselves to students as they become aware of language at a metalinguistic level:

- Awareness of speech sounds in familiar and new words.

- Awareness of meaning, and layers of meaning.

- Awareness of how words change, their sounds and how those sounds are linked to letters and combinations of letters.

- Awareness of how words are arranged into sentences.

- Awareness of morphemes, their meanings, what they sound like in general English (plurals: tents /s/ and boys /z/) and how they are spelled.

- Awareness of our use of language in social settings, language pragmatics.

Let's explore ways to fully appreciate the language our students speak and understand as they are learning to read and write. All language varieties are full of morphemes! Children's awareness of these morphemes evolves over many years. Explicitly integrating morphology awareness within our oral language, reading, and writing instruction, is a sure way to build a solid language foundation.

See Appendix for an informative chart that outlines key features of African American English (AAE): Verb Morphology, Syntax, and Phonology.

MORPHEMES FOR LITTLE ONES – THE RESEARCH BEHIND IT

The lesson design in **Morphemes for Little Ones** is firmly based in Structured Literacy (IDA, 2018). Teachers are directed to explicitly teach the morphemes, model the use of language, provide opportunities for students to hear, read, write and use the vocabulary providing exposure to the morphology being taught. A dominant focus is on oral language with a strong written language component intended to strengthen the oral-written language linkage.

The following instructional principles are built into the lessons and are isolated here to remind teachers of effective teaching processes that we all strive to master (IDA, 2018):

1. Instructional tasks are modeled, when appropriate.

2. Explicit instruction is provided.

3. Meaningful interactions with language occur during the lesson.

4. Multiple opportunities are provided to practice instructional tasks.

5. Corrective feedback is provided after initial student responses.

6. Student effort is encouraged.

7. Lesson engagement during teacher-led instruction is monitored.

8. Lesson engagement during independent work is monitored.

9. Students successfully complete activities at a high criterion level of performance.

Effective reading instruction in primary classrooms should address necessary elements associated with teaching decoding – phoneme awareness and phonics. Teaching morphemes is a natural companion to this instruction for this very reason.

> We know that learning about the written code is easier for students who know more about the sounds and meanings of the spoken words they are learning to read. Individual student differences in knowledge of these characteristics of spoken language at the start of formal instruction have an enormous impact on students' progress (Hulme, Nash, Gooch, Lervag, & Snowling 2015).

Before we proceed let's make sure we are all on the same page with the terminology associated with teaching reading and morphology.

Teaching awareness of phonemes, morphemes, and orthography, can happen seamlessly during our reading lessons.

Phoneme = phon (sound) + eme (little bit). The smallest sound unit within a word

Phoneme Awareness – The awareness that words are composed of speech sounds that can be isolated.

Morpheme = morph (form) + eme (little bit). The smallest unit of meaning within a word, or a word itself.

Morphological Awareness – The awareness that words are composed of meaningful units.

Orthography – The written form of a word is its orthography or, in other words, its spelling.

Early lessons in *Morphemes for Little Ones* focus on *free morphemes,* the words students can read, as bases for teaching the common suffixes. Later lessons introduce students to bound morphemes when affixing prefixes and suffixes to bases.

Free morphemes – Units of meaning that can stand alone without being combined with other morphemes to make a word. Examples: function words – and, is, are. These are mostly Anglo Saxon words: house, woman, blue, run, large.

Bound morphemes – Morphemes that cannot stand alone and be a word. These morphemes need to be combined with other morphemes to make a word. Examples: un- must be combined with another morpheme to make a word. The same is true of -ject, and -ing.

The morphemes taught in *Morphemes for Little Ones* focus mostly on the affixes, suffixes and prefixes.

Inflectional Suffixes – Added to words, they do not change the part of speech. These include -s for plurals and present tense, -ing for progressive tense, -ed for past tense, -er for comparatives, and -est for superlatives.

Derivational Suffixes – Added to words, they do change the part of speech. These include -ly, -er, -al, -ion, and multiple others.

Example: The comparative -er is inflectional in kinder because kind and kinder are both adjectives. The suffix -er meaning one who or that which is derivational in trainer, because train is a verb (in this sense) and trainer is a noun.

Justification for attending to morphology in the early grades is readily located in the literature (Apel, et. al., 2021). There is now very strong evidence that learning to appreciate the relationship between spelling and sound is fundamental in the initial stages of reading acquisition (Lervag, et. al., 2018). The reason that learning this relationship is so important is because it provides the developing reader with access to their spoken language knowledge about the meanings of words. Students bring their robust spoken language knowledge to the classroom. Early reading instruction establishes a beginning link to meaning through the ability to decode words. Additional attention to the fundamental sounds (phonemes, syllables, morphemes) and graphemes of familiar words can support learning of specific grapheme-to-language mappings and may also lead to generalizations about how their written forms map to their language.

We now know that morphological awareness is growing and developing beginning in kindergarten and continues throughout the school years (Kirby et al., 2012; Mahony, Singson, & Mann, 2000; Nagy, Berninger, & Abbott, 2006). As early as 6 and 7 years old, morphological processing is influencing how students spell words (Breadmore & Deacon, 2019). Children apply the patterns that exist in the orthography and morphology of words when they spell (Treiman, 2017). Furthermore, morphemes play a role in the development of lexical memory for meanings of words (Nation, 2009, Perfetti, 2007).

In addition, morphological awareness predicted significant unique variance on spelling measures for both 1st and 2nd grades and on a word-level reading measure for children with typical skills (Apel & Lawrence, 2011).

Intervention studies in Grades K, 1, and 2 wherein morphological awareness was taught resulted in significant improvements in reading, spelling, and reading comprehension. The groups in these intervention studies were low socioeconomic children. The researchers' recommendation is that student populations demonstrating difficulty learning to read may benefit from morphological instruction (Wolter & Green, 2013).

Research – Why is morphological awareness so important? Morphological awareness:

- Makes a powerful contribution to word reading abilities. (Apel & Diehm, 2014)
- Explains 4 to 15 percent of students' reading abilities as measured by literacy assessments. (McCutchen, Green & Abbot, 2008)
- Impacts reading comprehension positively. (Nagy, Berninger, & Abbot, 2006; Wolter & Dilworth, 2014)
- Improves spelling and written compositions. (McCutchen et al., 2008)
- Positively impacts students' literacy skills when taught during intervention. (Bowers et al., 2010)
- Uniquely predicts reading and writing skills even when other linguistic awareness skills are considered. (Apel et al., 2012)

In some cases, morphological awareness is the sole or strongest predictor for reading and spelling ability. (Apel et al., 2012)

HOW TO USE THIS BOOK

LESSON CONTENT AND DESIGN

The lessons in **Morphemes for Little Ones** are designed with a strong emphasis on the language components (phoneme awareness, orthography, morphology, and syntax) which, along with systematic explicit instruction, lead to the development of morphological awareness.

Instruction begins with the most basic morphemes such as plurals and past tense. These morphemes are easily incorporated into early decoding lessons by making CVC nouns plural (pups) and CVC verbs past tense (hopped). The morphemes chosen for the lessons are based on the most common inflectional suffixes first, and then the most common prefixes. Bases upon which the affixes are affixed, are initially common Anglo-Saxon words e.g., **quick**-ly and pre-**set**. In upper Level 2 and Level 3 lessons, root meanings are provided for teachers to share with students when the stem is not a free base, e.g., pre-**tend** (tens, tend – Latin meaning to stretch).

Word lists provide options for teachers to match words to their students' reading and vocabulary levels. These word lists are meant to get teachers started and it is recommended that the target morpheme be integrated into classroom reading program lessons using words that students are learning to read.

- Choose words students are able to decode and those to which target morphemes, suffixes and prefixes, can be affixed.

- Choose a selection of words that students are familiar with and others that would be good for them to add to their listening and speaking vocabularies. Use these word lists to grow student vocabularies.

- Model how to use the words in sentences. Some words change part of speech when we add a morpheme, or words may be unique enough that students need to hear how they are used to help them formulate their own sentences.

- Follow decoding practice with encoding (spelling) practice. Dictate the words students decoded for them to spell.

- Provide sentence frames that set kids up for success using newly formed words.

- Give students many opportunities to use words orally and then to write the sentences they speak.

LEVEL 1 PAST TENSE

-ed, /ed/

Lesson Goal:

Past tense is spelled -ed and in this lesson, we say /ed/ adding another syllable.

Teachers know:

When the verb base ends in /t/ or /d/, the past tense -ed says /ed/.

Word Bank

lifted
acted
blasted
drifted
trusted
twisted
floated
dented
gusted
added
folded
counted

Double It Spelling

jotted
patted
potted
dotted
budded
skidded
plodded

INTRODUCTION

DAY ONE: EXPLORE THE MORPHEME

Introduce the concept of action verbs to students. T
learning about how verbs change when we are talkin
happened before right now.

"Say **nod**." Students clap as they say **nod.**" "**Nod** yo
me."

"You just **nodded** your heads! Say **nodded** (clap the two syllables)." Students say **nodded** and clap the syllables. Say and clap the syllables **nod** and **nodded**. "How did **nod** change when we talked about what you had already done?" Clap the two parts again: **nod-ed**. The verbs we will work with today will change and say /ed/at the end when we are talking about action that we are finished doing. You **nodded** your heads a few minutes ago.

EXPLORE THE PHONEMES

The ending we say for this lesson's past tense verbs
/d/ are voiced adding an additional syllable because
om the Word Bank that match your
els (beginning and ending blends a
e it in a brief sentence, say the word
segment the phonemes. Emphasiz
s will double the final consonant w
onant is not voiced, i.e., **jotted** = /
er.

─ READING AND SPELLING

guage Exercises if students are not yet decoding words.
e It rule prior to this part. See the **Spelling with Suffixes**
oduction.

nodded on the board. "When I read this word, my eyes see
od if you see it too**." Circle **nod** and decode it. "I also see the new word part /ed/ that is spelled -ed". Say the base **nod** and ending -**ed**. "**Nodded.** We doubled the final consonant to protect t
adding -ed."

Follow the same process with other words to help st
word parts with /ed/. Make sure the words you choo
and will form a regular past tense verb, i.e. **sit** is not
Review the Double it Rule process for each word.

ENCODE: Dictate the words you used in the decodi
write. "Say **pot**. I will **pot** my plants. What is the past tense of **pot**?" "**Potted.**"
Spell **potted.**" Use response boards and ask student
after each word. Provide corrective feedback. Emph
work with in this lesson are spelled -ed and we say /

Begin the lesson with an introduction to the morpheme through oral language. Engage the children.

Word Banks provide words for decoding and spelling. Choose words that match your students' phonics knowledge and additional words from your reading and spelling lessons.

Explore the morpheme's phonemes. This part provides a phoneme segmentation activity.

Every lesson includes decoding and spelling.

Kng will engage with morphemes through oral language exercises.

ACTIVITIES

MORPHEME GRABBER - WORD EQUATION OR DRAW AND LAB[EL]

Direct students to create a new page in their Morpheme Grabber.

WORD + -ed	= NEW WORD	PICTURE OR SE[...]
lift + ed	lifted	
nod + ed	nodded	

Adjust the following exercises for your students' language and reading[...]

I jotted a thank you note to my friend.
Your Turn: If you jotted a note, who would you send it to? Use the word jotted.
© Morpheme Magic

THE MORPHEME CARD

Display the Morpheme Card. Instruct students to say the past tense word for each picture. Segment the phonemes. Use the words in sentences to tell about the picture. REVIEW: Teach **Double It Rule** if needed. Level Two - say and write the words. Level Three - say and write the words and a sentence for each.

NOTE: Irregular past tense verbs are addressed in Level 3.

ORAL LANGUAGE AND WRITE

After students finish the Connect to the Classroom[...] the -ed verbs and spell them if appropriate.

Oral and written language activities will engage students with the morphemes being taught. Apply these activities over 1-3 weeks.

More Word Bank Words

CONNECT TO THE CLASSROOM

Past Tense Art Project: Give every student a piec[...] the paper up, and **fold** it in half and then to **fold** it [...] think of someone they can send a Thank You Note [...] **provide** ideas: teacher, parent, playground person[...] a friend what they will write, then to **jot** it in the not[...] **jot** the note inside. When students are done, revie[...] "We **lifted** the paper and **folded** it. Our friends **pro**[...] our note and **decorated** it! We are finished and ca[...]

twisted

scripted

granted

cheated

grafted

painted

invented

suggested

corrected

directed

REVIEW AND PRACTICE

Non-reader and Reader: Use words from the Word Bank. Say the present tense for a word, and ask students to say the past tense. Direct students to use the past tense words in sentences. Provide assistance if needed. Ask, "How did the [...] word change to show we already did it?" Draw attention t[...] hear in the words.

Reader: Display one past tense word from this lesson eac[...] lesson. Model how to read the word, circle the base, and [...] plural suffix -ed. Use words from the Word Banks or from [...]

Review is important. A daily word problem to solve and sound spelling can become regular morpheme routines.

[...]hing the [...] are in [...]**uffixes** [...]the Introduction.

Thank you!

Lesson Goal:

Learn that -FUL can be added to words to make new words. It means full of.

Teachers know:

Full is a free morpheme – a word that can stand alone. -FUL is a suffix that cannot stand alone and is affixed to primarily Anglo-Saxon words.

Word Bank

spoon – spoonful

fork – forkful

plate – plateful

cup – cupful

taste – tasteful

rest – restful

wonder – wonderful

hope – hopeful

wish – wishful

youth – youthful

waste – wasteful

awe – awful

beauty – beautiful

bounty – bountiful

harm – harmful

hurt – hurtful

joy – joyful

INTRODUCTION

DAY ONE: EXPLORE THE MORPHEME

Today we are going to use some familiar words and [...] suffix, we will use the words in sentences in a differe[...] as the two examples are introduced.) Say **spoon**. I u[...] soup. Say **spoonful**. A **spoonful** of soup warms me [...] we change **spoon** to a word meaning **full of**? Spoon[...] explain they added -**ful** to **spoon** to make **spoonful**. -**FUL** added to the noun **spoon** helps us use **spoon** in new way. -**FUL** means full, or when we have **"a spoonful"** our **spoon** is full! Do the same with **fork**. Will this **fork** hold mashed potatoes? Add -**ful** to **fork**. **Forkful**. The **forkful** of potatoes will not fit into my mouth! We add -**ful** to **fork** and have another word to help us talk about **fork**. **Forkful** – a full fork.

EXPLORE THE PHONEMES

We just learned a new word ending, -**ful**. Say -**ful**. Sa[...] vowel /u/ will coarticulate with /l/. Help students isol[...] phoneme.) -**FUL** means… full! Lots of something, fill [...] word part? -**FUL**.

ORTHOGRAPHY – READING AND SPELLING

DECODE: Teach the orthography of -**ful**. Write **spoon**. Read it with the students. "We can use a **spoon** to eat ice-cream." Add -**ful** to **spoon**. "**Spoonful** is a spoon full of something." Read **spoonful**. Teach: When we spell and read the *word* full, we spell it f-u-l-l – write it, read it. When spelling and reading words with the suffix -ful, we spell it -**FUL** – write it and read it.

Do the same with other words in the Word Bank or words from your current reading lesson. Direct students to use the words in sentences. Emphasize how the meanings change when we add -**ful**. The new words we make mean **full**.

ENCODE:

Dictate pairs of words: **spoon** and **spoonful**, **fork** and **forkful** and other words for students to spell. Use response boards and ask students to share their spellings after each word. Emphasize that -**f**[...] in sentences and means a **full** ____. (fill in [...] Use the -**ful** words in sentences – model s[...] of the words as needed.

Begin the lesson with an introduction to the morpheme through oral language. Engage the children.

Segment the phonemes in the target morpheme after teaching the meaning.

Teach a decoding lesson with words that reflects known graphemes. Then dictate the same words for students to spell in their Morpheme Grabbers.

90

ACTIVITIES

MORPHEME GRABBER - WORD EQUATION OR DRAW AND LABEL

Direct students to create a new page in their Morpheme Grabber.

WORD + ful	= NEW WORD	MEANING
spoon + ful =	spoonful	a spoon full of something

Adjust the following exercises for your students' language and reading levels.

THE MORPHEME CARD

Display the Morpheme Cards. Instruct students to say the focus **-ful** word for each picture, explore the meanings, use the words in sentences to tell about the pictures. REVIEW: Level Three – Reteach the morpheme. Say and write the words and a sentence for each.

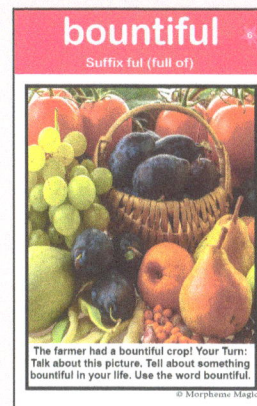

ORAL LANGUAGE AND WRITE

Display a list of **-ful** words provided below along w
into which the words can fit. Ask students to create
Morpheme Grabber for the categories and spell th
Ask students to be ready to share their thinking!

Categories: Parts of the Body and Words that Mak

Word List: **earful**, **joyful**, **beautiful**, **headful**, **mout**
OTHERS)

CONNECT TO THE CLASSROOM

Ask students to think of examples of when the clas
following: **earful**, **headful**, **thankful**, **handful**, **hope**
students use the target -ful word in their respon

REVIEW AND PRACTICE

Display one **-ful** word each day you are on this lesson. Model how to
word, circle the base, and then underline the suffix -
Word Banks or from your reading program.

Use sound spelling boxes to map and spell **-ful** words. Circle the m
Switch it out and display a word from previous week's lessons for re

bountiful
Suffix ful (full of)

The farmer had a bountiful crop! Your Turn:
Talk about this picture. Tell about something
bountiful in your life. Use the word bountiful.

© Morpheme Magic

More Word Bank Words

ear – earful

eye – eyeful

head – headful

hand – handful

mouth – mouthful

thank – thankful

Oral and written language activities will engage students with the morphemes being taught. Apply these activities over 1-3 weeks.

A daily review is important. Regular use of sound spelling boxes and a daily problem to solve, with a focus on meaning, will work to establish morphological awareness.

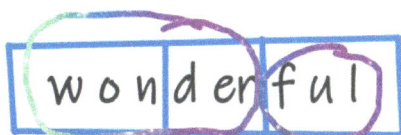

w o n d e r f u l

Lesson Goal:

Learn that -ABLE can be added to words to make adjectives. It means can do or be.

Teachers know:

-IBLE is a variant of -able. It is mostly used with Latin roots. See Word Bank on next page for word examples.

Word Bank

believable

fixable

eatable

kissable

drinkable

floatable

trainable

likeable

lovable

payable

answerable

excitable

enjoyable

comfortable

allowable

forgivable

respectable

supportable

suitable

notable

INTRODUCTION

DAY ONE: EXPLORE THE MORPHEME

Today we are going to learn a new suffix. Write **-able**▮ students to read it with you. **–ABLE** means **can do**. board. Students read it with you. Underline **-able,** ci the word **believable**, I know that the **-able** means c▮ means **can be believed**. **Is it believable that it will s▮**

> Begin the lesson with an introduction to the morpheme through oral language. Engage the children.

ORTHOGRAPHY – READING AND SPELLING

DECODE: Teach the orthography for **-able**. Create a list of 5-10 words from the Word Bank. Display the words one at a time creating a column of words for reading and spelling instruction. Model decoding, word meaning, and word use.

TEACHER	STU▮
Write and read **-able**. **ABLE** means **can do or be**.	Read **-able** and ▮ meaning to a pa▮
Write and read **believe**. Erase e and add **able**. **believable**. Circle and say **believe**. Underline **-able**. Read the parts. Say **believable – can be believed. The story we are reading is believable.** Reteach the Drop It rule for bases ending in e.	Read **-able**, ble▮ read **believable.** a senten▮e (assi▮
Follow the same process with 5-10 words. After reading the words, direct students to read them again with you. Prompt students to say **-able** and word meanings each time.	Read through th▮ directed by the t▮ and word meanings as directed. Use the words in sentences. Teacher provides sentence frames as needed.

> The decoding lesson is systematic and explicit. Follow the process left to right in each row. Teacher Says then Student Says.

be liev able

Leave the words displayed. Read them again pri▮ to the encoding lesson.

ENCODE:

Dictate **-able** words for students to spell. Use response boards or the Morpheme Grabber and ask students to sh▮ word, provide corrective feedback. Ask stu▮ meaning after each spelling. Work with stu▮ **-able** words.

> Follow the decoding lesson with spelling practice. Students spell the same words they decoded above. Students use the Morpheme Grabber to spell the dictated words.

136

ACTIVITIES

MORPHEME GRABBER - WORD EQUATION

Direct students to create a new page in their Morpheme Grabber.

WORD + -ABLE	= NEW WORD	-ABLE MEANS
believe + able =	believable	can do or be

Adjust the following exercises for your students' la~~...~~

THE MORPHEME CARDS

Display the Morpheme Cards. Instruct students to ~~...~~
picture, explore the meanings, and use the words ~~...~~
pictures. Add the cards to your Morpheme Wall for ~~...~~

ORAL LANGUAGE AND WRITE

Post a set of **-able** words for students to read and ~~...~~
to. Direct students to write the heading **Pet ___** in ~~...~~
Grabbers and fill in the blank with a pet of their choi~~...~~
(dog, cat, hamster, etc). Then choose -**able** - words that
could describe the pet they chose. Ask students to share
their answers with a partner with reasons and examples for
their word choices.

kissable
likeable
excitable

CONNECT TO THE CLASSROOM

Over the course of the week, see how many **-able** words
students can use to discuss and write about what they are
learning. Pose a brief list of words that you think may apply.
Add to the list each day. Consider all content areas including
aspects of the social classroom. Model your use of the **-able** words. Tally the
number of times words are used. Ask for a classroom helper to assist with this.

REVIEW AND PRACTICE

Daily Morpheme Problem to Solve: Display one **-able** w~~...~~
on this lesson. Model how to read the word, circle the bas~~...~~
-**able**. Use words from the Word Banks or from your read~~...~~

ex press i ble
out + make a + can do
permanent image

Use sound spelling boxes to map and spell **-able** words. Circle the
morphemes. Switch it out and display a word from previous week's lessons for
review.

irrestible
Suffix -able -ible (can do or be)

~~...~~dow full of treats is irresistible.
~~...~~rn: What would you do if you
~~...~~this display? Use irresistible.

© Morpheme Magic

~~...~~ord Bank Words

~~...~~Words

~~...~~flexible
legible
resistible
irresistible
responsible
sensible
terrible
accessible
compatible
comprehensible
eligible

These activities provide ideas for creating the language rich classroom as students build their morpheme vocabulary through oral language and writing.

A daily review is important. A daily problem to solve and encoding words with a focus on meaning will work to establish morphological awareness.

~~...~~about ~~-able words~~ ~~...~~ this lesson.

137

17

DETERMINING WHICH LEVEL IS RIGHT

The lessons in **Morphemes for Little Ones** are presented in levels, **Level One, Level Two** and **Level Three**. These levels are not meant to be directly interpreted as grade levels. The level you choose for your students will depend on their language and decoding abilities. All levels are built upon a strong oral and written language foundation which slowly increases in complexity as students work through the lessons in each level.

A Note About Kindergarten: It is recommended that Level 1 Lessons be used to enrich language exercises in kindergarten classrooms. Each lesson provides a focus that will guide teachers and students in an exploration of words, their meanings, and creating sentences. Once students begin to decode and encode, writing the words and sentences that stem from these lessons can be incorporated into the reading curriculum. Students who explore language through Level 1 lessons in kindergarten, will be ready to engage more deeply with Level 1 morphemes again in first grade.

Typical placement for grade levels in the **Little Ones** lessons:

LEVEL ONE L-1	• Kindergarten (oral language only) and most first grade students; intervention groups first through third grades. ELs. • First grade students may or may not be decoding for the early lessons in L-1. Decoding is necessary for later lessons in L-1.
LEVEL TWO L-2	• Advanced first grade and second grade; intervention groups first through third grades. ELs. • Early lessons review basic morphemes taught in L-1 and later lessons introduce new affixes and stems.
LEVEL THREE L-3	• Advanced second grade and third grade; intervention groups and into intermediate grades. ELs. • Word items become more sophisticated. Roots are introduced through word study of the affixes.

Once students have begun morpheme awareness instruction, take your time! There is no hurry. Most important is that students are building vocabulary, becoming aware of words, their meanings and the important roles morphemes play.

We want students to spend lots of time applying the words they learn in the lessons to their spoken and written language.

We want teachers to gradually realize the many times throughout the day morphemes surface and present teaching opportunities.

When a Level is completed, teachers can move onto the next level, or work to reinforce what has been taught through frequent reference to the **Morpheme Wall** and **Morpheme Grabber**, continual reference to the spelling charts, and continuing to add to the **Morpheme Grabber** collection of morphemes and words that students have been creating.

A lesson can take one to two weeks to complete. Take your time!

We are never finished with this instruction and can never underestimate the repetition that our students need in order to master the seamless integration of language components. "What I say, I can write. What I read I can talk about the write about." Weave the components together to take advantage of how phonology, orthography, and meaning work together toward reading success.

THE MORPHEME GRABBER

Let's **GRAB** those morphemes and words we learn.

Let's write them down so we remember them!

That's the message we want to send to our students. When we write something down, we are more apt to learn it. The process teachers establish should set students up to collect their learning over time. Use the morpheme booklets to record all morpheme awareness activities, writing, spelling, and art work related to learning the lesson vocabulary.

Consider and choose what will work best for you and your students. Read through the following ideas to provide direction for setting students up to create a long-lasting collection of language learning.

Decide What the Class Will Call their Morpheme Grabbers

- *Morphemes for Little Ones* lessons refer to the booklets students make as *Morpheme Grabbers*. It is kind of catchy, "Get out your *Morpheme Grabbers*!

We have morphemes and words to write down!" The booklet can be renamed if desired: Word Collection, Vocabulary Notebook, NAME'S Word and Activity Book (student's name), Morpheme Collection, etc. Choose a title that will stick and become a regular part of your daily word work with students.

Kindergarten and First Grade – The Morpheme Grabber:

- Little ones do best with more consolidated formats. For first grade, a week or two worth of sheets of appropriate, primary lined paper, landscape, stapled together at the long end, work just fine. Two pages per day is a good target. Put a colored cover on the "booklet" and ask students to put their names on their "Word Books". When the booklet is full, place it in a safe place and start over again. A new book is always captivating and reengaging. Pull out the used-up booklets for review. Combine the booklets in sets of 4 and 5 or more over time.

- Locate blackline masters of lined paper in the Appendix which can be used for creating the *Morpheme Grabber*.

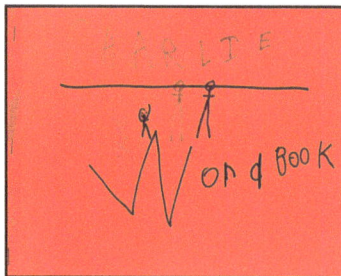

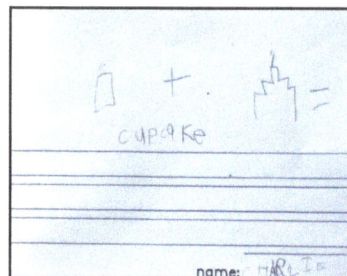

Second Grade – The Morpheme Grabber:

- Second grade students can use the same format as first grade with paper adapted for their writing levels. Create booklets that will hold their learning for a month or two. Choose and print a black line master located in the back of this book. Include several of these in the booklet. Collect the booklets after a month or two, and then begin again. Return to the used booklets for review.

- Find backline masters of lined paper in the Appendix that can be used for creating the *Morpheme Grabber.*

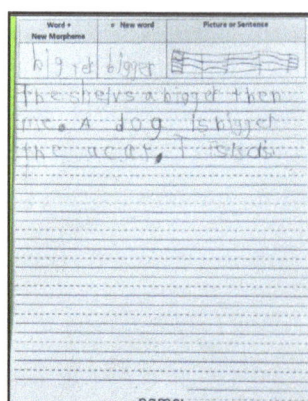

Third Grade – The Morpheme Grabber:

Choose and print a Morpheme Grabber heading located in the back of this book.

- Most third graders are ready to take on a notebook in which they can record their morpheme learning over several months. If desired, Composition Booklets available in most office supply stores can be used. Make sure the booklets have wide rule paper. Choose and print a Morpheme Grabber Heading located in the back of this book. Students can cut out the heading used for recording morphemes and glue it into their notebooks. Alternatively (sometimes cutting and gluing take too much time and creates frustration) model the Morpheme Grabber format provided in the lessons for students and ask them to follow your lead to record the morphemes in their notebooks.

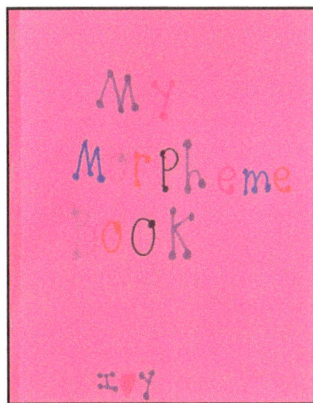

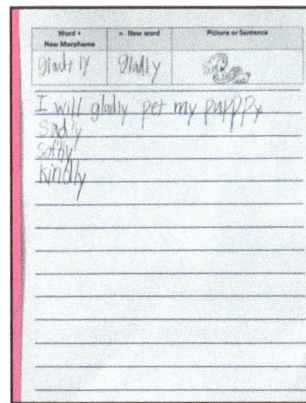

- The Morpheme Grabber is a wonderful way to begin building early study skills and organization habits. Make it simple at first and gradually build in more structure. When students get to 4th grade, **Morpheme Magic** will set them up with creating a Table of Contents and inserting page numbers in their *Morpheme Lexicons*. The work students do with the simpler models now, scaffolds to a more complex process when they are older.

CREATING THE MORPHEME WALL

Wall space is a premium in classrooms. Spare wall space is rare real estate in our classrooms so talking about putting up a **Morpheme Wall** may seem over the top for most teachers. If you can swing it, a **Morpheme Wall** can be the next best educational tool you provide for yourselves and your students!

Following are tips and steps to help teachers get started:

- Designate a location for the **Morpheme Wall** that is within easy access for students, i.e., eye level, cards can be reached and easily seen. The **Morpheme Wall** will need to be in a location that lends itself to frequent reference and updates.

- Preserve a space that will accommodate a growing set of cards. You will be adding one card per lesson and there are 17 lessons per level. Post a lesson card of your choice. Over time, a card may be switched out with one of the other lesson cards.

- Leave room below the morpheme for students to post additional word items that reflect the target morpheme.

- Create a label for each column as shown in the photo below. Build the Wall from left to right in rows.

- Add the spelling charts to the **Morpheme Wall** as you begin to teach the spelling rules for Double It! Drop It! and Change It! See the end of this section to locate the charts.

- Refer to the wall often: for review purposes; to help correct spelling; to help students find a word to use in their speaking and writing, i.e., "Use a plural word to tell your partner about your favorite part of the story."

- Add words under each of the Morpheme Wall Cards that the class uses to practice the morpheme. Write each word on a separate index-type card or write words on one card. Words from your reading program are a great resource for this. Make sure these words are words that incorporate the grapheme-phoneme spellings your students have learned and can decode.

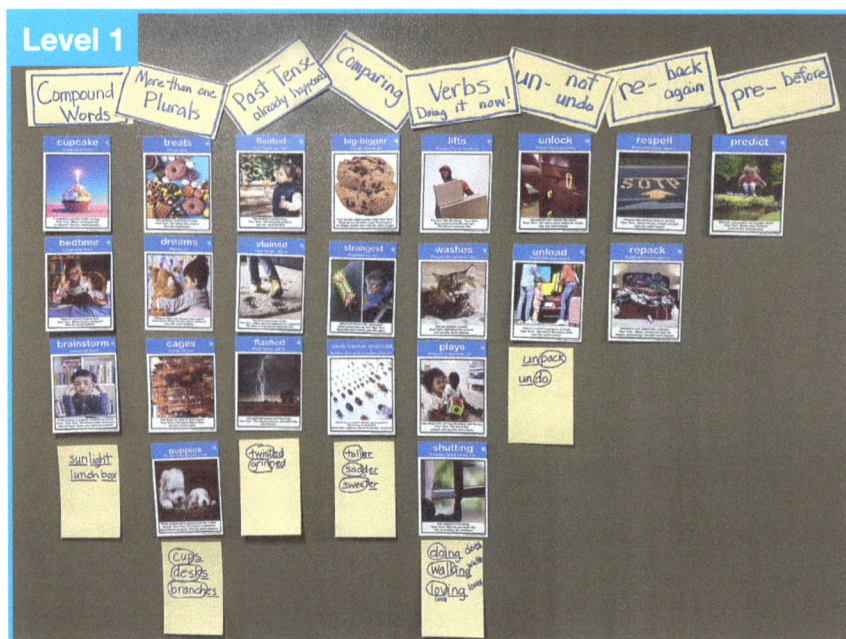

The Morpheme Wall serves as a reminder to **REVIEW**. There are several ways review sessions can be done and creativity abounds when planning review lessons:

1. Begin your review by referring to the **Morpheme Wall**. Reteach the target morpheme. Allow students to provide as much information as they can during the review. "One way we change words, is when we are talking about more than one. This is called a ___. The ending on these words can sound like ___. Or it can sound like ____. We spell this ending that tells more than one ___."

2. Create a class **Morpheme Card** for the morpheme. Find your own picture to illustrate the word students choose. Project the new card using your classroom technology.

3. Put students in pairs and instruct them to come up with a **Morpheme Card** for one word from of a set of words the class brainstorms. They can work together to illustrate a card, or each create their own.

4. Direct students to create and illustrate their own **Morpheme Cards** and create it in the section for the target morpheme in their **Morpheme Grabber**.

5. Be aware and encourage students to also be aware of words that surface in their reading materials and in read alouds. Add these words to the **Morpheme Wall** and also the students' **Morpheme Grabbers**.

6. Include a few words with the morphemes that have been taught in weekly spelling assignments and add them to spelling lists. If one of the spelling rules needs to be applied, remind students to look up at the Spelling Charts. If the suffix starts with a vowel, STOP and check it out using the checklist. If the suffix starts with a consonant, GO and add the suffix to the base without any changes.

INFORMAL CRITERION MORPHOLOGICAL AWARENESS ASSESSMENTS

There are a handful of formal normed morphological awareness assessments that are working their way through technical validation and publication. When these assessments are available, classroom teachers will be able to administer them to students for whom a deeper understanding of morphological knowledge and awareness is desired. These formal assessments can provide a substantial picture of a student's morphological awareness.

For purposes of gaining information about students' oral language and morphological knowledge 'at a glance' *Morphemes for Little Ones* criterion assessments can be used. Teachers gain a quick picture of their students' comfort with words and tasks that mirror what we ask of students in the lessons. The assessment is helpful, but not necessary for placement, as the suggested placements in the chart presented earlier can be used for determining an entry Level in the program.

The *Morphemes for Little Ones Assessments* are located in the Appendix in this book. Please read the information below to become familiar with the assessment design and how to administer and use the results.

The questions on the *Little Ones* assessments, are based on the types of questions developed for assessment research (Apel, 2021; Reed, 2022). To gain a more accurate indication of morpheme knowledge, many normed assessments will use nonsense words i.e, This is a wog. This is two (<u>wogs</u>). The assessments in this book use real words.

Alternatively, teachers may want to informally assess students one-on-one using the following suggestions:

- Say a compound word, backpack. Ask student to say it. Ask, "What words make up the word backpack?" Repeat with other compound words: sunshine, housefly, pinecone.

- If students are reading, ask them to circle bases in compound words. *(Perceiving two meaningful units).*

- Present a word such as **rewrite** orally or in writing. **Ask**: "What does this word mean?" Other words you could use are: boys (which part means more than one?) floated (which part means it happened in the past?). *(Word meaning and morpheme recognition-meaning)*

- Present a word orally or in writing such as **hopeless**. **Ask**: "What is the main part of this word?" Other words you could use are: forkful, cloudy, kindness. *(Morpheme segmentation and meaning)*

- Ask students to read a list of words with affixes and roots. See word items on the Level 2 and Level 3 assessments. (*Morphology-orthography word recognition, consolidation*)

- If appropriate for students' reading abilities, give students a written list of words with bases and affixes. **Ask**; Find the bases and affixes: **unlikable**, **misplaced**, etc. (*morpheme awareness, word recognition*)

- Analyze students' writing samples for indicators of morphological knowledge.

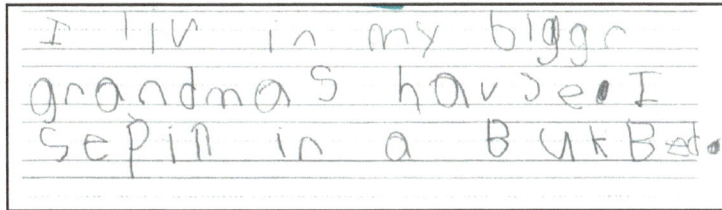

This 1st grade student is using **comparatives** (bigger), **possessives** (grandma's), and **compound words** (bunkbed). This writing sample also presents a helpful picture of the student's phoneme segmentation level. She needs more instruction on segmenting the initial and final phonemes in consonant blends (<u>s</u>leep /s/l/ and bu<u>nk</u> /ng/k/).

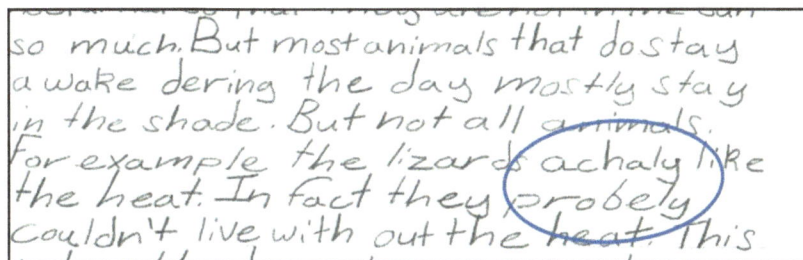

This 3rd grade student has not internalized the word family that can be built around **act** (**actually**). She is spelling **probably** (probable+ly) the way she most likely says the word, with two syllables, instead of demonstrating knowledge of **probable**.

Purpose and Caution: Use the ***Morphemes for Little Ones*** assessments to obtain a general understanding of morpheme knowledge and assess readiness for lessons in Levels 1, 2, and 3. Interpret these assessments with caution. They are meant to assess general language knowledge. We know that even if students provide correct answers, that does not necessarily mean they are ready to advance beyond the related lessons which will create awareness of the morpheme elements and enrich oral language.

Remember, the criterion assessments included in this book are informal. Their purpose is to help teachers gain a basic understanding of their students' morphological knowledge. Use your best judgement when scoring students' answers.

ASSESSMENT	RECOMMENDED GRADE	SCORING
Level 1 Assessment	(Kinder) Grade 1 Administer One-on-One.	Stop assessment when 3 consecutive errors occur. Each question is worth 1 point if correct, and 0 points if incorrect. The assessment is worth 16 points.
Level 2 Assessment	Grade 2 Administer one-on-one for questions 1-8. Questions 9 and 10 can be administered to a group or one-on-one.	Stop administering Part 1 of the assessment if students miss 3 consecutive questions. Move to **Reading Words** and **Spelling Words**. If students miss the first 3 questions, give the Level 1 Assessment. The assessment is worth 34 points.
Level 3 Assessment	Grade 3 Administer one-on-one or as a group assessment with students submitting written responses. The Reading Words section will need to be administered individually.	If students are unable to answer any of the first 5 questions correctly, move to the **Reading Words** and **Spelling Words** portions of the assessment. Teachers may also discontinue Level 3 assessment and choose to administer Level 2. Level 3 Assessment is worth 53 points.

Use the **Student Scoring Sheets** to record students' performance on the assessments or use the individual student scoring form, the assessment itself. Interpret the scores to obtain a picture of your *class* performance and then individual performance.

The Administration Guidelines, Scoring Sheets, and Assessments can be located in the Appendix.

MORPHOLOGICAL AWARENESS ACTIVITIES TO USE OVER AND OVER

Everyone loves a good activity. When teachers tell me that their students had a lot of fun doing a particular activity, I know that students were engaged in their learning. Activities serve the purpose of practicing what was taught. Practice makes permanent. The more active, engaged time spent thinking about what is taught, the stronger the memory is for that learning (Willingham, 2008). What better way to engage in practice is there than with a well-designed and fun activity!

Teachers do not need LOTS of activities, in fact we can have too many to choose from. When we have too many activities to choose from the focus becomes on the activity not the learning focus. Be mindful of this. Just a few trusted activities that can be used over and over again, switching out the learning focus, is all we need. Some of the following activities are already built into the lessons, but can be used in any of the lessons or for review.

1. SOUND OR SYLLABLE SPELLING BOXES – CIRCLE THE MORPHEMES

Find Blackline Masters at the end of this book.

Teacher prepares word list. Choose words with the target morpheme and reflect students' knowledge of phoneme-grapheme correspondences. Make sure students have practiced decoding the words before initiating this practice activity. If the list is long, use a sampling of the words for whole group and then use the rest of the words during small group lessons.

Use sound spelling for students in Level 1 and early Level 2 lessons. Use syllable spelling for students who are chunking syllables when they read.

Teachers model the process along with students as students are engaged in the process.

1. Teacher says a word. Students repeat the word.

2. "Dot and say the sounds (*syllables*, if using syllable spelling)." Students and teacher together, say each phoneme (*syllable*) as they place a small dot in the bottom of a spelling box.

3. Teacher, touching the first box, "What sound (*syllable*)?" Students say the sound (*syllable*). "Spell it." Students and teacher spell the phoneme (*syllable*) in the dotted box.

4. Repeat for each phoneme-grapheme (or syllable) until the word is spelled. Write the word in the final column.

5. Point out the phonic elements that are being taught, and the target morpheme and its meaning. Circle the base and then the affixes while saying the meanings of each. Include any other information that will help students recall the sound-spelling connections (i.e., "We double the P in hop because we are adding the ending -ING that starts with a vowel and we need to protect that short /o/!"

See sample sound and syllable spellings throughout the lessons.

2. SENTENCE STARTERS

Many of our students have difficulty getting started with forming sentences during oral language exercises. Here are a variety of sentence starters for young and older students. Choose the ones that fit your students' language abilities. Create a display of these sentence starters for your students to choose from when they need some help starting their sentences to demonstrate their new morphological awareness!

Maybe…	Possibly…	I'm confident…
I learned…	I was surprised…	I think…
In my opinion…	I'm surprised…	This reminds me…
If…	Although…	I believe…
I question…	When…	An important…

3. SEED SENTENCES

Used with permission from Top 10 Tools, and Tools 4 Reading.

The SEED process teaches students how to expand a simple sentence into a richer lengthier sentence. Provide a short list of target morpheme words from a lesson. Read the words and discuss the morphemes and their meanings (base and affix). Provide a simple sentence to get the students started. Explain, that the simple sentence is a seed and our job is to water and grow the seed into a richer sentence that gives us more information.

STEPS SEED	DESCRIPTION	MORPHEME FOCUS AND GROWING THE SENTENCE	SENTENCES
S	Simple Sentence. A simple sentence has a subject and a predicate.	Target Morpheme: **-er**, one who or that which. Also **plurals** review.	Teach**ers** teach.
E	Expand. Grow the predicate – Did or Do what?	Teachers teach what? When? Why. Ask a question or questions that will lead to creating a complex sentence.	Teach**ers** teach **sub**trac**tion** after lunch because student**s** are settl**ed** down.
E	Extend. Tell more about the subject to extend your reader's thinking about the subject. Describe or add information about your subject.	Can you think of any comparative or superlative to describe Teachers?	The smart**est** teach**ers** teach **sub**trac**tion** after lunch because student**s** are settl**ed** down.
D	Decide. Students will rehearse different ways to bring the ideas together into a sentence and decide on their final sentence.	Teachers and students can suggest additional words using the Morpheme Wall as a reference for ideas.	*Students work independently, with the class or with a partner to decide on what the final sentence will sound like.*

Student**s** are settl**ed** down after delici**ous** lunches, so the smart**est** teach**ers** teach **sub**trac**tion** follow**ing** lunch.

4. SENTENCE FRAMES

The sentence frame is a supportive tool to help low language students build self-confidence with their oral and written responses. The sentence frame is a common tool which most teachers are familiar with, but seldom use. Teachers are more likely to use sentence frames if they have a few good, simple frames available that they can give their students to use when practicing using the words in the morpheme lessons.

Here is one that has wide application to using the Morpheme Lessons word items. Add to your bank of sentence frames as you think of them and match them up with the lesson vocabulary.

Sample Lesson: - Focus on the morpheme past tense verbs.

Word Lists: Provide a word list, or create one with them, for students to choose from. Or direct them to refer to the **Morpheme Wall** for ideas.

Who or What	Name a character from our story. List a few options for students to choose from. Or, brainstorm a list with students.
Did what _____ Present tense will ask, *"Does what ___."*	Brainstorm past tense verbs describing the character's actions ending with -ed.
Where? When? Why? How? _____	Answer one or more of the questions to finish the sentence. Limit the questions asked depending on students' language skills and the context from which the sentence is being developed.

Students say and write their whole sentence in their **Morpheme Grabber.**

Example: (Who?) The gardeners (Did what?) planted flowers (Where?) in the new garden (When?) last week (Why?) to help make the park a beautiful place to visit.

5. GO FISH

Prepare the Cards:
Work with students over the course of two or three lessons to create playing cards. When encoding during the lesson, ask students to spell their words on cards. Provide corrective feedback if needed. Students collect the cards in zip bags that they keep for playing games. Alternatively, teachers can create sets of cards: make one set, copy the set, and cut the copies to create cards.

Prepare for the Game:
Direct students to remove cards from their pack to leave 10 that they will play with. Extra cards are place in a pile in the middle to create the "fishing pond". Students can remove any words they want. This will create sets of cards students are holding that are not identical. If students want their own cards back after the game is over, they can put their initials on the bottom of each of their cards.

Play!

Students play in partners or small groups of 3 or 4. Each student has his or her own cards.

All kids know how to play go fish! (if not, teach them) The object is to get pairs of words that share the same morpheme. "Do you have any past tense verbs? Only one word is given up at a time, in other words, if the student has two past tense verbs, he only gives one of them to the requester. If the person does not have any past tense verbs, they Go Fish!

6. CONCENTRATION

Concentration is an old standby and always a favorite! Students can play with a partner to match words.

Prepare the Cards:
Use the same process to prepare playing cards outlined above in Go Fish.

Prepare for the Game:
Partners sit next to each other at a desk or table. Each of the students places their word cards face down in a column creating two columns of words.

Play!
Students take turns turning over one card in one column, reading it and then turning over a card in the next column and reading it. If the two do not match, both cards are turned face down again in the same locations. This play continues with students taking turns and reading the cards until a match is made. When a match is made, the student finding the match *reads the word and then says the morphemes and their meanings* to keep the set and takes another turn.

7. ROLL A WORD

Larger size cubes (dice) upon which words can be written on the six sides, are available through school supply outlets. Use these to create morpheme game cubes.

Prepare the Cubes:
Write suffixes and/or prefixes that the students have learned on the sides of one cube. Write and display a short list of nouns, adjectives, and verbs.

Prepare for the Game:
Students can work independently, with partners, or small groups. Give students a cube and read through each of the morphemes written on the sides. There may be more than one of the same morpheme. Direct students to read through the list of bases displayed.

Play!

One student rolls the cube and reads the morpheme. Then the individual or group of students determine which base to affix the morpheme to and say the new word. All students write their new word in their morpheme grabbers. Then, ask students to use the word in a sentence. Play continues until it is time to stop. Then students read all of their words to the class.

Optional: students can think of their own bases to which they add the morphemes they roll.

8. GRAPH IT!

This activity may be tied to the math concept of creating and interpreting a graph.

Directions: Explain to students on Monday that they're going to work all week to find examples of the morphemes they have been working on. State which morphemes you want them to focus on. Write the target morphemes on the board.

Direct students to create *three* (however many morphemes they will be watching for) columns on a dedicated page in their Morpheme Grabber. Write the target morphemes, one at the top of each column.

Students note words in their reading materials that apply the target morphemes, and write them on a special page under the headings they created. At the end of each day, students report out the number of words they found and the number of words is recorded under the displayed morpheme on the board.

At the end of the week, the numbers are tallied and a class graph can be created to show visually the most 'popular' morpheme. Alternatively, students can create their own graphs.

Optional: Students can compare their word collections for duplicates and adjust their numbers accordingly.

9. PAIR UP AND SHARE UP!

This simple exercise can be used to fill time with some effective review of the morphemes students have learned. In addition to valuable review, this activity helps students build pride in their **Morpheme Grabbers**.

Directions: Pair students and ask them to take their **Morpheme Grabbers** with them for their partner work. Ask students to take turns sharing their sentences they wrote, the pictures they might have created, reading through the morphemes they have learned, asking and answering questions about the morphemes and words. Give the students a goal such as:

1. Add another word to each new morpheme page.

2. Decide which morpheme page is your favorite and be ready to explain why.

3. Choose one morpheme to write a new sentence and draw a picture for the sentence.

SPELLING WITH SUFFIXES - DOUBLE IT - DROP IT – CHANGE IT

It is important to teach the orthography for decoding and encoding when suffixes are added to bases. The spelling rules **Double It, Drop It,** and **Change It** require lots of practice over an extended period of time before the orthographic mapping is secure – sometimes a few years! We can make the process more streamlined by presenting these spelling processes explicitly and systematically.

1. **Start by adding suffixes to words that will not require any spelling changes.** This is tough to do when students are spelling cvc words and adding suffixes that start with vowels! There are a few suffixes, however that we can use in the beginning that will not require changes. One of these is plurals and present tense verbs.

2. Introduce the Green-Light and Red-Light concept to students. Copy the Red Light-Green Light poster below and post it with the Spelling Rules on your Morpheme Wall.

3. If the suffix begins with a consonant – **GREEN LIGHT!** Go ahead and add the suffix.

4. If the suffix begins with a vowel – **RED LIGHT!** Stop and check. Do we have to change the spelling of the base?

5. **Teach the Double It rule first**. Display the Double It checklist found on the Spelling Poster. Use a sample word to demonstrate the steps. Ask: Are we adding a vowel suffix? If yes, give the step a check mark. Ask: Is there one syllable? If yes, give it a check mark. Ask each question in the checklist. If all steps have a check, then DOUBLE IT! Repeat the process with another word.

6. **Teach the Drop It rule next** when students have begun decoding and spelling silent e, c_e words. Follow the same process to teach this rule, checking the steps as outlined in Double It, step 6.

7. **Teach the Change It rule last.** When students begin encountering words that end in -y introduce the third rule. A few high frequency words fit this category: try – tried, trying (***Two i's together are not wise!).*** Follow the same process to teach this rule, checking the steps as outlined in Double It, step 6.

8. **Copy and make a wall chart for each of the spelling rules**. Post the charts on your Morpheme Wall. Direct students to place copies of the Spelling Charts in their Morpheme Grabbers.

If the suffix starts with a VOWEL, **STOP** do the checklist

If the suffix starts with a CONSONANT, **GO!**

SPELLING PLURAL NOUNS

TO MOST NOUNS, ADD -S.

tree = trees   giraffe = giraffes

WHEN NOUNS END IN A VOWEL + Y, ADD -S.

monkey = monkey   sunray = sunrays

WHEN NOUNS END IN CONSONANT + Y, CHANGE THE Y TO I AND ADD -ES.

lady = ladies   facility = facilities

WHEN BASES END IN S, X, CH, SH, AND Z, ADD -ES TO CREATE ANOTHER SYLLABLE.

boss = bosses   box = boxes   batch = batches
wish = wishes   buzz = buzzes

Morpheme Magic - Deb Glaser

SPELLING PLURAL NOUNS
WHAT ABOUT WORDS THAT END IN -O?

WHEN NOUNS ARE SHORT FOR OTHER NOUNS, ADD -S.

kilogram = kilo = kilos

photograph = photo = photos

WHEN NOUNS END IN A VOWEL + O, ADD -S.

video = videos   kangaroo = kangaroos

WHEN NOUNS COME FROM OTHER LANGUAGES, ADD -S.

burrito = burritos   kimono = kimonos

SOME -O WORDS TAKE -ES, JUST BECAUSE! HERE ARE ALL OF THEM.

echoes, embargoes, heroes,
potatoes, tomatoes, torpedoes, vetoes

AND FEW WORDS CAN BE SPELLED EITHER WAY, JUST BECAUSE!

buffalos/buffaloes, dominos/dominoes,
mosquitos/mosquitoes, tornados/tornadoes,
volcanos/volcanoes, zeros/zeroes

Morpheme Magic - Deb Glaser

DOUBLE IT!
SPELLING CHECKLIST TO DOUBLE IT

✓ Adding a vowel suffix? (ing, ed, er, est, y, en)
___ One syllable?
___ One vowel?
___ Base ends in one consonant?

skip+ed = skipped   whisper+ing = whispering

DROP IT!
SPELLING CHECKLIST TO DROP THE "E"

___ Adding a vowel suffix? (ing, ed, er, est, y, en)
___ Base ends in silent "e"?

forgive+ing=forgiving
move+ment = movement

Silent e

CHANGE IT!
SPELLING CHECKLIST TO CHANGE "y" to "i"

___ Base ends in "y" with a consonant before the "y"?
___ Suffix does not begin with "i"? Two "i"s are never wise!

carry+er = carrier   supply+ing = supplying

ends in consonant y

Morpheme Magic - Deb Glaser

DOUBLE IT!

land + ing = ?   hum + ed = ?

✔ Adding a vowel suffix?   ✔ Adding a vowel suffix?
✔ (ing, ed, er, est, y, en)   (ing, ed, er, est, y, en)
✔ One syllable?   ✔ One syllable?
✔ One vowel?   ✔ One vowel?
🚫 Base ends in one   ✔ Base ends in
   consonant?   consonant?

DROP IT!

wave + ing = ?   name + less = ?

✔ Adding a vowel suffix?   🚫 Adding a vowel suffix?
   (ing, ed, er, est, y, en)   (ing, ed, er, est, y, en)
✔ Base ends in silent   ✔ Base ends in silent
   "e"?   "e"?

CHANGE IT!

joy + ous = ?   fry + ed = ?

🚫 Base ends in "y" with a ✔ Base ends in "y" with a
   consonant before the   consonant before the
   "y"?   "y"?
✔ Suffix does not begin   ✔ Suffix does not begin
   with "i"? Two "i"s are   with "i"? Two "i"s are
   never wise!   never wise!

Morpheme Magic - Deb Glaser

REFERENCES

Anderson, J. (2006). Zooming in and zooming out: Putting grammar in context into context. *The English Journal, 95* (5), pp. 28-34.

Anderson, R.C., & Nagy, W.E. (1992). The vocabulary conundrum, *American Educator, 16*(4), 14-18, 44-47.

Apel, K., & Dieham, E. (2014). Morphological awareness intervention for kindergarteners and first and second grade students from low SES homes: A small efficacy study. *Journal of Learning Disabilities,* 47, 65-75.

Apel, K., Wilson-Fowler, E.B., Brimo, D., & Perrin, N.A. (2012). Metalinguistic Contributions to reading and spelling in second and third grade students. *Reading and Writing, 25, 1283-1305.*

Apel, K, Henbest, V.S., & Petscher, Y.(2021). Morphological awareness performance profiles of first- through sixth- grade students. *Journal of Speech Language and Hearing, ASHA.*

Apel, K., Brimo, D., Diehm, E., & Apel, L. (2012). Morphological awareness intervention with kindergarteners and first- and second -grade students from low socioeconomic status homes: A feasibility study. *Language, speech, and Hearing Services in Schools, 44,* 161-173.

Apel, K. & Lawrence, J., (2011). Contributions of morphological awareness skills to word-level reading and spelling in first-grade children with and without speech sound disorder. *Journal of Speech, Language, and Hearing Research, 54*(5), 1312–1327.

Bowers, P.N., Kirby, J.R., & Deacon, S.H. (2010). The effects of morphological instruction on literacy skills: A synthesis of the literature. *Review of Educational Research, 80,* 144-179.

Breadmore, H.L., & Deacon, H (2019) Morphological processing before and during children's spelling *Scientific Studies Of Reading* V 23, No. 2, 178–191.

Ehri, L.C. & Snowling, M. (2004). Developmental variation in word recognition. In A.C. Stone, E.R. Silliman, B.J. Ehren, & K.Apel (Eds.) *Handbook of language and literacy: Development and disorders,* 443-460. New York: Guilford Press.

Foorman, B.R., Chen, D., Carlson, C., Moats, L.C., Francis, D.J., & Fletcher, J.M. (2003). The necessity of the alphabetic principle to phonemic awareness instruction, *Reading and Writing: An Interdisciplinary Journal, 16,* 289-324.

Goodwin, A.P., & Ahn, S. (2013). A meta-analysis of morphological interventions in English: Effects on literacy outcomes for school-age children. *Scientific Studies of Reading, 17(*4), 257-285.

Henry, M.K. (2010). Unlocking literacy: Effective decoding & spelling instruction, 2nd Ed. Baltimore, MD: Paul Brookes Publishing Co.

Hooper, S.R., Roberts, J.E., Nelson, L., Zeisel, S., & Kasambria Fannin, D. (2010). Preschool predictors of narrative writing skills in elementary school children. *School Psychology Quarterly, 25*(1), 1-12.

Hulme, C., Nash, H.M., Gooch, D., Lervåg, A., & Snowling, M.J. (2015). The foundations of literacy development in children at familial risk of dyslexia. *Psychological Science*, 26(12), 1877–1886.

International Dyslexia Association. (2018). *Knowledge and Practice Standards for Teachers of Reading.* https://dyslexiaida.org/knowledge-and-practices/

Kuo, L.J., & Anderson, R.C. (2006). Morphological awareness and learning to read: A cross-language perspective. *Educational Psychologist, 4*(3), 161-180.

Kirby, J. R., Deacon, S. H., Bowers, P. N., Izenberg, L., & Wade-Woolley, L., & Parrila. R., (2012). Children's morphological awareness and reading ability. *Reading Writing: An Interdisciplinary Journal*, 25, 389– 410.

Lervag, A., Hulme, C., & Melby-Lervag, M. (2018). Unpacking the developmental relationship between oral language skills and reading comprehension: It's simple, but complex. *Child Development.* 89(5):1821-1838.

Ludo Verhoeven & Charles Perfetti (2021): Universals in Learning to Read Across Languages and Writing Systems, *Scientific Studies of Reading*.

Mahony, D., Singson, M., &Mann, V. (2000). Reading ability and sensitivity to morphological relations. *Reading and Writing: An Interdisciplinary Journal*, 12, 191–218.

McCutchen, D., Green, L., & Abbott, R.D. (2008). Children's morphological knowledge: Links to literacy. *Reading Psychology, 29*(4), 289-314.

Nagy, W.E., Berninger, V.W., Abbot, R.D. (2006). Contributions of morphology beyond phonology to literacy outcomes of upper elementary and middle-school students. *Journal of Educational Psychology, 98,* 134-147.

Nation, K. (2009). Form–Meaning links in the development of visual word recognition. *Philosophical Transactions of the Royal Society B: Biological Sciences*, 364(1536), 3665–3674.

Perfetti, C. (2007). Reading ability: Lexical quality to comprehension. *Scientific Studies of Reading, 11*(4), 357–383.

Singson, M., Mahony, D., & Mann, V. (2000). The relation between reading ability and morphological skills: Evidence from derivational suffixes. *Reading and Writing: An Interdisciplinary Journal, 12,* 219-252.

Treiman, R. (2017). Learning to spell words: Findings, theories, and issues. *Scientific Studies of Reading, 21*(4), 265–276.

Washington, J. A. & Seidenberg, M. S. (2021). Teaching reading to African-American children: When home and school language differ. *American Educator*, Spring 2021.

Willingham, D. (2008). What will improve a student's memory? *American Educator*, Winter 2008-2009.

Wolter, J.A. & Green, L. (2013). Morphological awareness intervention in school-age children with language and literacy deficits: A case study. *Topics in Language Disorders*, 33, 27-42.

Wolter, J. A., Wood, A., & D'zatko, K. W. (2009). The influence of morphological awareness on the literacy development of first-grade children. *Language, Speech, Hearing Services in Schools*, 40, 286–298.

LEVEL 1 LESSONS
– The Magic of Language

WELCOME TO THE BEGINNING OF TEACHING MORPHOLOGICAL AWARENESS:

1) If desired, determine a morphological readiness for your students using the **Informal Criterion Assessment** found in the Appendix. Read about the Assessments in the Introduction prior to administering them.
2) If your students are not yet decoding, follow the directions in the lessons to engage students to explore and apply the morpheme and words within oral language exercises.
3) If students are just beginning to decode, choose words for decoding and encoding that reflect the phoneme – grapheme relationships they have learned. Return to more word examples as students acquire more decoding skills.

TIPS FOR TEACHING LEVEL 1 LESSONS

- Level 1 lessons can be taught during circle time. Your students' attention will be focused and they can be given lots of opportunities to apply orally the words you present.
- Pay attention to your read alouds for example words reflecting the morphemes you teach. Draw explicit attention to these words, draw students into discussions about the words and the "word parts that change meaning" (plurals, past tense, etc.)
- Begin writing the words and sentences as soon as your students have developed phoneme grapheme correspondence.

REMINDERS:

Use all language learning processes in your **Morphemes for Little Ones** lessons:

★ Model how the morphemes and words **sound** and how they are used.

★ Direct student to **say** the focus morphemes and words aloud.

★ Share **meanings** using student accessible definitions and examples.

★ Ask students to **read** the focus morphemes and words.

★ Provide opportunities for students to **practice** using the words they learn in meaningful sentences. It is best to apply the words to topics they are studying.

★ **Write!** Direct students to put into words what they are learning using the words in the lessons.

★ **Model** how to use words in sentences when students struggle to use the words correctly.

★ **Provide sentence frames** when students are not sure how to use a word.

Lesson Goal:

Create awareness that words have meaning. Some words have more than one meaningful part!

Word List

cupcake
a cake made in a cup.

backpack
a pack on your back

pinecone
a cone on a pine tree

bedtime
time to go to bed

housefly
a fly in your house

sunlight
light from the sun

lunchbox
a box for a lunch

pancake
a cake made in a pan, or flat like a pan.

brainstorm
a storm of thinking in your brain

INTRODUCTION

EXPLORE THE MORPHEME

Words have meaning. We use words to explain and tell about our needs and experiences. Each single word has meaning, but sometimes a word has more than one part that means something.

Say **cup**. Students say **cup**. "A cup is a small round container."

Say **cake**. Students say **cake**. "A cake is a dessert, usually with frosting. **Cup** and **Cake** are two separate words that each mean something."

"Let's put those two words – **cup** and **cake** – together to make one word." Hold your fists out in front of you. Nod your left fist and say "**cup**". Nod your right fist and say "**cake**". Put your fists together and say "**cupcake**! What's our new word?" Students say **cupcake**. Say, "A **cupcake** is a **cake** made in a **cup**. Two words go together to make one word!" Students hold their fists out with you and say, "**cup** has meaning, and **cake** has meaning, put the two together and we have one big word with two parts - **cupcake**!"

Tell students that they just learned what a **compound word** is! A **compound word** is two words put together to make one word.

ORAL LANGUAGE

Follow the same procedure as above with a couple more words in the **Word List**. Engage students to say each separate word, say what the word means, and then put them together to say one word. Students use their fists or linking cubes for the separate words, and then put the two words together and say the compound word.

Show a picture of one of the compound words. Ask students to say the compound word and use it in a sentence orally. Repeat with additional pictures.

ORTHOGRAPHY - READING AND SPELLING

Present this section as an Oral Exercise if students are not yet decoding.

Say **cupcake**. Students repeat. Write the word on the board. Scoop the two base words. Decode each and say **cupcake**. Students decode **cupcake**. Instruct students to write cup on a slip of paper and cake on a second. Repeat with a selection of words appropriate for the students' decoding levels. Working in pairs, students place their own sets of cards face side down, and take turns pulling up two cards, reading each. When a compound word can be created, the student writes the word in their Morpheme Grabber. Students may create their own compound words from the card combinations, but they have to say what their new word means!

ACTIVITIES

MORPHEME GRABBER - WORD EQUATION OR DRAW AND LABEL

Direct students to create a new page in their Morpheme Grabber.

WORD + WORD	= NEW WORD	PICTURE OR SENTENCE
cup + cake	cupcake	

Adjust the following exercises for your students' language and reading levels.

THE MORPHEME CARD

Display the Morpheme Card. Point to the first photo. Say the two words that make up the compound word. Ask students to say the words and combine them to say the compound word. Lead students to create sentences about the pictures using the target compound words, orally, and in writing if appropriate.

ORAL LANGUAGE

Play *Compound Word Riddle*. Provide a couple of examples for the students: "A pack you wear on your back. What am I?" (**backpack**) "Light that comes from the moon. What am I?" (**moonlight**). Display photos depicting compound words. Ask students to create the riddles for others to solve.

WRITE

Display compound words separated into two columns of words. Column one, first word in a compound word and in the second column, the second word of the compound word. Make sure that the words presented are spelled with graphemes the students have learned and can decode (short vowels, silent-e, consonant blends, digraphs, etc.). Ask students to find the matches, one word from each column, and write the compound words they create.

If students are just beginning to decode cvc words, explore compound words using oral language exercises.

cup | mark
pine | cake
book | cone

MORPHOLOGICAL PROBLEMS TO SOLVE - REVIEW AND PRACTICE

Post one of the compound words daily. Ask students to write the word in their Morpheme Grabber, circle each separate word. Ask students to be ready to share the words' meanings with the class or partner. Ask them to orally use the word in a sentence and then write the sentence.

cupcake
Compound Word

A cupcake is a cake made in a cup.
Your Turn: When would you eat a cupcake? Use the word cupcake.
© Morpheme Magic

Did You Know?

Some word combinations are hyphenated:

six-pack

runner-up

merry-go-round

short-term

full-scale

old-fashioned

More Words

boxcutter

fishhook

screwdriver

wristwatch

Questioning Minds

What does **hotdog** mean? A dog that is hot?

What does **catnip** mean? Nip for a cat?

What does **strawberry** mean? A berry that grows in straw?

Lesson Goal:

Plurals can be pronounced /s/ spelled -s.

Teachers Know:

If the base ends in an unvoiced phoneme, the plural will be pronounced /s/. If the base ends in the unvoiced /s/ or /sh/, the plural will be spelled es and pronounced /ez/.

Word Bank

pup - pups

kit - kits

lip – lips

jet - jets

cup – cups

dot – dots

net - nets

cat – cats

hat – hats

lock – locks

rock – rocks

sack – sacks

cake – cakes

note – notes

mitt – mitts

ship - ships

truck - trucks

INTRODUCTION

DAY ONE: EXPLORE THE MORPHEME

Explain to students that words can change when we speak. Say, "If I am talking about a **pup** (show picture of **pup**) I say **pup**. But if I am talking about more than one **pup** (show picture of **pups** playing) I say **pups**.

1) Show picture of single pup. Say "**pup**". Students say **pup**.
2) Show picture of the group of **pups**. Say "**pups**". Students say "**pups**".
3) Show picture of the single **pup**. Say a sentence, "This **pup** likes to play with his tail." Elicit sentences from the students using singular **pup**.
4) Show the picture of the group of **pups**. Say a sentence, "These **pups** enjoy playing with each other." Elicit sentences from the students using plural **pups**.

EXPLORE THE PHONEMES

Count the phonemes in **pup**. Let's figure out how the word **pup** changed! Show the picture of **pup**. Students say **pup**. Direct students to say and show with their fingers the phonemes in **pup** - /p/u/p/. Lead students to say there are three sounds in **pup**.

Count the phonemes in **pups**. Show the picture of **pups**. Direct students to say and show with their fingers the phonemes in **pups**. /p/u/p/s/.

Count the phonemes in each - **pup** and **pups** again.

Discuss how **pup** changed. Discuss the differences. Point out the word **pups** has /s/ at the end that helps us know we are talking about more than one **pup**.

Review: Ask students to turn to a partner and explain how the word **pup** changes when we are talking about more than one **pup**, *pups*.

ORTHOGRAPHY - READING AND SPELLING

Move to Oral Language Exercises if students are not yet decoding.

DECODE: Write **pup**. Students decode and read it. Explain that **pup is one**. Use the term **singular** if your students are ready.
Write **pups**. Students decode and read it. Explain that **pups is more than one (use the term plural if your students are ready). Circle pup and circle -s.**

Do the same with other words in the **Word List** or use your program's words.

ENCODE: Dictate singular and plural words for students to spell. Use response boards and ask students to show their spellings after seach word. Provide corrective feedback if needed, i.e., model the correct spelling and ask students to correct theirs.

ACTIVITIES

pups
Plural s /s/

Several pups were waiting for their dinner. Your Turn: Compose a sentence about these pups. Use the word pups.

© Morpheme Magic

MORPHEME GRABBER - WORD EQUATION OR DRAW AND LABEL

Direct students to create a new page in their Morpheme Grabber. Display the Lesson Morpheme Card and ask students to create their Morpheme Equation. Provide a sample if needed. Alternatively, younger students can draw a picture and label it with the plural form.

WORD + s	NEW WORD	PICTURE OR SENTENCE
pup + s	pups	

Adjust the following exercises for your students' language and reading levels.

THE MORPHEME CARD

Display the Morpheme Card. Instruct students to say the singular and plural forms for each picture, explore the phonemes, and use the words in sentences to tell about the picture. REVIEW: Level Two - say and write the words. Level Three - say and write the words and a sentence for each.

ORAL LANGUAGE AND WRITE

1. Teacher says a singular or plural /s/ word. Students say the word, say the phonemes, thumbs up if the word is plural, thumbs down if it is not plural. Write the words.

2. Display two plural words. Ask students to read the words, compose a sentence orally using both words, and write their sentence. EXAMPLE: **chips**, **sacks**. We will need five **sacks** of potato **chips** for the picnic.

CONNECT TO THE CLASSROOM

Ask students to look around the classroom. Is there one **light** (students say the phonemes with you, /l/igh/t/) or many **lights**, /l/igh/t/s/a/? Count the **lights** and fill in the sentence frame: There are _____ **lights** in our classroom. Do the same with **book** and **books**, and **desk** and **desks**. State that words change when we are talking about one or more of something. Lead students to say how words change. "There is a /s/ on the ends of the words that talk about more than one."

REVIEW AND PRACTICE

Non-reader and Reader: Engage students in dialogue about a picture displaying the plural forms for objects in the Word Bank. Be explicit about the plural forms.

Reader: Display one plural word each day you are on this lesson. Model how to read the word, circle the base, and then underline the plural suffix /s/. Use words from the word lists or from your reading program.

Did You Know?

Some plurals are noncountable plurals: **rice**, **corn**, **deer**, **sand**, and **elk** are examples of some of the noncountable nouns. The plural form is the same as the singular. Can you think of others?

More Word Bank Words

chip – chips

lamp – lamps

boat – boats

step – steps

shape - shapes

goat – goats

flight – flights

light - lights

wrist – wrists

wart – warts

Lesson Goal:

Lesson Goal: Plurals can be pronounced /z/ spelled -s.

Teachers Know:

If the base ends in a voiced phoneme, the plural will be pronounced /z/. If the base ends in the voiced /z/ such as *rose*, the plural will add another syllable, /ez/. This will be introduced in Lesson 4.

Word Bank

pig – pigs

pan – pans

tag – tags

pad - pads

peg – pegs

bib – bibs

cob – cobs

drum – drums

shed – sheds

bun – buns

lid – lids

train - trains

jar – jars

INTRODUCTION

DAY ONE: EXPLORE THE MORPHEME

Remind students that they just learned that words change when we talk about more than one – /p/u/p/ pup changes to /p/u/p/s/ pups. The ending sound on the words we explored was /s/. Today our words will end with a different sound.

1) Show picture of single *pig*. Say "*pig*". Students say "*pig*".
2) Show picture of the group of *pigs*. Say "*pigs*". Students say "*pigs*".
3) Show picture of the single *pig*. Say a sentence, "A *pig* has a funny nose." Elicit sentences from the students using singular *pig*.
4) Show the picture of the *pigs*. Say a sentence, "These *pigs* are very cute." Elicit sentences from the students using plural *pigs*.

EXPLORE THE PHONEMES *(Locate photos of a pig and pigs to use.)*

Count the phonemes in **pig**. "Let's figure out how the word **pig** changed!" Show the picture of **pig**. Students say **pig**. Direct students to say and show with their fingers the phonemes in **pig** - /p/i/g/. There are three sounds in **pig**.

Count the phonemes in **pigs**. Show the picture of **pigs**. Direct students to say and show with their fingers the phonemes in **pigs**. /p/i/g/z/.

Count the phonemes in each - **pig** and **pigs** again.

Discuss how **pig** changed. Point out that **pigs** has /z/ at the end that helps us know we are talking about more than one **pig**. Last time, pups had /s/ at the end.

Review: Ask students to turn to a partner and explain how the word **pig** changes when we are talking about more than one **pig**; *Pigs has a /z/ sound at the end*.

ORTHOGRAPHY - READING AND SPELLING

Move to Oral Language Exercises if students are not yet decoding words.

DECODE: Explore the orthography of singular and plural nouns with /z/.

Write **pig**. Students decode and read it. Explain that **pig tells us there is one (use the term singular if your students are ready)**.

Write **pigs.** Students decode and read it. Explain that **pigs is more than one and the S makes the /z/ sound (use the term plural if your students are ready)**. Circle **pig** and underline -s, say /z/**. We hear /z/ but we spell it S because there is more than one.**

Do the same with other words in the Word List or words from your current reading lesson. Make sure the words you choose end with a voiced phoneme and reflect the /z/ sound for the plural spelling.

ENCODE:

Dictate singular and plural words for students to write. Use response boards and ask students to share their spellings after each word. Emphasize the plural spelling is S and sometimes it sounds like /z/.

ACTIVITIES

MORPHEME GRABBER - WORD EQUATION OR DRAW AND LABEL

Direct students to create a new page in their Morpheme Grabber.

WORD + s	NEW WORD	PICTURE OR SENTENCE
COW + S	COWS	

Adjust the following exercises for your students' language and reading levels.

THE MORPHEME CARD

Display the Morpheme Card. Instruct students to say the singular and plural forms for each picture, explore the phonemes, and use the words in sentences to tell about the picture. REVIEW: Level Two - say and write the words. Level Three - say and write the words and a sentence for each.

ORAL LANGUAGE AND WRITE

1) Teacher says a singular or plural /z/ word. Students say the word, say the phonemes, thumbs up if the word is plural, thumbs down if it is not plural.
2) Students orally share their answers to the Morpheme Card questions then write them in their Morpheme Grabber. Ask students to highlight the plural words they write.

CONNECT TO THE CLASSROOM

Ask students to look around the classroom. Is there one **wall** (students say the phonemes with you, /w/a/ll/) or many **walls**, /w/a/ll/z/? Count the **walls** and fill in the sentence frame: There are ____ **walls** in our classroom. Do the same with **pen** and **pens**, and **window** and **windows**. State that words change when we are talking about one or more of something. Lead students to say how words change. "/z/ is on the ends of these words that talk about more than one, spelled S." Optional: Students write the sentences

REVIEW AND PRACTICE

Non-reader and Reader: Engage students in dialogue about a picture displaying the plural forms for objects in the Word Bank and words from Lesson 2. Ask students to identify /s/ or /z/ in their words.

Level One reader: Post one of the following plural words each day you are on this lesson. Model how to read the word, circle the base, and then underline the plural suffix /z/: tags, fans, bags, buns, beds. Direct students to record their work in their Morpheme Grabber.

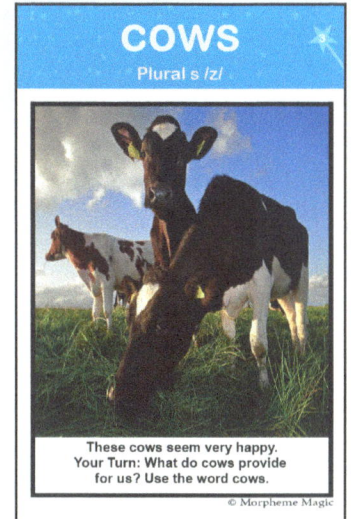

COWS
Plural s /z/

These cows seem very happy.
Your Turn: What do cows provide
for us? Use the word cows.

© Morpheme Magic

Did You Know?

Morphological awareness includes being aware of the phonemes in words. The phonemes provide initial access to meaning.

More Word Bank Words

rags

cans

pills

sheds

trees

names

dimes

homes

roads

shells

beads

holes

germs

trains

thumbs

gyms

Lesson Goal:

Some plurals are spelled -es and pronounced /z/ as in flies, or /ez/ as in wishes.

Teachers know:

When a base ends in /s/, /z/, /j/, /sh/, /zh/, /ch/, the plural will be spelled -es and pronounced /ez/. If the base ends in consonant -y, y changes to i and -es is added. This is taught in Level 2.

Word Bank

bus
buses

wish
wishes

dress
dresses

batch
batches

ditch
ditches

match
matches

INTRODUCTION

DAY ONE: EXPLORE THE MORPHEME

Remind students that they just learned that words change when we talk about more than one – /p/u/p/ pup changes to /p/u/p/s/ pups and /p/i/g/ pig changes to /p/i/g/z/ pigs! Today let's explore other words that say more than one.

1) Show picture of a **bus**. Say "**bus**". Students say "**bus**".
2) Show picture of buses. Say "**buses**" as you clap the syllables. Students say "**buses**" and clap the syllables. Tell them that the words they work with today will say /ez/ and might add a syllable to the word: "**buses**"
3) Show picture of the single **bus**. Say a sentence, "A **bus** can take you home." Elicit sentences from the students using singular **bus**.
4) Show the picture of the **buses**. Say a sentence, "These **buses** are full of people." Elicit sentences from the students using plural **buses**.
5) Do the same with **dress/dresses**, **wish/wishes**, and **finch/finches (a type of little bird)**.

EXPLORE THE PHONEMES

Listen for /ez/ at the ends of some more words. Choose words from the Word Bank or from your program that apply the -es plural spelling pronounced /ez/. Say the word, students say the word and segment the phonemes.

ORTHOGRAPHY - READING AND SPELLING

Move to Oral Language Exercises if students are not yet decoding words.

DECODE: Explore the orthography of singular and plural nouns with /ez/.

Write **bus**. Students decode and read it. Explain that **bus tells us there is one (use the term singular if your students are ready)**.

Write **buses**. Students decode and read it. Explain that **buses is more than one and the -es says the /ez/ sound(s)** (use the term plural if your students are ready). Circle **bus** and underline -es, say /ez/. **We hear /ez/ but we spell it -es because there is more than one.**

Do the same with other words in the Word Bank or words from your current reading lesson. Make sure the words you choose end with one of the phonemes listed under Teachers Know.

ENCODE:

Dictate singular and plural words for students to write. Use response boards and ask students to share their spellings after each word. Emphasize the plural spelling is -es and sounds like /ez/.

ACTIVITIES

MORPHEME GRABBER - WORD EQUATION OR DRAW AND LABEL

Direct students to create a new page in their Morpheme Grabber.

WORD + -es	= NEW WORD	PICTURE OR SENTENCE
dish + es	dishes	

Adjust the following exercises for your students' language and reading levels.

THE MORPHEME CARD

Display the Morpheme Card. Instruct students to say the singular and plural forms for each picture, explore the phonemes, and use the words in sentences to tell about the picture. REVIEW: Level Two - say and write the words. Level Three - say and write the words and a sentence for each.

ORAL LANGUAGE AND WRITE

Say the target plural word in parentheses below – students say the word. Read the sentence and pause for students to say the target plural word in the sentence. If writing, direct students to write the target plural words before reading the story to them. (**Words**: flies, buses, wishes, dresses)

Marissa and her brother James were waiting for the bus to take them to their gramma's home. It was hot outside and a finch kept landing on James' head. And another finch kept landing on Marissa's shoulder.

("finches") Marissa noticed that many ____ were flying around. Maybe they were waiting for the bus too!

("buses") Many ____ went by, but none of them were the right bus to take the children to gramma's house. James made a wish, "I wish that the right bus would come soon!"

("wishes") Marissa replied, "While we wait, we can make more ____, ok? One of my ____ is that I get a new t-shirt."

("dresses") "My dress is too small so I also wish for three new ____."

("wishes") James thought about his ____ and said, "I have two ____"

("buses") "I wish that all the ____ would go to gramma's."

("finches") "I also wish that these ____ would stop bugging me! They are annoying!"

REVIEW AND PRACTICE

Non-reader and Reader: Engage students in dialogue about a picture displaying the plural forms for words in the Word Bank. Draw attention to the phonemes.

Reader: Display one written plural word each day you are on this lesson. Model how to read the word, circle the base, and then underline the plural suffix -es. Use words from the Word Banks or from your reading program.

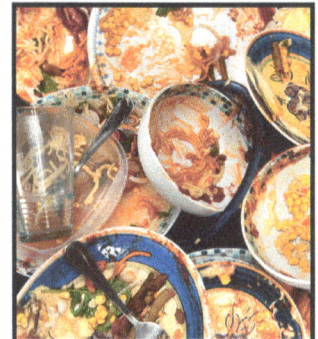

dishes
Plural -es /ez/

Be careful not to break the dishes when you wash them. Your Turn: What do we use dishes for? Use the word dishes.

© Morpheme Magic

More Word Bank Words

bench
benches

flash
flashes

branch
branches

house
houses

circus
circuses

cactus
cactuses

NOTE: Level 1 will create plurals with bases that do not require a spelling change. Level 2 will learn change Y to i and add -es.

Lesson Goal:

Students will review plurals – phonemes and spelling.

Teachers know:

Building word sense for reading and spelling begins with awareness of oral language: word meanings, phonemes, syntax. It takes a lot of review over time to build morphological awareness.

Word Bank

/s/

dots

ships

stacks

flocks

shops

drops (of rain)

stumps

lumps

rafts

husks

/z/

jobs

screws

ponds

grins

clods

webs

INTRODUCTION

DAY ONE: EXPLORE THE MORPHEME

This lesson focuses on the three previous plurals lessons for cumulative review. Remind Students: We learned about how words change when we are talking about more than one. The words we use help others know if we are talking about one or more than one.

We also learned that there are three different sounds we hear at the ends of these plural words.

EXPLORE THE PHONEMES

Use the Morpheme Cards from Lessons 2-4 and this Lesson 5 to initiate review. Say one of the plurals as students look at the card. Ask students to say the word, segment the phonemes, and say the ending plural sound: /s/ /z/ or /ez/. Say the singular and then the plural. Compare and contrast the two being explicit about the plural and word meaning - more than one.

ORTHOGRAPHY - READING AND SPELLING

Move to Oral Language Exercises if students are not yet decoding words.

DECODE: Review the orthography of plural suffixes. Write **pet**. Decode with students. "Listen. The children brought their **pets** to school. What did the children bring?" When they say "**pets**" ask, "What do I need to do to make **pet** say **pets**?" Add the **S** and ask children to read the word.

Do the same with other words in the Word Bank or words from your current reading lesson. Choose words that are decodable for your students.

ENCODE: Dictate plural words for students to write providing a quick simple sentence for context. Choose words that spell the plural with -s and -es. Use response boards and ask students to share their spellings after each word. Provide corrective feedback: model correct spelling and ask students to make corrections.

If Levels 2 and 3 students are reviewing plurals, use these word items for oral and written exercises.

/s/		/z/		/ez/	
hips	pits	hams	beds	lunches	branches
naps	mops	lids	tubs	inches	matches
sacks	blimps	crabs	drums	crutches	bridges
cakes	ropes	brims	cribs	benches	notches
dates	milk-shakes	drills	lambs	wishes	ditches

ACTIVITIES

MORPHEME GRABBER - WORD EQUATION OR DRAW AND LABEL

Direct students to create a new page in their Morpheme Grabber.

WORD + PLURAL MORPHEME	= NEW WORD	PICTURE OR SENTENCE
Select words from the Word Bank that reflect the three plural sounds		

Adjust the following exercises for your students' language and reading levels.

THE MORPHEME CARD

Display the Morpheme Cards. Instruct students to say the plural for each picture, explore the phonemes, and use the words in sentences to tell about the picture. REVIEW: Level Two - say and write the words. Level Three - say and write the words and a sentence for each.

ORAL LANGUAGE AND WRITE

Silly Sentences: Provide the prompts below. Students think of a word and respond orally with their plural word. Say the sentence frame and ask students to take turns repeating the sentence with their word to make a Silly Sentence.

1) Something you see on the streets. (cars, trucks, buses, cleaners, taxis)
   My pet loves to eat _____.
2) Something to eat (plural). (pizzas, apples, potatoes, nuts, salads)
   When I opened my desk in the morning I found _____.
3) Something you wear. (pants, shirts, shoes, socks, coats)
   Mother asked me to set the table for dinner with _____.
4) Something I see on the way to school. (birds, cars, buses, friends, parents)
   There are many _____ growing on the trees at my house.

Have fun making up other plural requests and silly sentences. If students are ready, ask them to create and **write** a silly sentence and ask classmates for plurals to complete them. Ask students to read their sentences to the class.

CONNECT TO THE CLASSROOM

Ask students to find items in the classroom and say the plural form, and then use the word in a sentence of 7 or more words – "Give me 7!" Ask the rest of the class to say the plural word and the phoneme they hear at the end.

REVIEW AND PRACTICE

Non-reader and Reader: Engage students in dialogue about a story you are reading. Use a picture from the story; ask students to use plurals in their responses.

Reader: Display one plural word each day you are reviewing. Model how to read the word, circle the base, and then underline the plural suffix -s or -es. Use words from the Word Banks or from your reading program.

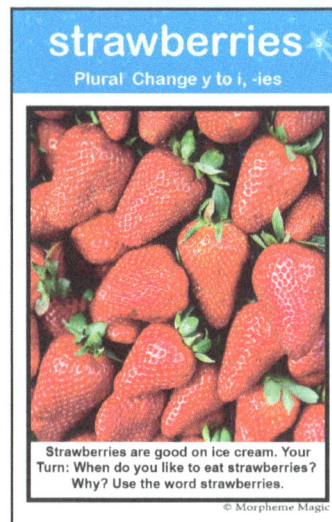

strawberries
Plural: Change y to i, -ies

Strawberries are good on ice cream. Your Turn: When do you like to eat strawberries? Why? Use the word strawberries.

© Morpheme Magic

More Word Bank Words

Multi-Syllable:

blankets

statues

tissues

uncles

movies

Legos

handles

giggles

ruffles

apples

axes

duplexes

relishes

secrets

robots

53

Lesson Goal:

Past tense is spelled -ed and in this lesson, we say /ed/ adding another syllable.

Teachers know:

When the verb base ends in /t/ or /d/, the past tense -ed says /ed/.

Word Bank

lifted

acted

blasted

drifted

trusted

twisted

floated

dented

gusted

added

folded

counted

Double It Spelling

jotted

patted

potted

dotted

budded

skidded

plodded

INTRODUCTION

DAY ONE: EXPLORE THE MORPHEME

Introduce the concept of action verbs to students. Tell them that they will be learning about how verbs change when we are talking about an action that happened before right now.

"Say **nod**." Students clap as they say **nod."** "**Nod** your head if you can see me."

"You just **nodded** your heads! Say **nodded** (clap the two syllables)." Students say **nodded** and clap the syllables. Say and clap the syllables **nod** and **nodded**. "How did **nod** change when we talked about what you had already done?" Clap the two parts again: **nod-ed**. The verbs we will work with today will change and say /ed/at the end when we are talking about action that we are finished doing. You **nodded** your heads a few minutes ago.

EXPLORE THE PHONEMES

The ending we say for this lesson's past tense verbs is /ed/. Both the /e/ and /d/ are voiced adding an additional syllable because the vowel e is voiced. Choose words from the Word Bank that match your students' phoneme segmentation levels (beginning and ending blends are harder to segment). Say the word, use it in a brief sentence, say the word again. Ask students to say the word and segment the phonemes. Emphasize the /e/d/ on the ends. NOTE: CVC words will double the final consonant when spelling the words. The doubled consonant is not voiced, i.e., **jotted** = /j/o/t/e/d/. She **jotted** a note to her teacher.

ORTHOGRAPHY - READING AND SPELLING

Move to Oral Language Exercises if students are not yet decoding words.

Teach the **Double It** rule prior to this part. See the **Spelling with Suffixes** section in the Introduction.

DECODE: Write **nodded** on the board. "When I read this word, my eyes see the verb **nod. Nod** if you see it too**."** Circle **nod** and decode it. "I also see the new word part /ed/ that is spelled -ed". Say the base **nod** and ending -**ed**. "**Nodded.** We doubled the final consonant to protect that short vowel before adding -ed."

Follow the same process with other words to help students see and say the word parts with /ed/. Make sure the words you choose end with a /t/ or /d/ and will form a regular past tense verb, i.e. **sit** is not **sitted**, but becomes **sat**. Review the Double it Rule process for each word.

ENCODE: Dictate the words you used in the decoding section for students to write. "Say **pot**. I will **pot** my plants. What is the past tense of **pot**?" "**Potted**." Spell **potted**." Use response boards and ask students to share their spellings after each word. Provide corrective feedback. Emphasize that the verbs we work with in this lesson are spelled -ed and we say /ed/.

ACTIVITIES

MORPHEME GRABBER - WORD EQUATION OR DRAW AND LABEL

Direct students to create a new page in their Morpheme Grabber.

WORD + -ed	= NEW WORD	PICTURE OR SENTENCE
lift + ed	lifted	
nod + ed	nodded	

Adjust the following exercises for your students' language and reading levels.

THE MORPHEME CARD

Display the Morpheme Card. Instruct students to say the past tense word for each picture. Segment the phonemes. Use the words in sentences to tell about the picture. REVIEW: Teach **Double It Rule** if needed. Level Two - say and write the words. Level Three - say and write the words and a sentence for each.

ORAL LANGUAGE AND WRITE

After students finish the Connect to the Classroom activity below, review orally the -ed verbs and spell them if appropriate.

CONNECT TO THE CLASSROOM

Past Tense Art Project: Give every student a piece of paper. Ask them to **lift** the paper up, and **fold** it in half and then to **fold** it in half again. Direct them to think of someone they can send a Thank You Note to. Brainstorm with them to **provide** ideas: teacher, parent, playground person, friend, etc. Ask them to tell a friend what they will write, then to **jot** it in the note. **Decorate** the front, and **jot** the note inside. When students are done, review the project using the verbs: "We **lifted** the paper and **folded** it. Our friends **provided** ideas for us. We **jotted** our note and **decorated** it! We are finished and can now deliver it."

REVIEW AND PRACTICE

Non-reader and Reader: Use words from the Word Bank. Say the present tense for a word, and ask students to say the past tense. Direct students to use the past tense words in sentences. Provide assistance if needed. Ask, "How did the word change to show we already did it?" Draw attention to the phonemes they hear in the words.

Reader: Display one past tense word from this lesson each day you are on this lesson. Model how to read the word, circle the base, and then underline the plural suffix -ed. Use words from the Word Banks or from your reading program.

jotted
Past Tense -ed /ed/

I jotted a thank you note to my friend. Your Turn: If you jotted a note, who would you send it to? Use the word jotted.
© Morpheme Magic

NOTE: Irregular past tense verbs are addressed in Level 3.

More Word Bank Words

twisted

scripted

granted

cheated

grafted

painted

invented

suggested

corrected

directed

interacted

Double It!

Instructions for teaching the Double It suffix rule are in the **Spelling with Suffixes** section following the Introduction.

Lesson Goal:

Past tense is spelled -ed and in this lesson, we say /d/.

Teachers know:

When the verb base ends in a voiced consonant the past tense -ed says /d/.

Word Bank

fanned
pinned
wagged
bagged
chugged
drummed
slugged
lugged
hummed
clubbed
dimmed
dragged
whammed
grinned
bobbed
lobbed
grabbed
drilled
hailed
chained
stained
claimed
sprained
played
stayed
prayed

INTRODUCTION

DAY ONE: EXPLORE THE MORPHEME

Remind students about action verbs. Today they will learn another way action verbs change when we talk about an action that is over and done.

"Say **fan**." Students clap as they say **fan.**" "**Fan** your face with your hand."

"You just **fanned** your faces! Say **fanned** (clap one syllable)." Students say **fanned** and clap one syllable. Say and clap the syllables **fan** and **fanned**. "How did **fan** change when we talked about what you had already done?" Clap the one part **fanned**. "We changed the word **fan** to **fanned** and still had one syllable."

EXPLORE THE PHONEMES

"Say **fanned**." Students say **fanned**. "Say the sounds in **fanned**: /f/a/n/d/. How did our action word **fan** change when we said **fanned**?" Say **fan**, then **fanned**. Work with students to discover how **fanned** is different from **fan**. "**Fanned** has a /d/ at the end which makes a new word. The verbs we will work with today will change and say /d/at the end when we are talking about action that we are finished doing. You **fanned** your faces a few minutes ago."

Repeat with a few more words from the Word Bank.

ORTHOGRAPHY - READING AND SPELLING

Move to Oral Language Exercises if students are not yet decoding words.

DECODE:
Teach the **Double It** rule prior to this part. See the **Spelling with Suffixes** section.

Write **fanned** on the board. "When I read this word, my eyes see the verb **fan**. **Fan** your face if you see it too.**"** Circle **fan** and decode it. "I also see the new word part that is spelled -ed just like the last words we worked with." Say the base **fan** and ending /d/. **Fanned.** "We doubled the final consonant to protect that short vowel before adding -ed. Even though we see -ed, we know the sound is /d/.

Follow the same process with other words in the Word Bank, or from your reading or spelling program, to help students see and say the base word and the part spelled -ed, sound /d/.

Review the Double it Rule process for each word.

ENCODE:
Dictate plural -ed, /d/ words for students to spell. Use response boards and ask students to share their spellings after each word. Emphasize: "We may only hear /d/ at the end when we say these words, but we know we will spell /d/ -ed because it changes the meaning of the verb to past tense!" Provide scaffolding for doubling the final consonant before adding -ed.

ACTIVITIES

MORPHEME GRABBER - WORD EQUATION OR DRAW AND LABEL

Direct students to create a new page in their Morpheme Grabber.

WORD + -ed	= NEW WORD	PICTURE OR SENTENCE
fan + ed	fanned	
play + ed	played	

Adjust the following exercises for your students' language and reading levels.

THE MORPHEME CARD

Display the Morpheme Card. Instruct students to say the past tense word for each picture, explore the phonemes with emphasis on the final phoneme. Use the words in sentences to tell about the picture. REVIEW: Teach **Double It Rule** if needed. Level Two - say and write the words. Level Three - say and write the words and a sentence for each.

ORAL LANGUAGE AND WRITE

Choose words from the Word Bank that your students will be able to connect to something the class is learning about or reading. Say a word. Ask students to use the word to share something they remember or recall from your study. This activity works well with fiction where students can use verbs to describe characters' actions.

Writing: Adapt the oral language activity. Ask students to say their sentences and then to write the sentences using the -ed verbs that say /d/. This is a good comprehension activity that engages students through language about what they have read or learned.

CONNECT TO THE CLASSROOM

Academic Language: Ask students to "survey" the room for items they might not have noticed before. "Survey means look around closely." Provide time for students to share what they saw. Tell the class that they just **surveyed** the room ask them to say **surveyed.** "I asked you to **survey** the room and you **surveyed** it!

REVIEW AND PRACTICE

Non-reader and Reader: Engage students in dialogue about a picture displaying past tense /d/. Draw attention to the phoneme for -ed, /d/.

Reader: Display one -ed, /d/ word each day you are on this lesson. Model how to read the word, circle the base, and then underline the plural suffix -ed. Use verbs from the Word Banks or from your reading program that end with a voiced consonant (except /d/).

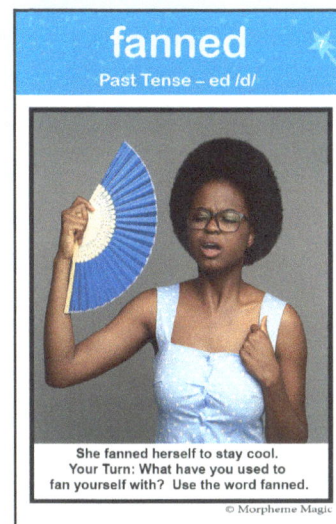

fanned
Past Tense – ed /d/

She fanned herself to stay cool.
Your Turn: What have you used to
fan yourself with? Use the word fanned.

© Morpheme Magic

More Word Bank Words

pledged

conveyed

displayed

obeyed

surveyed

employed

Lesson Goal:

Past tense is spelled -ed and in this lesson, we say /t/.

Teachers know:

When the verb base ends in an unvoiced consonant (except /t/) the past tense -ed says /t/.

Word Bank

zipped

mixed

fixed

zapped

mopped

lugged

clapped

dimmed

tossed

jumped

skipped

limped

flapped

dripped

High Frequency Words

looked

laughed

talked

walked

INTRODUCTION

DAY ONE: EXPLORE THE MORPHEME

Remind students about action verbs. Today they will learn another way action verbs change when we talk about an action that is over and done.

"Say **zip**." Students clap as they say **zip." "Zip** up your jacket."

"You just **zipped** up your jacket! Say **zipped** (clap one syllable)." Students say **zipped** and clap one syllable. Say and clap the syllables **zip** and **zipped**. "How did **zip** change when we talked about what you had already done?" Clap the one part **zipped**. "We changed the word **zip** to **zipped** and still had one syllable."

EXPLORE THE PHONEMES

"Say **zipped**." Students say **zipped**. "Say the sounds in **zipped**: /z/i/p/t/. How did our action word **zip** change when we said **zipped**?" Say **zip**, then **zipped**. Work with students to discover how **zipped** is different from **zip**. "**Zipped** has a /t/ at the end which makes a new word. The verbs - doing words - we will work with today will change and say /t/ at the end when we are talking about action that we are finished doing. "You pretend **zipped** your jackets up."

Repeat with a few more words from the Word Bank. Ask students to note how the verb changes when we talk about something that is done and over.

ORTHOGRAPHY - READING AND SPELLING

Move to Oral Language Exercises if students are not yet decoding words.

DECODE:

Teach the **Double It** rule prior to this part. See the **Spelling with Suffixes** section.

Write **zipped** on the board. "When I read this word, my eyes see the verb **zip**. **Zip** up your jacket**."** Circle **zip** and decode it. "I also see the new word part that is spelled -ed just like the last words we worked with." Say the base **zip** and ending /t/. **Zipped.** "We doubled the final consonant to protect that short vowel before adding -ed. Even though we see -ed, we know the sound is /t/."

Follow the same process with other words in the Word Bank, or from your reading or spelling program, to help students see and say the base word and the part spelled -ed, sound /t/. Review the Double it Rule process for each word.

ENCODE:

Dictate the plural -ed, /t/ words used in the decoding section for students to spell. Use response boards and ask students to share their spellings after each word. Emphasize: "We hear /t/ at the end when we say these words, but we know we will spell /t/ -ed because -ed changes the meaning of the verb to past tense!" Provide scaffolding for doubling the final consonant before adding -ed.

ACTIVITIES

MORPHEME GRABBER - WORD EQUATION OR DRAW AND LABEL

Direct students to create a new page in their Morpheme Grabber.

WORD + -ed	= NEW WORD	PICTURE OR SENTENCE
zip + ed	zipped	

Adjust the following exercises for your students' language and reading levels.

THE MORPHEME CARD

Display the Morpheme Card. Instruct students to say the past tense word for each picture, explore the phonemes with emphasis on the final phoneme, /t/. Use the words in sentences to tell about the pictures. REVIEW: Teach **Double It Rule** if needed. Level Two - say and write the words. Level Three - say and write the words and a sentence for each.

ORAL LANGUAGE AND WRITE

Create a set of present tense verb cards from the Word Bank or your reading program words (zip, fix, limp, etc.).

1) **Oral language activity**: A student is chosen, pulls a card, and the teacher reads it into the student's ear, "**Zip**". The student acts out the word. When done, the group guesses the word and says the word past tense in a sentence. "Derrick **zipped** up his coat." All students say the past tense verb and segment the phonemes. "How did **zip** change? Why did **zip** change to **zipped**?"

2) **Writing activity**: Students take turns choosing a verb card. After reading the card, the student acts out the verb. The other students guess the verb and write it past tense on their response boards. One student tells what the student acted out in a sentence, same as above. Students may also be asked to write the sentence.

REVIEW AND PRACTICE

Non-reader and Reader: Dictate a word from the Word Bank and use it in a sentence. Ask students to say the word and then segment the phonemes into sound boxes with sound markers. Readers: Spell each phoneme (double it letters in one box, /t/ is spelled ed in one box).

Reader: Display one -ed, /t/ word each day you are on this lesson. Model how to read the word, circle the base, and then underline the plural suffix -ed. Use verbs from the Word Banks or from your reading program that end with an unvoiced consonant (except /t/).

zipped
Past Tense -ed /t/

He zipped up his coat.
Your Turn: Tell about when you zipped up something. Use the word zipped.
© Morpheme Magic

More Word Bank Words

forced

hoped

shaped

dropped

tipped

camped

helped

splashed

thanked

patched

hatched

clasped

tramped

flashed

stacked

stamped

blessed

worshiped

whispered

gossiped

Lesson Goal:

Students will review **past tense phonemes and spelling.**

Teachers know:

It is important to know students' word recognition phases to plan appropriate instruction. See Introduction for more information.

Word Bank

Short Vowel:

skip – skipped

pin – pinned

dent - dented

clap – clapped

chug – chugged

chant – chanted

wink - winked

beg – begged

mend – mended

bump – bumped

fill – filled

nod – nodded

wash – washed

> **TIP:** Teachers may use the term "verb" and or "doing word"or "action word" when working with past tense.

INTRODUCTION

DAY ONE: EXPLORE THE MORPHEME

This lesson focuses on the three previous past tense lessons for cumulative review. Remind Students: We learned about how words change when we are talking about something that is done and over. The words we use help others know if we are talking about action that happened before now.

We also learned that there are three different sounds we hear at the ends of these past tense words.

EXPLORE THE PHONEMES

Use the Morpheme Cards to initiate the review. Say one of the past tense verbs as students look at a card, or ask students to recall the verbs for the pictures. Ask students to say the word, segment the phonemes, and say the ending past tense sound: /ed/ /d/ or /t/. Use the words in sentences.

Continue this exercise with words from the Word Bank or words from your reading program.

ORTHOGRAPHY - READING AND SPELLING

Move to Oral Language Exercises if students are not yet decoding words.

DECODE:

Display present tense verbs. Work with students to decode them one by one. After reading a word, change the word to past tense. Decode again. Determine the sound of /ed/. Review doubling rule if needed.

ENCODE:

Ask students to fold a paper in half lengthwise. Label the two columns: **Verb** and **Past Tense.** Dictate the words students read in the DECODE section, direct them to spell the word in the Verb column and then spell the past tense form in the Past Tense column.

Review the **Double It!** rule with appropriate word items. Introduce the **Drop It!** rule for cvc-e words if students have not yet learned it (hope = hoped).

Do the same with other words in the Word Bank or words from your current reading lesson. See the **Spelling with Suffixes** section at the end of the Introduction if needed.

/ED/		/D/		/T/	
heated	planted	<u>pinned</u>	stayed	<u>skipped</u>	soaked
shouted	squirted	<u>chugged</u>	joined	<u>clapped</u>	marched
tasted	melted	snowed	sailed	<u>hoped</u>	squeaked
twisted	lifted	bloomed	smelled	<u>liked</u>	clanked
hunted	acted	scrubbed	planned	hooked	reached

ACTIVITIES

MORPHEME GRABBER - WORD EQUATION OR DRAW AND LABEL

Direct students to create a new page in their Morpheme Grabber.

WORD + -ed	= NEW WORD	PICTURE OR SENTENCE
Select words from the Word Bank that reflect the three sounds of -ed		

Adjust the following exercises for your students' language and reading levels.

THE MORPHEME CARD

Display the Morpheme Cards for Lessons 6-8 and 9. Instruct students to say the past tense for each picture, segment and explore the phonemes, use the verbs in sentences to tell about the picture. REVIEW: Review Suffix Spelling rules as needed. Level Two - say and write the words. Level Three - say and write the words and a sentence for each.

ORAL LANGUAGE AND WRITE - ACTION WITH JACKSON

Introduce students to Jackson: Jackson is a puppy with a lot of energy. You know what that means? We can use verbs to describe his various activities.

Teachers: Access the videos for this activity using the **QR code on this page**.

1) Before watching a video, ask students to observe Jackson to see him do many actions. Tell them that they will see him **chew** on something, **pick** something up, etc. See margin for lists of verbs to get you going. The students and you will probably come up with other verbs.

2) After viewing a video, ask student to describe what they saw and use a past tense word. You can also stop the video and engage language using the past tense verbs.

3) Ask students to write about Jackson using many past tense verbs.

REVIEW AND PRACTICE

Non-reader and Reader: After students come in from recess, brainstorm verbs to describe their actions while playing. Record the verbs they think of, and add others to enrich the list (skip, toss, laugh, jump, wish, yell, listen, etc). If students say verbs that become irregular when past tense, use the opportunity to teach, i.e., run – ran, we don't say runned! Hit – past tense is also hit. Always use words in sentences, for context and grammar sense. "During recess, she **hit** the ball out of the field!"

Once the list is composed, say a verb. Students say it. Ask students to change the word to past tense. Skip – skipped. Use each in a sentence. Ask students to put the words in sentences.

Readers: Direct students to sort their verbs into three columns, each grouped by -ed phoneme: /ed/, /t/, /d/.

melted
Review Past Tense -/ed/

My ice cream melted! Your Turn: Tell about a time you had something melt. Use the word melted.

© Morpheme Magic

Verbs for the Action with Jackson Videos

Preview the videos, lists of verbs provided in the videos, and the verbs listed below. Use these verbs to guide students' discussion about Jackson.

rest - rested
carry - carried
wait - waited
drop – dropped
fetch – fetched
wade – waded
play - played
trot – trotted
hunt – hunted
flop - flopped (ears)
enjoy – enjoyed
sway - swayed

https://youtu.be/7XWme9JEkRw

Lesson Goal:

Learn how words (adjectives) change when we compare things.

Teachers know:

When working with comparatives, be sensitive to your students' self concepts. Using words like smarter, richer, etc. to compare students is not recommended. Stick with comparing animals and things in your oral language exploration.

Word Bank

big - bigger

tall – taller

short – shorter

sweet – sweeter

high – higher

strong – stronger

weak – weaker

short – shorter

bright – brighter

light – lighter

happy – happier

sad – sadder

green - greener

INTRODUCTION

DAY ONE: EXPLORE THE MORPHEME

Explain to students that words can change when we speak. Say, "I know that you all like cookies. Use the Morpheme Card. Look at this picture of two cookies. Which one would you choose to eat?" Point to each cookie, "This cookie is **big**, but this one is **bigger**." Point to each and say **big** and **bigger** again. Ask students to say the two adjectives with you. We change the word **big** to **bigger** when we are talking about the cookie you probably want!"

EXPLORE THE PHONEMES

Count the phonemes in **big**. Let's figure out how the word **big** changed! Show the picture of the cookies on the Morpheme Card. Students say **big**. Direct students to say and show with their fingers the phonemes in **big** - /b/i/g/. Lead students to say there are three sounds in **big**.

Count the phonemes in **bigger**. Show the pictures of cookies again. Direct students to say and show with their fingers the phonemes in **bigger**. /b/i/g/er/.

Count the phonemes in each - **big** and **bigger** again.

Discuss how **big** changed. Discuss the differences. Point out that **bigger** has /er/ at the end that helps us know we are talking about something that is larger in size.

Review: Ask students to turn to a partner and explain how the word **big** changes when we are comparing the sizes of two things – **big** and **bigger**.

ORTHOGRAPHY - READING AND SPELLING

Move to Oral Language Exercises if students are not yet decoding words.

If students are decoding CVC words explore the orthography of simple comparatives. Move to Oral Language Exercises if students are not yet decoding.

DECODE:

Write **big**. Students decode and read it. Explain that **big describes the size of something**.

Write **bigger.** Students decode and read it. Explain that **bigger** is a word we use when we compare two things. Circle **big** and circle **-er.** Review the Double It rule.

Do the same with other words in the **Word Bank** or use your program's words.

ENCODE: *Reteach the Suffix Spelling Rules as needed.*

Dictate comparative -er words for students to write. Use response boards and ask students to show their spellings after each word. Provide corrective feedback if needed, i.e., model the correct spelling and ask student to correct theirs. Include an oral language component by using the words in sentences.

ACTIVITIES

MORPHEME GRABBER - WORD EQUATION OR DRAW AND LABEL

Direct students to create a new page in their Morpheme Grabber.

WORD + -er	= NEW WORD	PICTURE OR SENTENCE
big + er	bigger	

Adjust the following exercises for your students' language and reading levels.

THE MORPHEME CARD

Display the Morpheme Card. Instruct students to say the two adjectives for each picture, explore the phonemes, use the words in sentences to tell about the pictures. REVIEW: Revisit the Suffix Spelling rules if needed. Level Two - say and write the words. Level Three - say and write the words and a sentence for each.

ORAL LANGUAGE AND WRITE

1) Say the following words and ask students to change the word to show comparison: tall, short, sweet, high, strong, weak, bright, light, quick, happy, mighty, sad, green. Ask students to explain how the word changed each time: "We added /er/ to the end of the word!" Use words in sentences.
2) Sound Spelling boxes. Provide a Sound Spelling grid. Dictate several -er words that match students' decoding abilities. Students identify the phonemes and spell each phoneme while working with you.

CONNECT TO THE CLASSROOM

Classroom Riddles – Ask students to use complete sentences when they answer. After each riddle, ask students to repeat the comparative and say the phonemes. Or, if students are capable, ask them to write their answers. Students may want to create their own riddles too!

What is **thicker**, a slice of bread or a cracker?

What is **taller**, a giraffe or this school?

What is **stronger**, a piece of rope of a piece of string?

What is **greener**, grass in the winter or grass in the summer?

What is **colder**, ice cream or a slushie?

REVIEW AND PRACTICE

Non-reader and Reader: Engage students in dialogue about pictures displaying comparatives in the Word Bank. Draw attention to the phoneme /er/ at the ends.

Reader: Display one comparative word each day you are on this lesson. Model how to read the word, circle the base, and then underline the plural suffix -er. Use words from the Word Banks or from your reading program.

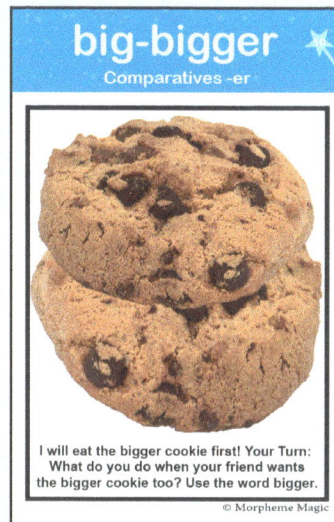

big-bigger
Comparatives -er

I will eat the bigger cookie first! Your Turn: What do you do when your friend wants the bigger cookie too? Use the word bigger.

© Morpheme Magic

More Word Bank Words

young – younger

old – older

wise – wiser

smart – smarter

thick – thicker

dirty – dirtier

easy – easier

itchy – itchier

cloudy – cloudier

shiny – shinier

funny - funnier

hungry –hungrier

mighty –mightier

b i gg er

Lesson Goal:

Learn how words (adjectives) change when describing the highest quality or degree.

Teachers know:

Not all superlatives add -est. The superlative of bad is worst, good (well) is best, beautiful is most beautiful.

Word Bank

hot-hotter-hottest

big-bigger-biggest

fast-faster-fastest

rich-richer-richest

quick-quicker-quickest

nice-nicer-nicest

old-older-oldest

young-younger-youngest

proud-prouder-proudest

brave-braver-bravest

quiet-quieter-quietest

INTRODUCTION

DAY ONE: EXPLORE THE MORPHEME

Explain to students that words can change when we speak. Use the Morpheme card. "Look at the flames in these pictures. Point to each flame in order: This flame is **hot.** This flame is **hotter**, and this one is **hottest**!" Talk a bit about how you can tell, ask students to share observations. Point to each and say, "**hot, hotter, hottest**." Ask students to say the three adjectives with you. We change the word **hot** to **hotter** and then we change it again when we are talking about highest level of **hot – hottest**!" Does this remind you of Goldilocks?

EXPLORE THE PHONEMES

Count the phonemes in **hot**. Let's figure out how the word **hot** changed! Show the photos on the Morpheme Card. Students say **hot**. Direct students to say and show with their fingers the phonemes in **hot** - /h/o/t/.

Count the phonemes in **hotter**. Point to the hotter flame. Direct students to say and show with their fingers the phonemes in **hotter**. /h/o/t/er/.

Finally, point to the **hottest** flame and say **hottest**. Students say **hottest** and say the phonemes: /h/o/t/e/s/t/.

Discuss how **hot** and **hotter** changed to **hottest**. Discuss the differences. Point out that **hotter** has /er/ at the end and **hottest** has /est/ on the end that helps us know we are talking about something that is the highest level of **hot – hottest.**

Review: Ask students to turn to a partner and explain how the word **hot** changes when we are comparing the heat of these flames – **hot, hotter,** and **hottest**.

Ask: What is something else we could use **hot, hotter** and **hottest** to describe?

ORTHOGRAPHY - READING AND SPELLING

Move to Oral Language Exercises if students are not yet decoding words.

DECODE: Write **hot**. Students decode and read it. Explain that **hot describes the heat level of something**. Reteach the Suffix Spelling Rules as needed.

Write **hotter and hottest**. Students decode and read the words. Explain that **hotter** is a word we use when we compare two things. Circle **hot** and circle **-er**. Explain that **hottest** is a word we use when we describe the highest level. Circle **hot** and circle **-est**.

Do the same with word sets in the **Word Bank** or use your program's words.

ENCODE: Reteach the Suffix Spelling Rules as needed.

Dictate superlative **-est** words for students to write. Use response boards and ask students to show their spellings after each word. Provide corrective feedback if needed, i.e., model the correct spelling and ask student to correct theirs. Include an oral language component by using the words in sentences.

ACTIVITIES

MORPHEME GRABBER - WORD EQUATION OR DRAW AND LABEL

Direct students to create a new page in their Morpheme Grabber.

WORD + -est	= NEW WORD	PICTURE OR SENTENCE
hot + est	hottest	

Adjust the following exercises for your students' language and reading levels.

THE MORPHEME CARD

Display a Morpheme Card. Direct students to discuss and compare the photos using -est, explore the phonemes, and use the questions to discuss the photos. REVIEW: Revisit the Suffix Spelling rules if needed. Level Two - say and write the words. Level Three - say and write the words and a sentence for each.

ORAL LANGUAGE AND WRITE

Say the following words and ask students to change the word to show comparison -er, and -est: **tall**, **short**, **sweet**, **high**, **strong**, **weak**, **bright**, **light**, **quick**, **happy**, **mighty**, **sad**, **green**. Ask students to explain how the word changed each time: "We added /er/ and /est/ to the end of the word!" Use the words in sentences.

Sound Spelling boxes. Provide a Sound Spelling grid. Dictate several -est words that match students' decoding abilities. Students identify the phonemes and spell each phoneme while working with you. Circle the base and circle the suffix.

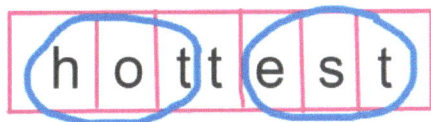

h o t t e s t

CONNECT TO THE CLASSROOM

Find ways to describe levels of comparison in the classroom. *"Let's have the* **quietest** *line up for lunch today!" I heard the* **kindest** *compliment today!"*

REVIEW AND PRACTICE

Non-reader and Reader: Engage students in dialogue about pictures displaying comparatives and superlatives in the Word Bank. Draw attention to the phoneme /er/ and /est/ at the ends.

Reader: Display one comparative/superlative word set each day you are on this lesson. Model how to read the words, circle the bases, and then underline the plural suffixes -er and -est. Use words from the Word Banks or from your reading program.

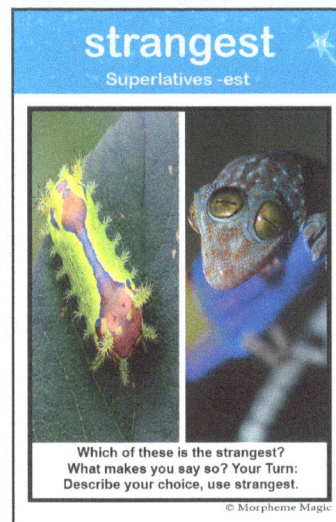

---

strangest
Superlatives -est

Which of these is the strangest?
What makes you say so? Your Turn:
Describe your choice, use strangest.

© Morpheme Magic

More Word Bank Words

thin-thinner-thinnest

safe-safer-safest

smooth-smoother-smoothest

simple-simpler-simplest

strange-stranger-strangest

great-greater-greatest

Lesson Goal:

Students will review how words change when we are making comparisons.

Teachers know:

It takes frequent exposures with direct instruction to build lasting memories for content.

Word Bank

loud-louder-loudest

kind-kinder-kindest

proud-prouder-proudest

bold-bolder-boldest

nice-nicer-nicest

ripe-riper-ripest

simple-simpler-simplest

smooth-smoother-smoothest

weird-weirder-weirdest

INTRODUCTION

DAY ONE: EXPLORE THE MORPHEME

This lesson will explore families of words built from a base using comparatives and superlatives. This lesson has one card associated with it.

Show a picture for this lesson. Point to a bug on the right. Say, "This bug is **small**." and direct students to say it. "If this is **small**, this one is _____" Guide students to say "**smaller**". "If this one is **smaller**, then this one is the _____" Guide students to say, "**smallest**". Point to each picture and say with students, "**small, smaller, smallest**".

EXPLORE THE PHONEMES

Show the picture of bugs again. Point to the pictures and say **small** – students segment phonemes /s/m/a/ll/ and say "**small**." Point to the next picture this one is _____. Students say "**smaller**". Segment the phonemes, /s/m/a/ll/ er/. Ask, "How did **small** change to help us describe this picture?" Elicit /er/ added to the end of **small**. Do the same for **smallest**. Point to picture, all say **smallest**, segment phonemes and verbalize how **small** changed to describe the **smallest**. End with all students saying , "**Small, smaller, smallest**!"

ORTHOGRAPHY - READING AND SPELLING

Move to Oral Language Exercises if students are not yet decoding words.

DECODE:

Write **small**. Students decode and read it. Explain that **small describes the size level of something**. . *Reteach the Suffix Spelling Rules as needed.*

Write **small, smaller, smallest.** Students decode and read the words. Circle the base and circle the suffix in each with the students. Explain that **smaller** is a word we use when we compare two things. Explain that **smallest** is a word we use when we describe the highest level of being **small**.

Do the same with word sets in the **Word Bank** or use your program's words.

ENCODE:

Reteach the Suffix Spelling Rules as needed. Choose words for which students have learned the phoneme-grapheme correspondences.

Dictate a base word for students to spell (**thin**). Ask students to spell the word again and add the ending to make it say **thinner**. Ask them to write **thin** again and make it say **thinnest**. Instruct them to circle and say the base, then circle and say the ending, then read the word for each. Repeat with other sets of words in the Word Bank. Use response boards and ask students to show their spellings after each word set. Provide corrective feedback if needed, i.e., model the correct spelling and ask student to correct theirs. Include an oral language component by using the words in sentences.

ACTIVITIES

MORPHEME GRABBER - WORD EQUATION OR DRAW AND LABEL

Direct students to create a new page in their Morpheme Grabber.

WORD + -er, -est	= NEW WORD	PICTURE OR SENTENCE
small smaller + er small + est	small smaller smallest	

Adjust the following exercises for your students' language and reading levels.

THE MORPHEME CARD

Display the Morpheme Card. Instruct students to compare the bugs in the picture cards using the base, comparative, and superlative. Explore the phonemes, use the words in sentences to tell about the pictures. REVIEW: Level Two - say and write the words. Level Three - say and write the words and a sentence for each.

ORAL LANGUAGE AND WRITE

Comparative – Superlative Art! Students create pictures and label, and or use sentence captions, to display in a classroom display.

1) Choose a set of base words. Display them for children to read if appropriate for decoding, or present a word orally. Students say the three words in the word family, i.e. **tall**, **taller**, **tallest**. Ask, "What is something we can use **tall** (or the word you or students choose) to describe?" (**trees**, **buildings**, **dogs**, **people**, etc.).

2) Give students half sheets of paper, cut horizontally. Fold into three sections. Direct students to label the bottom of each section with the descriptors: **tall-taller-tallest**. Provide a model if needed. Ask students to decide what they will draw, and create their three drawings. Oral Language: Students talk about their pictures using the -er, -est forms. Or, ask them to write sentences.

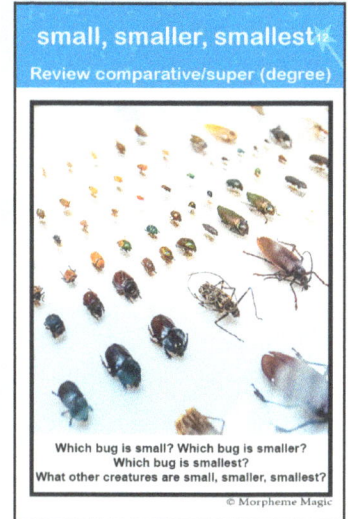

tall | taller | tallest

REVIEW AND PRACTICE - FUN

Find a source online for **strange** or **weird** animal (or other) facts. Choose a topic your students will enjoy. Read about the topic. Discuss. Then, ask students to decide which was **strange (weird)**, **stranger (weirder)**, and **strangest (weirdest)**. Students' opinions will emerge! Ask for reasons to support their thinking. Direct an oral language activity and then lead students to write about what they learned and use the base, -er, and -est forms. Have fun!!

small, smaller, smallest
Review comparative/super (degree)

Which bug is small? Which bug is smaller? Which bug is smallest? What other creatures are small, smaller, smallest?

© Morpheme Magic

More Word Bank Words

Deep-deeper-deepest

Shallow-shallower-shallowest

Change the -y to i and add -er, or -est

funny-funnier-funniest

scary-scarier-scariest

heavy-heavier-heaviest

easy-easier-easiest

shiny-shinier-shiniest

windy-windier-windiest

cloudy-cloudier-cloudiest

dirty-dirtier-dirtiest

scary-scarier-scariest

curly-curlier-curliest

Lesson Goal:

Present verb tense is spelled ––s or -es and we say /s/, /z/, or /ez/.

Word Bank

s = /s/

rest-rests

work-works

clap-claps

sleep-sleeps

jump-jumps

write-writes

protect-protects

s = /z/

hold-holds

tell-tells

win-wins

guard-guards

care-cares

dream-dreams

read-reads

s = /ez/

pass-passes

quiz-quizzes

wish-wishes

wash-washes

search-searches

INTRODUCTION

DAY ONE: EXPLORE THE MORPHEME

Review the concept of action verbs with students. Briefly review past tense verbs. Tell students that today, we will discover another way verbs change when we are talking and reading.

"Say **help**." Students clap as they say **help.**" "Can this class **help** each other?"

"This class **helps** their friends! Say **helps** (clap the one syllable)." Students say **helps** and clap the syllable. Say and clap the syllables **help** and **helps**. "How did **help** change when we talked about what you do now?" Students say **help** and **helps**, segment the phonemes in each, and isolate the final sounds. "Yes, **helps** says /s/ at the end."

EXPLORE THE PHONEMES

The verbs we will work with today will say /s/, /z/, or /ez/ to show the action is happening right now. "She **helps** her friends and **washes** and **cleans** with a smile." Explore the bold words: **helps** /s/, **washes** /ez/, **cleans** /z/. Students say the forms of each word (**help-helps**, etc.) and segment the phonemes in each. Lead them to tell you how they two words are the same and how they are different. Do the same with a selection of words from the Word Bank.

ORTHOGRAPHY - READING AND SPELLING

Move to Oral Language Exercises if students are not yet decoding words.

DECODE:

Write **helps** on the board. "When I read this word, I can sound out **help.** Circle **help** and decode it. "I also see the new word part /s/ that is spelled -s. Say the base **help** and ending -**s**. **Helps.** That little -**s** on the end of **helps** is very important and *helps* us know that *help* is happening right now!" Do the same, decode and discuss, with a selection of words from the Word Bank.

ENCODE:

Dictate -s and -es words for students to spell. Ask students to spell their words in a column and to leave their words on their boards when they are done. Use response boards and ask students to share their spellings after each word. After dictating several words, ask students to read the words they spelled and find two words that can go together to talk about (fill in the blank with a concept, such as 'football game' – **jumps** and **claps**). Repeat with other concept sorts. This activity will integrate vocabulary, spelling, and decoding. It is also a great verbal reasoning exercise when you ask, "What made you choose those words?"

ACTIVITIES

MORPHEME GRABBER – WORD EQUATION OR DRAW AND LABEL

Direct students to create a new page in their Morpheme Grabber.

WORD + -s, -es	= NEW WORD	PICTURE OR SENTENCE
help + s wish + es	helps wishes	

Adjust the following exercises for your students' language and reading levels.

THE MORPHEME CARD

Display the Morpheme Cards. Instruct students to say the present tense verb for each picture, explore the phonemes, use the words in sentences to tell about the picture. REVIEW: Level Two - say and write the words. Level Three - say and write the words and a sentence for each.

ORAL LANGUAGE AND WRITE · TONGUE TWISTERS!

Many present tense verbs ending in -s and -es can also be used as plural nouns. Use this grammar element to create *tongue twisters*. Substitute your students' names for the pronouns to personalize the activity. Read the sentence – students repeat it. Help students identify the verb and the noun in each, and the ending phoneme too. Expand to a writing activity.

She **wishes** she had more **wishes** to make.
He **meets** her at the swim **meets** after schools.
She **twists** her pretzel dough making five **twists** before baking it.
His car **turns** on the sharp **turns** in the road.
The actor **acts** in several **acts** in the play.
He **folds** the towels on the previous **folds**.

ADVENTURES WITH JACKSON! QR CODE IN LEVEL 1 LESSON 9

Revisit the puppy Jackson videos. Assist your students to identify present tense verbs to describe Jackson's actions. Use the list you created in Lesson 9. Guide students to express what they see using present tense verbs – Ask for 7 or more words in a sentence – Give me 7!

https://youtu.be/7XWme9JEkRw

REVIEW AND PRACTICE

Non-reader and Reader: Use words from the Word Bank. Say a word and ask students to use it in a sentence to tell about something they are learning or reading. Choose words that lend themselves to making the connections to learning content.

Reader: Display one present tense word each day you are on this lesson. Model how to read the word, circle the base, and then underline the suffix -s, or -es. Use words from the Word Banks or from your reading program.

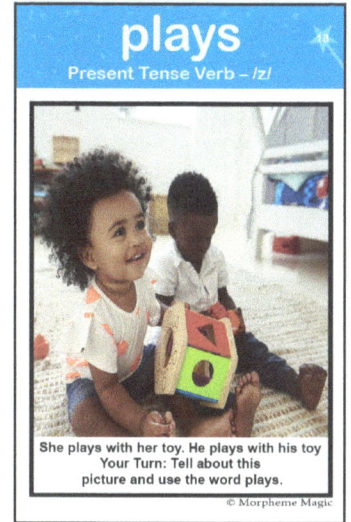

---

plays
Present Tense Verb – /z/

She plays with her toy. He plays with his toy
Your Turn: Tell about this
picture and use the word plays.
© Morpheme Magic

More Word Bank Words

other verb-noun combos for tongue twisters!

lifts – to lift

lifts – elevators

blasts – to blast

blasts – dynamite explosion

dots – make dots

dots – the shape

dents – to dent

dents – more than one dent

Can you think of more?

Teachers know:

The -s means something different when affixed to verbs (present tense) than it means when affixed to nouns (plural). Be explicit about this with your students. This is more important when students begin to read and write.

Lesson Goal:

Learn how words change when we add -ing.

Teachers know:

The vowel phoneme in -ing is a lax (short) /i/. Our mouths are preparing for the nasal /ng/ that follows it and assumes more of an /ee/ position tricking us. Teach the vowel as /i/ for spelling and reading – "I_N_G spells -ing!"

Word Bank

tip-tipping

mop-mopping

sit-sitting

rub-rubbing

zip-zipping

shut-shutting

jump-jumping

hit-hitting

pat-patting

swim-swimming

toss -tossing

step-stepping

fish-fishing

track-tracking

rush – rushing

flash-flashing

swell-swelling

INTRODUCTION

DAY ONE: EXPLORE THE MORPHEME

Explain to students that they will be working with a new ending on words. It is a common ending that is familiar to them. They use it all the time!

"Say **hop**." Students clap as they say "**hop.**" "Show me how you can **hop** on one foot" While students hop, say, "You are **hopping**! Please stop **hopping**."

"Everyone say **hop** (clap)**.** Say **hopping** (clap the two syllables)." Say and clap the syllables **hop** and **hopping**. "How did **hop** change when I asked you to stop?" Clap the two parts again: **hop-ing**. The words we will work with today will change and say **/ing/** at the end. What will they say?   "-ing."

EXPLORE THE PHONEMES

The word-ending we say for this lesson's words is /ing/. The sounds we say for /ing/ are /i/ng/. Explore the phonemes, ask students to watch your mouth say each sound, but when we say /ing/ quickly, our lips stay the same! Choose words from the Word Bank. Say the base and -ing word form. Students repeat. Use the -ing form in a brief sentence, say the word again. Ask students to say the word parts – **swim-ing** NOTE: CVC words will double the final consonant when adding -ing. The doubled consonant is voiced once, i.e., **hopping** = /h/o/pp/i/ng/. The kids stopped **hopping**."

ORTHOGRAPHY - READING AND SPELLING

Move to Oral Language Exercises if students are not yet decoding words.

Review the *Spelling Rules* as needed. See the *Spelling with Suffixes* section.

DECODE: Write **hopping** on the board. "When I read this word, my eyes see the base **hop. Hop** if you see it too**."** Circle **hop** and decode it. Circle -ing. "I also see the new word part /ing/ that is spelled -ing. Say the base **hop** and ending -**ing**. **Hopping**." We doubled the final consonant to protect that short vowel before adding -ing.

Follow the same process with other words to help students read the word parts with /ing/.

ENCODE: Dictate words from the Word Bank and from your reading program for students to spell. Say **mop**. We will mop the floor. Spell **mop**. Say **mopping**. They are **mopping** the floor. Write **mopping**. Use response boards and ask students to share their spellings after each word. Provide corrective feedback. Emphasize that they are adding the ending -ing, /ing/ to words in this lesson.

ACTIVITIES

hopping
Present Tense Verbs -ing

The bunny is hopping.
You Turn: Tell about the picture
and use the word hopping.
© Morpheme Magic

MORPHEME GRABBER - WORD EQUATION OR DRAW AND LABEL
Direct students to create a new page in their Morpheme Grabber.

WORD + -ing	= NEW WORD	PICTURE OR SENTENCE
hop + ing	hopping	

Adjust the following exercises for your students' language and reading levels.

THE MORPHEME CARD
Display the Morpheme Cards. Instruct students to say the -ing words for each picture. Segment the phonemes. Use the words in sentences to tell about the picture. REVIEW: Teach **Spelling Rules** if needed. Level Two - say and write the words. Level Three - say and write the words and a sentence for each.

ORAL LANGUAGE AND WRITE
Create Rhymes! Use as an oral activity and if appropriate a writing activity.

Provide an -ing verb. Ask students to think of a rhyming word. Then, use the two words to fill in the sentence frames to create funny sentences.

Turning – (*burning*): The tree was _____ colors as it was _____!

Crunching – (*lunching*): She was _____ as she was _____.

Sleeping – (*peeping*): The lions were _____ while the monkeys were ____.

Crying – (trying): They were _____ while they were _____.

CONNECT TO THE CLASSROOM

ACTION REVIEW!
Give students a verb from the Word Bank, or others that reflect current activity in the classroom, what they see and hear (orally or written depending on students' reading levels). Guide students to create word families from the base. **Smile**-smile**s**-smil**ed**-smil**ing**. Wow! Four words that all have **smile** in them! Unless you are ready to address irregular past tense verbs, avoid the past tense forms for eat (ate), give (gave), read (read), write (wrote), drive (drove), sit (sat), etc.

REVIEW AND PRACTICE
Non-reader and Reader: Engage students in dialogue about a picture displaying a lot of action. Direct students to talk about what they see happening and use -ing words.

Reader: Display one -ing word each day you are on this lesson. Model how to read the word, circle the base, and then underline the suffix -ing. Use words from the Word Banks or from your reading program.

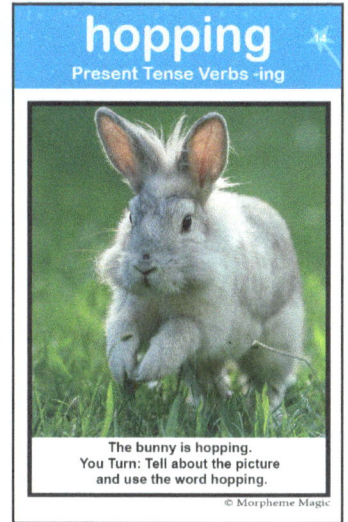

Teachers Know:

Sometimes -ing words are adjectives: **Swimming** meet, **Jumping** beans. Sometimes -ing words are nouns: He put a sweet **topping** on the cake.

More Word Bank Words

crunch-crunching

lean-leaning

slip-slipping

turn-turning

write-writing

sleep-sleeping

read-reading

eat-eating

cook-cooking

cry-crying

drive-driving

hide-hiding

give-giving

lie- lying

smile-smiling

Lesson Goal:

Un- can be affixed to the beginning of words to change their meaning. Un-means not or to undo or reverse.

Teachers know:

Un- is the most common prefix.

Word Bank

un- means not:

unfed

unlit

unable

unfair

unhappy

unhealthy

unsafe

unwise

unable

unafraid

unbeatable

un means to undo or reverse:

unzip

unpack

undo

unfix

unfold

unchain

unload

unlock

unstick

unlatch

INTRODUCTION

DAY ONE: EXPLORE THE MORPHEME

"We have been working with word parts that come at the ends of words to change their meanings, When we add – s /s/ to the end of **pup**, we get **pups!** Now we are talking about more than one! Can you remember any other word parts we have been adding to the ends of words?" Lead students to recall past tense -ed, -plural -es, -ing. Pull samples from earlier lessons to review.

Introduce **un**-. Today we are going to learn a word part we hear at the beginnings of words. Say "**zip**" Students say **zip**. "**Zip** up your jacket." Students show the action for "**zip**". I am going to add our new word part to **zip**. Listen. **Unzip.** Say the new word**.** How did **zip** change in our new word, **unzip**? Lead students to identify **un-** was added to make a new word. **Un-** means reverse – the opposite. A minute ago, you showed me, **zip** up your jacket. Now, do the opposite, **UNZIP** your jacket! We added **un** to the beginning of **zip**, what's our new word? **Unzip!**

Un means opposite or reverse, but it can also mean **NOT**. **Fair** (students say it) **unfair** (students say it). **Unfair** means **NOT** fair. Say happy. Change **happy** to a new word if you are NOT happy. Lead students to say **Unhappy** – **not happy**. **Un** is an important word part that changes the meanings of words!

EXPLORE THE PHONEMES

The new word part we learned is **un**. Say it. Say the sounds in **un**, /u/n/ **un**. **Un** means the **OPPOSITE**. We can **zip** up and when we **zip** down, we ___ (students say **unzip**). Segment the phonemes in **un** on the left hand then segment the phonemes in **zip** on the right hand. Close each fist and say, "**un**" "**zip**" "**unzip**." Do the same with a couple more examples from the Word Bank. **Un** also means **NOT**. **Safe** means you feel secure, it is a good feeling. Change **safe** to a new word if you do not feel **safe** – you feel ___ **unsafe**. Not safe. What is our new word part? "**Un**!"

ORTHOGRAPHY - READING AND SPELLING

Move to Oral Language Exercises if students are not yet ready to decode these words.

DECODE:
Present the bases of several words. Decode each with students. Then add **un**-to one word at a time, decode, and then discuss the meanings. Use each in a sentence.

ENCODE:
Dictate **un**- words from the word bank for students to spell. Use response boards and ask students to share their spellings after each word. Emphasize **un**- and the meanings of each word. "**Un**-means ____ and so the word means ____."

ACTIVITIES

MORPHEME GRABBER – WORD EQUATION OR DRAW AND LABEL

Direct students to create a new page in their Morpheme Grabber.

un + WORD	= NEW WORD	PICTURE OR SENTENCE
un + lock	unlock	

Adjust the following exercises for your students' language and reading levels.

THE MORPHEME CARD

Display the Morpheme Card. Instruct students to say the **un-** word for each picture, explore the phonemes, morphemes and word meaning. Use the words in sentences to tell about the picture. REVIEW: Level Two - say and write the words. Level Three - say and write the words and a sentence for each.

ORAL LANGUAGE AND WRITE

Ask a question below. Say the **un**-word and students say it. Discuss the word meaning, then children answer the question and use the word in their answers. Create additional questions.

When might you be **unlucky**? When might you be **uncertain**? When would you **unlace** something? What might you **undo**? When would you be **unhealthy**?

CONNECT TO THE CLASSROOM

The prefix -un lends itself to creating pairs of opposites. Use the following sentence riddles and students provide the un-word. If appropriate, students can write their own riddles and share with the other students.

You could make a **wise** decision or an _____ decision. (**unwise**)

Lock the door when you leave and ___ it when you return. (**unlock**)

A **fed** baby is content but an ____ baby might cry! (**unfed**)

We **fold** the towels to put them away and ___ them when we swim. (**unfold**)

This bridge is **safe**, but the broken one is ____. (**unsafe**)

We **latch** the gate to keep it closed, and _____ it to open it. (**unlatch**)

REVIEW AND PRACTICE

Non-reader and Reader: Students hold their touching fists in front of them. Say a word from the Word Bank, "**Unwise**." Students say it, then segment the two word parts while separating the fists, "**Un----** Wise." Put the fists back together and say the word, "**Unwise**!" Use it in a sentence.

Reader: Display one **un-** word each day you are on this lesson. Model how to read the word, circle the base, and then underline the prefix **un-**. Use words from the Word Banks or from your reading program. Discuss meaning and use in sentences. If you can tie the word to content students are learning – even better!

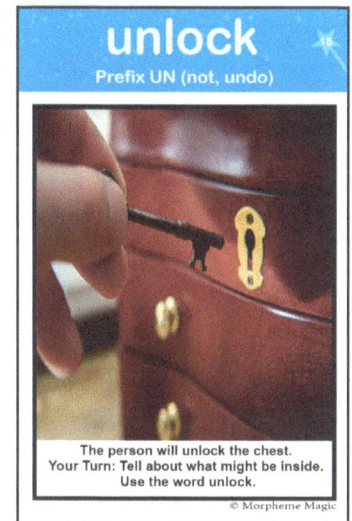

unlock
Prefix UN (not, undo)

The person will unlock the chest.
Your Turn: Tell about what might be inside.
Use the word unlock.
© Morpheme Magic

More Word Bank Words

unable

unacceptable

unanswered

unappetizing

unavailable

unlucky

unclean

uncertain

unlace

unglue

unknown

unwilling

untruthful

unacceptable

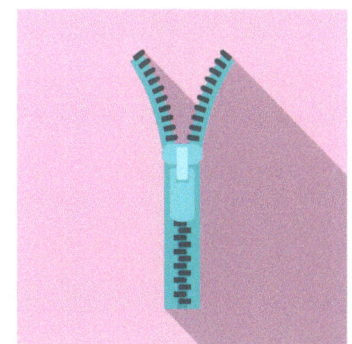

Lesson Goal:

Re- can be affixed to the beginning of words to change their meaning. Re—means back or again.

Teachers know:

RE- is the second most common prefix.

Word Bank

Re- means again:

respell-spell again

review-view again

redo –do again

reset – set again

recut – cut again

redig – dig again

repat pat again

recast -cast again

rezip – zip again

repin – pin again

remix - mix again

repick – pick again

repack–pack again

rewrite–write again

respread-spread again

rework-work again

rejoin-join again

retrace-trace again

reorder-order again

INTRODUCTION

DAY ONE: EXPLORE THE MORPHEME

Introduce **re**-. Today we are going to learn another word part we hear at the beginnings of words. Say "**spell**" Students say **spell**. I am going to add our new word part to **spell**. Listen. **Respell**. Say the new word. How did **spell** change in our new word, **respell**? Lead students to identify **re-** was added to make a new word. **Re-** means again. If we **spell** a word incorrectly, we stop, erase, and **respell** the word right! We spell it again. We added **re** to the beginning of **spell**, what's our new word? **Respell!**"

Re means again, but it can also mean **BACK**. Say **Capture**. Students say **capture**. I am going to add our new word part, **recapture** (students say it). **Recapture** means **to capture back**. What are some games you play where your **capture** something or someone and when they get away, you get them back – you **RECAPTURE** them! **RE** is an important word part that changes the meanings of words! It means back or again.

EXPLORE THE PHONEMES

The new word part we learned is **re**. Say it. Say the sounds in **re**, /r/ee/ **re**. **Re** means **AGAIN**. We can **spell** words and when we fix our spelling we (students say **respell**). Segment the phonemes in **re** on the left hand then segment the phonemes in **spell** on the right hand. Close each fist and say, "**re**" "**spell**" "**respell**." Do the same with a couple more examples from the Word Bank. **Re** also means **BACK**. **Move** your pencil into your desk. Change **move** to a new word. When you take the pencil **back** out you **remove** it.

ORTHOGRAPHY - READING AND SPELLING

Move to Oral Language Exercises if students are not yet decoding words.

DECODE
Present the bases of several words that your students can decode. Decode each with students. Then add **re-** to one word at a time, decode, and then discuss the meanings. Use each in a sentence.

ENCODE:
Dictate **re-** words from the word bank for students to spell. Use response boards and ask students to share their spellings after each word. Emphasize **re-** and the meanings of each word. "**Re**-means _____ and so the word means _____."

ACTIVITIES

MORPHEME GRABBER - WORD EQUATION OR DRAW AND LABEL

Direct students to create a new page in their Morpheme Grabber.

re- + WORD	= NEW WORD	PICTURE OR SENTENCE
re + spell	respell	

Adjust the following exercises for your students' language and reading levels.

THE MORPHEME CARD

Display the Morpheme Card. Instruct students to say the **re-** word for each picture, explore the phonemes, morphemes and use the words in sentences to tell about the picture. REVIEW: Level Two - say and write the words. Level Three - say and write the words and a sentence for each.

ORAL LANGUAGE AND WRITE -

Work with students to create words with the prefix -**re**. Beware – kids will have a lot fun with this! Say **make**. Say it again and add **re**-to the front. **Remake**. To **make** again. Discuss meaning and use in sentences related to the classroom, the students' bedroom, a kitchen. Say **visit**. Say it again and add **re**-to the front. **Revisit**. To **visit** again. Discuss meaning and use in sentences related to students' lives. After a few of these let kids start to think of their own verbs and add **re**, say the new word, and then what it means! Ask student who can, to write their new words, a sentence, and illustrate them.

CONNECT TO THE CLASSROOM

Several **re**-words can be used to discuss supportive classroom communities. Use the following words to discuss the positive values in your classroom:

respect (-spect means look), **relationship** (form of relate means to build back) **rebuild** (build again), **respond**, **regain**, **refrain**, **return**, **remind**, **recall**, **reject.**

REVIEW AND PRACTICE

Non-reader and Reader: Introduce the word **remember**. **Re** (back) and **member** (mind). When we **remember** something, we put the memory back in our minds. What can we do to help us **remember** that **re**-means back or again?

Reader: Display one **re**- word each day you are on this lesson. Model how to read the word, circle the base, and then underline the prefix -**re**. Ask students to be ready to tell the meaning. Use words from the Word Banks or from your reading program. Tie the word to content you are studying or reading about.

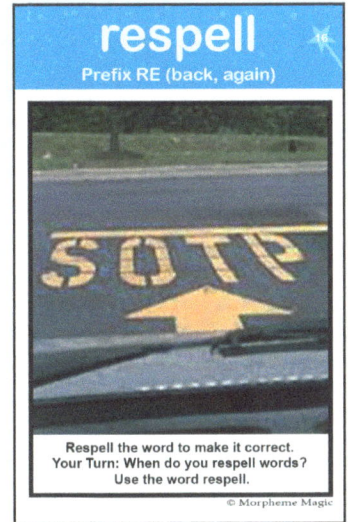

respell
Prefix RE (back, again)

Respell the word to make it correct.
Your Turn: When do you respell words?
Use the word respell.

© Morpheme Magic

More Word Bank Words

Re- means back

recall-call back

recapture – capture back

remove-move back

recollect-collect back

repay-pay back

reflect-bend back (*flect means bend*)

relax-loose back (*lax means loose*)

relieve—raise back (*lieve means raise*)

reverse - turn back (*verse means turn*)

revive – life back (*vive means life*)

TIP: If a prefix is added to a root with an unknown meaning, usually Latin, you can look it up on etymonline.com

Lesson Goal:

PRE- can be affixed to the beginnings of words to change their meanings. PRE- means before or earlier.

Teachers know:

When developing morphological awareness with prefixes, affix the prefix to a known word. Always discuss meaning!

Word Bank

Pre- means before or earlier:

premix – mix before

preview-view before or earlier

preset – set before

precut – cut before

predig – dig before

prezip – zip before

prepack–pack before or earlier

prewrite–write before

prespread-spread before

preorder-order before

INTRODUCTION

DAY ONE: EXPLORE THE MORPHEME

Introduce **pre**-. Today we are going to learn another word part we hear at the beginnings of words. Say "**mix**" Students say **mix**. "I am going to add our new word part to **mix**. Listen. **Premix**. Say the new word. How did **mix** change in our new word, **premix**"? Lead students to identify **pre**- was added to make a new word. **Pre** means before. Before I paint, I **premix** my paints to get the right color. I mix them before I begin - **premix**. We added **pre** to the beginning of **mix**, what's our new word? **premix!**

EXPLORE THE PHONEMES

The new word part we learned is p**re**. Say it. Say the sounds in p**re**, /p/r/ee/ p**re**. **Pre** means **BEFORE**. We can **mix** paints while we paint, or we can **premix** them before we begin. **Premix**. Students say it. Segment the phonemes in **pre** on the left hand then segment the phonemes in **mix** on the right hand. Close each fist and say, "**pre**" "**mix**" "**premix**." Do the same with a couple more examples from the Word Bank.

ORTHOGRAPHY - READING AND SPELLING

Move to Oral Language Exercises if students are not yet decoding words.

DECODE:

Present the bases of several words that your students can decode. Decode each with students. Then add **pre**- to one word at a time, decode, and then discuss the meanings. Use each in a sentence.

ENCODE:

Dictate **pre**- words from the word bank for students to spell. Use response boards and ask students to share their spellings after each word. Emphasize **pre**- and the meanings of each word. "**Pre**-means ____ and so the word means _____."

ACTIVITIES

MORPHEME GRABBER - WORD EQUATION OR DRAW AND LABEL

Direct students to create a new page in their Morpheme Grabber.

pre + WORD	= NEW WORD	PICTURE OR SENTENCE
pre + mix	premix	

Adjust the following exercises for your students' language and reading levels.

THE MORPHEME CARD

Display the Morpheme Card. Instruct students to say the **pre-** word for each picture, explore the phonemes, morphemes and use the words in sentences to tell about the picture. REVIEW: Level Two - say and write the words. Level Three - say and write the words and a sentence for each.

ORAL LANGUAGE AND WRITE -

Provide practice creating words with the prefix **pre**-. Use these sentence frames:

When I **zip** my coat *before* I put it on, I _____. (**prezip** it)

When I **set** the channels on my TV *before* I watch my show I ___. (**preset** them)

When I **view** (watch) some of a movie to see if I like it, I _____ (**preview** it)

When I **pack** my lunch the night *before* I ___ my lunch. (**prepack**).

Create others. If students are ready, ask them to write these kinds of **pre**-sentences for their classmates to figure out.

CONNECT TO THE CLASSROOM

Tell students they are going to **prewrite** some sentences using a variety of words you provide. Then they will review (discuss from earlier lesson *re+view*) the sentences and make any corrections needed in spelling and word choice. Then they will have their final sentences to share. Choose words from the Word Bank, and words that students can connect to their learning.

REVIEW AND PRACTICE

Non-reader and Reader: Introduce the word **prename**. Ask what **prename** means (to name before). Lead students to use **prename** to talk about baby siblings or pets that were **named BEFORE** they came into their homes. "If you were getting a new pet, would you **prename** it? What would it be?" I would **prename** a pup _____."

Reader: Display one **pre**- word each day you are on this lesson. Model how to read the word, circle the base, and then underline the prefix -**pre**. Ask students to be ready to tell the meaning. Use words from the Word Banks or from your reading program. Tie the word to content you are studying or reading about.

---

predict
Prefix PRE (before, earlier)

What do you predict will happen next?
Your Turn: Share your thinking and use the word predict.
© Morpheme Magic

More Word Bank Words

Pre- means before or earlier

prepay-pay before

prepaid – paid before

prearrange – arrange before or earlier

predict – to say before

preflight – the flight before

prename – to name before

prepackage package before

TIP: It is always a good idea to reinforce morphology when spelling. Use sound boxes at least 2-3 times per week - segment phonemes, spell with graphemes, and circle the morpheme!

Lesson Goal:

Maintain a focus on developing morphological awareness. Develop curiosity about words and their meaningful parts.

Teachers know:

When developing morphological awareness with little ones, affix prefixes and suffixes to known words. Always discuss how the base word changed and the new meaning!

TIP: It is always a good idea to reinforce morphology when spelling. Use sound boxes at least 2-3 times per week. Segment phonemes, spell with graphemes, circle the morphemes!

Congratulations! You have completed Level 1 with your students. Your students' development of morphological awareness has just begun. Keep up the focus on morphology through lots of P&R – Practice and Review.

1) Keep your Morpheme Wall dynamic. This means you change out the Morpheme Cards occasionally; refer your students to the wall when they are searching for a word to use, or need a refresher about the meanings of morphemes.

2) Guide students to use their Morpheme Grabbers as a reference, and to continue to collect words they find under the headings they created in Level 1.

3) See Review Tips and Additional Activities in the Introduction Section for ideas to keep you and your students focused on building morphological awareness.

4) Apply the following systematic approach with any vocabulary instruction. It keeps us focused on the language components to ensure a Language Rich Classroom.

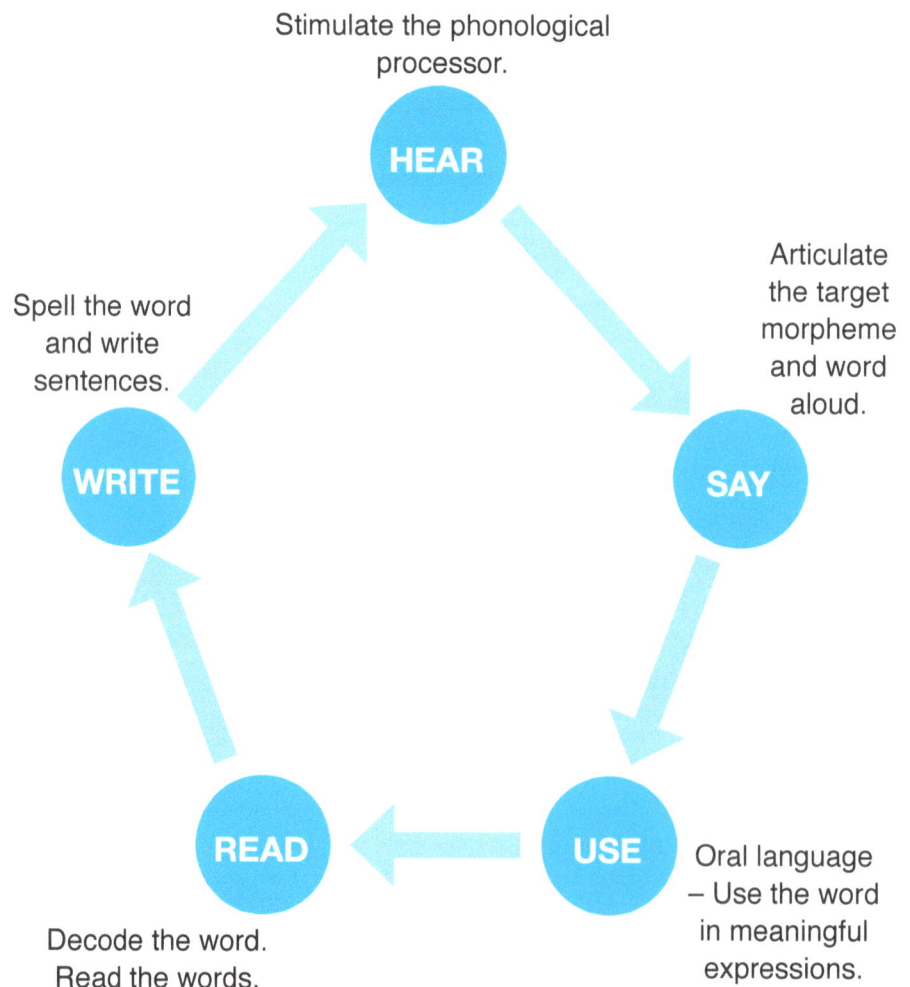

Stimulate the phonological processor.

HEAR

Articulate the target morpheme and word aloud.

SAY

Spell the word and write sentences.

WRITE

Oral language – Use the word in meaningful expressions.

USE

READ

Decode the word. Read the words.

LEVEL 2 LESSONS
– The Magic of Language

WELCOME TO A DEEPER FOCUS ON MORPHOLOGICAL AWARENESS:

1) Level 2 Lessons begin with a review. Use the Lessons in Level 1 as indicated on the following few pages to guide your planning for the first several weeks of word study and review. Level 1 and/or Level 2 Assessments can provide information about students' current morphological awareness.

2) Choose word items from the lists that reflect the grapheme -phoneme relationships your students have learned. When appropriate, apply the morphemes to words in your reading program. For example, can any of the words in your reading/spelling lessons take on the morpheme you are teaching? **Plan** can become **preplan** (teaching **pre-**), **plate** can become **plates** (teaching plurals).

3) If students are just beginning to decode, choose words for decoding and encoding that reflect the phoneme – grapheme relationships they have learned.

TIPS FOR TEACHING LEVEL 2 LESSONS

- Teach Level 2 lessons during your reading – writing block. Make sure students are given lots of opportunities to apply orally and in writing the words they learn.

- Watch your read alouds for example words reflecting the morphemes you teach. Draw explicit attention to these words, draw students into discussions about the words and the "word parts that change meaning" (suffixes and prefixes).

- Model how to use words in sentences. Provide sentence frames to assist students with applying the words. WHO or WHAT- DID WHAT – WHEN, WHY, HOW.

REMINDERS:
Use all language learning processes in your **Morphemes for Little Ones** lessons:

★ Model how the morphemes and words **sound** and how they are used.

★ Direct student to **say** the focus morphemes and words aloud.

★ Share **meanings** using student accessible definitions and examples.

★ Ask students to **read** the focus morphemes and words.

★ Provide opportunities for students to **practice** using the words they learn in meaningful sentences. It is best to apply the words to topics they are studying.

★ **Write!** Direct students to put into words what they are learning using the words in the lessons.

★ **Model** how to use words in sentences when students struggle to use the words correctly.

★ **Provide sentence frames** when students are not sure how to use a word.

Lesson Goal:

Learn that suffixes can be added to words to change meaning. Suffixes in this lesson include: plurals, past tense verbs, and present tense verbs.

Teachers know:

It is important to teach the spelling rules for adding suffixes to bases and review the rules often.

NOTE: The word items on the Review Morpheme Card for this lesson represent the varying phonemes for the morpheme spellings. Draw explicit attention to this. The words are also chosen to relate to the pictures for oral language practice.

TIP: Draw attention to how phonemes and stress change: When we add **-al to nature**, the A in **nature** sounds like /ae/ but in **natural**, the A sounds like /a/. Be explicit, compare and contrast phonemes when morphemes are added or changed in words.

LEVEL 2 REVIEW CONTENT

PLURALS AND PAST TENSE WITH SPELLING CHANGES

Note: Refer to the Level 1 Lessons noted below to plan your lessons for review.

The main focus for this review is to teach the spelling rules when adding suffixes that begin with a vowel. If your students did not receive instruction with Level 1 content, then it is recommended that they also receive instruction in the following:

1) **Compound Words** – An effective way to teach the concept of morphemes. See Level 1 Lesson 1.

2) **Comparatives and Superlatives (-er, -est)**– Spelling changes are needed with many of these words. See Level 1 Lessons 10-12.

PLURALS

WEEK 1 PLURALS	TEACH: A plural is formed when we add -s or -es to a noun. The morphemes -s and -es can sound like /s/, /z/, /ez/ or /eez/.	REVIEW: Level 1 Lessons 2-5.
Teach the Drop It, Change It, and Double It Spelling Rules		

| Word Items: /s/ cups, desks, tickets, trucks, goats, lamps, plants, belts, hips, scoops, weights | Word Items: /z/ storms, rules waves, bugs, eggs, cards, roads, poles, goals, bills, papers, stores | Word Items: /ez/ wishes, glasses, dishes, fences, lunches, purses, lenses, inches | Word Items: /eez/ **Don't change y to i. Add -s** key, donkey valley, kidney, chimney, journey

Word Items: /eez/ **Change y to i, add -es** baby, candy, copy, duty, story, fairy, family, party, library |

MORPHEME GRABBER - PLURALS

Direct students to create a new page in their **Morpheme Grabber**:

WORD + S, ES	= NEW WORD	PICTURE OR SENTENCE
cliff + s =	cliffs	
paper + s =	papers	
house + es =	houses	
candy +es =	candies	

Choose one word from each category of plurals to enter into the **Morpheme Grabber** as shown. Model the process for students as they create their page.

PAST TENSE VERBS

WEEK 2 Past Tense -ed and Irregular	TEACH: We affix -ed to verbs to indicate something finished and done. Irregular verbs do not add -ed, and these are one morpheme.		REVIEW: Level 1 Lessons 6-8.
Teach the Drop It, Change It, and Double It Spelling Rules			
-ed = /ed/	**-ed = /d/**	**-ed = /t/**	**/d/ Change y to i**
need	brew	pass	carry - carried
wait	rain	work	bury - buried
act	snow	talk	try - tried
cheat	scribble	slip	study - studied
greet	topple	erase	cry - cried
print	plug	wish	apply - applied

MORPHEME GRABBER - PAST TENSE

Choose one word from each category of past tense to enter into the **Morpheme Grabber**. Model the process for students as they create their page.

PRESENT TENSE VERBS - -ING, -S, -ES

WEEK 3 Present Tense -ing, -s, -es	TEACH: Verbs change when we add -s, -es, or -ing to them. The morphemes -s and -es can sound like /s//z/ /ez/or /eez/.		REVIEW: Level 1 Lessons 13-14.
Teach the Drop It, Change It, and Double It Spelling Rules			
Add -ing, -s to these verbs. Be careful of spelling changes!		Add -ing and -es to these verbs. Change the y to i when adding es	
s = /z/	**s = /s/**	**-es = /z/ and /eez/**	Fold a page in the Morpheme Grabber to make three columns. Write the base verb in column one, add -s or -es in the next column and then add -ing in the last column.
drive	like	cry	
need	work	fly	
become	make	try	
leave	write	wish	
remember	speak	study	
show	wait	carry	
hear	sit	apply	
stands	talk		

MORPHEME GRABBER - PRESENT TENSE

Choose one word from each category of present tense to enter into the **Morpheme Grabber**. Model the process for students as they create their page.

Review and Learn
Compound Words, Plurals, Past
Tense, Comparatives, Verb Suffixes

Plurals – -s, -es more than one
scoops, cones, faces

Past Tense Verbs -ed
printed, scribbled, worked, tried

Present Tense -s, -es, -ing
talks, shows, wishes, speaking

© Morpheme Magic

Use Morpheme Cards from Level 1 as needed.

Morpheme Grabber:

This is the first time students will use their Morpheme Grabber. Read through the directions in the introductory pages to prepare to create this morpheme dictionary. Students will add to this resource during every lesson.

Lesson Goal:

Learn the suffix -LY can be added to adjectives to become adverbs – telling how.

Teachers Know:

When affixing **-ly** to words ending in -y, change the -y to i and add **-ly**.

Word Bank

sad – sadly

mad – madly

glad – gladly

quick – quickly

soft – softly

dim – dimly

fond – fondly

last – lastly

close – closely

like – likely

late – lately

loose – loosely

shy – shyly

free – freely

light – lightly

loud – loudly

slow – slowly

nice – nicely

proud – proudly

kind – kindly

happy – happily

merry – merrily

INTRODUCTION

DAY ONE: EXPLORE THE MORPHEME

Explain that the class has been reviewing basic suffixes, the parts we add to ends of words that change the meanings of the stem words. Provide a few examples from Lesson 1 – plurals, past tense, -ing, etc. "Today we will study how words change when we add a different suffix, one that is familiar to you. Say "**quick**". Students say "**quick**." She was a **quick** runner. She ran **quickly**." *How* did she run? Students say, "**quickly**". How did we change **quick** to describe *how* she ran? Guide students to explain they added -**ly** to **quick** to make **quickly**. -**LY** added to adjectives and some nouns helps us explain **HOW** we do something. Do the same with glad. "**Glad**. The class was **glad** to be in school. They **gladly** entered the classroom. How did the class enter the room? **Gladly**." We add -**ly** to ends of words to describe **HOW**.

EXPLORE THE PHONEMES

Say **quick** as you clap. Students repeat. Now say **quick-ly** as you clap the syllables. Students repeat. How did **quick** change? She ran **quick-ly**? **Quick** is one syllable and when we added /l/ee/ to the end, we added another syllable. **Quick-ly** has two syllables and now tells **HOW** someone or something moves. What are the sounds in our new ending? /l/ee/. Do the same with **glad** and **gladly**.

ORTHOGRAPHY – READING AND SPELLING

DECODE: Teach the orthography of -ly. Write **quick**. Read it with the students. "I want to change **quick** to **quickly**." When you hear /ee/ on the end of a two syllable word, it will be spelled y. What do you hear at the end of **quickly**? /ee/. How do we spell our new suffix, -**ly**? Add -**ly** to **quick**. Read **quickly**.

Do the same with other words in the Word Bank or words from your current reading lesson. Direct students to use the words in sentences. Emphasize how the meanings change when we add -**ly**. The new words we make tell HOW.

ENCODE:
Dictate pairs of words: **quick** and **quickly**, **glad** and **gladly** and other words for students to spell. Use response boards and ask students to share their spellings after each word. Emphasize the spelling of -**ly**, and that this word part let us know that the word tells **HOW** something is done.

ACTIVITIES

MORPHEME GRABBER - WORD EQUATION OR DRAW AND LABEL

Direct students to create a new page in their Morpheme Grabber. Display the Lesson Morpheme Card and ask students to create their Morpheme Equation. Provide a sample if needed. Alternatively, younger students can draw a picture and label it with the **-ly** form.

WORD + ly	NEW WORD	MEANING
quick + ly =	quickly	**-LY** means **how** we do it

Adjust the following exercises for your students' language and reading levels.

THE MORPHEME CARD

Display the Morpheme Cards. Instruct students to say the focus **-ly** word for each picture, explore the meanings, use the words in sentences to tell about the pictures. REVIEW: Level Three – Reteach the morpheme. Say and write the words and a sentence for each.

ORAL LANGUAGE AND WRITE

Use the following sentence frames to engage students in using adverbs with **-ly**. Ask students "How" questions after each, i.e., *How* was he following his friend?" Write the words and or sentences after the oral responses. Ask students to expand the sentences.

He stayed **close** to his friend. He followed his friend ____. (**closely**)

The students were **loud**. They were talking ___. (**loudly**)

She was **proud** of her work. She displayed her art work ___. (**proudly**)

She was a **wishful** thinker. She gazed out the window ____. (**wishfully**)

CONNECT TO THE CLASSROOM

Substitute your students' names for the pronouns in the activity above. Present a list of words from the Word Bank. Ask students to create adverbs that tell how by adding **-ly**. Then work with students to create sentences applying their new words to their classroom and school. "**Thankfully**, we had our favorite substitute yesterday!"

REVIEW AND PRACTICE

Display one **-ly** word each day you are on this lesson. Model how to read the word, circle the base, and then underline the plural suffix **-ly**. Use words from the Word Banks or from your reading program.

Use sound spelling boxes to map and spell **-ly** words. Circle the morphemes.

slowly
Suffix -ly (how)

The turtle moved slowly across the sand.
Your Turn: When do you move slowly?
Use the word slowly.

© Morpheme Magic

More Word Bank Words

foolish – foolishly

reluctant – reluctantly

complete – completely

Why do the following words have a double -L when adding -ly?*

wishful – wishfully

thankful – thankfully

hopeful – hopefully

fitful – fitfully

regretful – regretfully

forgetful – forgetfully

careful – carefully

*Because the base ends in l and we add -ly

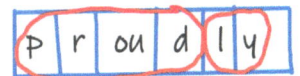

Lesson Goal:

Learn the suffix -LESS means without. It can be added to words to describe things and people.

Teachers Know:

-LESS is a good suffix to teach early because it only requires spelling changes when some bases end in y.

Word Bank

leaf – leafless

sleep – sleepless

help – helpless

hat – hatless

friend-friendless

joy – joyless

care – careless

cloud – cloudless

rest – restless

sleeve – sleeveless

voice – voiceless

life – lifeless

penny – penniless

pain – painless

INTRODUCTION

DAY ONE: EXPLORE THE MORPHEME

Let's study another suffix that changes the meaning of a base. Clap the syllables as the two examples are introduced. Say **care**. When we take **care** with our work, we can be proud of it. Say **careless**. When we are **careless** with our work, it does not turn out as good. How did we change **care** to describe *without* **care**? Guide students to explain they added -**less** to **care** to make **careless**. -LESS added to nouns helps us say **without it.** **Careless** means without **care**. Do the same with **sleep**. We need our **sleep** at night. How do you feel after a **sleepless** night? **Sleepless**." We add -**less** to ends of words to help us say **without it.**

EXPLORE THE PHONEMES

Say **care** as you clap. Students repeat. Now say **care-less** as you clap the syllables. Students repeat. How did **care** change? They were **care-less**? **Care** is one syllable and when we added /l/e/ss/ to the end, we added another syllable. **Care-less** has two syllables and now means **without care.** What are the sounds in our new ending? /l/e/ss/. Do the same with **sleep** and **sleepless**.

ORTHOGRAPHY - READING AND SPELLING

DECODE: Teach the orthography of -**less**. Write **care**. Read it with the students. "I want to change **care** to **careless,** meaning without **care."** Add -**less** to **care**. Read **careless.**

Do the same with other words in the Word Bank or words from your current reading lesson. Direct students to use the words in sentences. Emphasize how the meanings change when we add -**less**. The new words we make mean **without**.

ENCODE:

Dictate pairs of words: **care** and **careless**, **sleep** and **sleepless** and other words for students to spell. Use response boards and ask students to share their spellings after each word. Emphasize that -**less** means **without** ____. (fill in with the base word)

ACTIVITIES

MORPHEME GRABBER - WORD EQUATION OR DRAW AND LABEL

Direct students to create a new page in their Morpheme Grabber.

WORD + less	NEW WORD	MEANING
sleeve + less =	sleeveless	without sleeves

Adjust the following exercises for your students' language and reading levels.

THE MORPHEME CARD

Display the Morpheme Cards. Instruct students to say the focus **-less** word for each picture, explore the meanings, use the words in sentences to tell about the pictures. REVIEW: Level Three – Reteach the morpheme. Say and write the words and a sentence for each.

ORAL LANGUAGE AND WRITE

We can add **-less** to almost any noun which can lend itself to fun with making up words. "If I went into a bedroom and didn't see a bed, the room would be bedless." Work with students to come up with their own **-less** words, say the words, and then tell their meanings. Ask students to write one of their words with a sentence and be ready to share their word creations with the class.

CONNECT TO THE CLASSROOM

Discuss the characters, settings, plots, timelines in a story the students have read or listened to. Work with students to come up with **-less** words to talk about the story elements. For example, "The character was **joyless** when he did not find his missing soccer ball." "The tree in the yard was **leafless** after the big storm."

REVIEW AND PRACTICE

Display one **-less** word each day you are on this lesson. Model how to read the word, circle the base, and then underline **-less**. Use words from the Word Banks or from your reading program. Switch it out and display a word from the last lesson for review.

Use sound spelling boxes to map and spell **-less** words. Circle the morphemes.

sleeveless
Suffix -less (without)

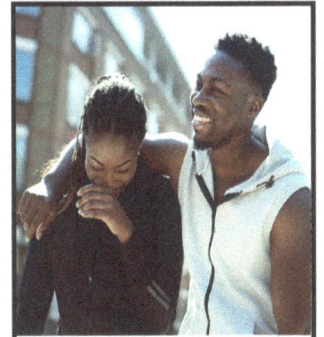

He was wearing a sleeveless hoodie.
Your Turn: Talk about this picture.
Use the word sleeveless.
© Morpheme Magic

More Word Bank Words

voice – voiceless

key – keyless

shape – shapeless

water – waterless

tune – tuneless

shapeless

Lesson Goal:

Learn the suffix -NESS means a state of. It can be added to words to say something is like the base. Words with -ness are nouns.

Teachers know:

An important part of building morphological awareness with young children is learning how to use words within sentences.

Word Bank

kind – kindness

sweet – sweetness

bold – boldness

sad – sadness

full – fullness

rich – richness

fit – fitness

well – wellness

glad – gladness

dark – darkness

short – shortness

INTRODUCTION

DAY ONE: EXPLORE THE MORPHEME

Today we are going to use some familiar words and when we add our new suffix, we will use the words in sentences in a different way. (Clap the syllables as the two examples are introduced.) Say **kind**. A **kind** person treats others with respect. Say **kindness**. **Kindness** makes our classroom a better place. How did we change **kind** to a word meaning being **kind**? **Kindness**. Guide students to explain they added -**ness** to **kind** to make **kindness**. -**NESS** added to **kind** helps us use **kind** in new way. -**NESS** means a state of, or when we have **kindness** we are being **kind**. Do the same with **sweet**. I like a **sweet** for dessert. Add -**ness** to **sweet**. **Sweetness**. The **sweetness** of chocolate cake makes me so happy! We add -**ness** to **sweet** and have another word to help us talk about **sweet - sweetness**.

EXPLORE THE PHONEMES

Say **kind** as you clap. Students repeat. Now say **kind-ness** as you clap the syllables. Students repeat. How did **kind** change? **Kindness** means being **kind**. **Kind** is one syllable and when we added /n/e/ss/ **ness** to the end, we added another syllable. **KIND-NESS** has two syllables and now means **being kind.** What are the sounds in our new ending? /n/e/ss/. Do the same with **sweet** and **sweetness.**

ORTHOGRAPHY - READING AND SPELLING

DECODE: Teach the orthography of -ness. Write **kind**. Read it with the students. "We will be **kind** to each other." Add -**ness** to **kind**. "**Kindness** is a good trait." Read **kindness.**

Do the same with other words in the Word Bank or words from your current reading lesson. Direct students to use the words in sentences. Emphasize how the meanings change when we add -**ness**. The new words we make mean **the way of being like the base.**

ENCODE:

Dictate pairs of words: **kind** and **kindness**, **sweet** and **sweetness** and other words for students to spell. Use response boards and ask students to share their spellings after each word. Emphasize that -**ness** changes how we use the word in sentences and means **being ____.** (fill in with the base word, **kind**, **sweet**). Use the -**ness** words in sentences – model sentences, and correct students' use of the words as needed.

ACTIVITIES

MORPHEME GRABBER - WORD EQUATION OR DRAW AND LABEL

Direct students to create a new page in their Morpheme Grabber.

WORD + ness	NEW WORD	MEANING
glad + ness =	to gladness	being glad

Adjust the following exercises for your students' language and reading levels.

THE MORPHEME CARD

Display the Morpheme Cards. Instruct students to say the focus -**ness** word for each picture, explore the meanings, use the words in sentences to tell about the pictures. REVIEW: Level Three – Reteach the morpheme. Say and write the words and a sentence for each.

ORAL LANGUAGE AND WRITE

Work with students to flex with word meanings to enrich their lexicons.

Rich – richness. – "The **richness** of the autumn color made me **breathless**."

Sweet – sweetness – "The **sweetness** of her singing voice made me so happy."

Furious – furiousness – "The **furiousness** of the dog's digging made a deep hole!"

Short – shortness – "The **shortness** of time caused us to hurry to finish!"

CONNECT TO THE CLASSROOM

What will these words sound like when we add -**ness**? These words name behaviors that help make our classroom a helpful learning environment. Do a T-Chart for each: What it sounds like, what it looks like.

alert - alertness, attentive – attentiveness, polite – politeness, careful – carefulness, busy – business, happy -happiness, neat – neatness, polite – politeness, swift – swiftness, responsive - responsiveness

responsiveness

Sounds Like	Looks Like
soft voices	follow directions

REVIEW AND PRACTICE

Display one -**ness** word each day you are on this lesson. Model how to read the word, circle the base, and then underline the -**ness**. Use words from the Word Bank or from your reading program.

Use sound spelling boxes to map and spell -**ness** words. Circle the morphemes. Switch it out and display a word from previous week's lessons for review.

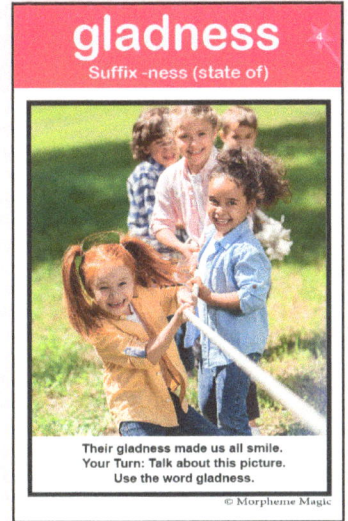

---

gladness
Suffix -ness (state of)

Their gladness made us all smile.
Your Turn: Talk about this picture.
Use the word gladness.

© Morpheme Magic

More Word Bank Words

swift – swiftness

tight – tightness

vast – vastness

busy – busyness

furious – furiousness

Questioning Minds:

Why is busy + ness spelled busyness and not business? Being busy, or a state of busy, is different than business which is commercial, or industrial dealings.

Lesson Goal:

Strengthen word knowledge with suffixes -LY, -LESS, and-NESS.

Teachers know:

Students learn new words incrementally over time. They need to hear how words are used, modeled by you, in many contexts. They need to practice using words to build knowledge of how words are used within sentences.

Word Bank

See Word Banks in Level 2 Lessons 2-4 and the Word Bank words on the next page.

-ly, -less, -ness meanings:

-ly = telling how

-less = without

-ness = like the base

INTRODUCTION

DAY ONE: REVIEW THE MORPHEMES, -LY, -LESS, -NESS

Write the review suffixes on the board. Say for each: When we add a suffix to a word we change the meaning of the word and how the word will be used. I will say a word, you say it. Then, when I pause while saying a sentence, say the word again.

Sweet – The cookies were ____. **Sweetly** – They thanked me very ____. (using a **sweet** voice) **Sweetless** – My sweet tooth can detect when a cookie is ____. **Sweetness** – We think ____ is a good thing!

Sweet can describe as an adjective (**sweet and sweetless**), adverb (**sweetly**), and noun (**sweet, sweetness**). **-LY** means *like* the base. **-LESS** means *without*. **-NESS** means *state of* being the base.

EXPLORE THE PHONEMES

Say one each of the words in the Word Banks with **-ly, -less, -ness**. Ask students to listen for the suffix on each word and whisper it to their elbow buddy. Then say the base and suffix as separate syllables.

ORTHOGRAPHY - READING AND SPELLING

DECODE: Prepare a variety of words using the review suffixes. Ensure that the words are spelled with graphemes your students have learned during your phonics lessons. Ask students to read the words together. Provide corrective feedback.

If you use words from your reading program, note them on this page for future use.

ENCODE:
Play the clue game with the words used above for decoding. Say, "Which word would I use when I see lots of smiling faces?" Students volunteer their answers, gladness, happily, friendly. Direct students to spell the word they are thinking of. Students can be asked to give clues for the class to answer.

ACTIVITIES

MORPHEME GRABBER - WORD EQUATION OR DRAW AND LABEL

Direct students to create a new page in their Morpheme Grabber.

WORD + REVIEW SUFFIX	= NEW WORD	MEANING
Choose a selection of **-LY**, **-NESS**, & **-LESS** words		

Adjust the following exercises for your students' language and reading levels.

THE MORPHEME CARDS

Display the Morpheme Cards for lessons 2-4. Instruct students to say the **-ly**, **-ness**, and **-less** word for each picture, and use the words in sentences to tell about the pictures. Challenge students to think of our other review suffix words to comment on the photos. For example, in the photo for **quickly**, we could use **fitness**, and **breathless**. Say and write sentences. REVIEW: Level Three – Reteach the morphemes. Say and write the words and a sentence for each.

ORAL LANGUAGE AND WRITE

Direct students to create three vertical columns on the next page in their Morpheme Grabber. Label each column with one of the three review suffixes and their meanings. Dictate a base word from the list on this page, and ask students to determine which suffixes they can add and then write the new words under the corresponding headings. If a student creates an awkward word such as *gladless*, ask the student to explain what the word would mean if it was a real word. Celebrate the morpheme awareness your students are gaining!

CONNECT TO THE CLASSROOM

Review the words students wrote in their three-column organizer. Ask students to work in small groups or partners to find words that describe their classroom. Ask them to be ready to share their thinking with the class.

REVIEW AND PRACTICE

Display a **-ly**, **-less**, and **-ness** word each day you are on this lesson. If needed, model how to read the word, circle the base, and then underline the suffix. Be ready to say what the suffixes means, the words mean, and use the words. Use words from the Word Banks or from your reading program.

Use sound spelling boxes to map and spell **-ly, -less, -ness** words. Circle the morphemes.

Use cards for Lessons 2-4 for review.

More Word Bank Words

glad: gladly, gladness

sweet: sweetly, sweetless, sweetness

swift: swiftly, swiftness

slow: slowly, slowness

light: lightly, lightless, lightness

happy: happily, happiness

fear: fearless, fearlessly

mad: madly, madness

polite: politely, politeness

price (N): priceless

love (N): lovely, loveless

friend (N): friendly, friendless, friendliness

Lesson Goal:

Learn that -FUL can be added to words to make new words. It means full of.

Teachers know:

Full is a free morpheme – a word that can stand alone. -FUL is a suffix that cannot stand alone and is affixed to primarily Anglo-Saxon words.

Word Bank

spoon – spoonful

fork – forkful

plate – plateful

cup – cupful

taste – tasteful

rest – restful

wonder – wonderful

hope – hopeful

wish – wishful

youth – youthful

waste – wasteful

awe – awful

beauty – beautiful

bounty – bountiful

harm – harmful

hurt – hurtful

joy – joyful

INTRODUCTION

DAY ONE: EXPLORE THE MORPHEME

Today we are going to use some familiar words and when we add our new suffix, we will use the words in sentences in a different way. (Clap the syllables as the two examples are introduced.) Say **spoon**. I use a **spoon** to eat my soup. Say **spoonful**. A **spoonful** of soup warms me on a cold day. How did we change **spoon** to a word meaning **full of**? **Spoonful**. Guide students to explain they added -**ful** to **spoon** to make **spoonful**. -**FUL** added to the noun **spoon** helps us use **spoon** in new way. -**FUL** means full, or when we have **"a spoonful"** our **spoon** is full! Do the same with **fork**. Will this **fork** hold mashed potatoes? Add -**ful** to **fork**. **Forkful**. The **forkful** of potatoes will not fit into my mouth! We add -**ful** to **fork** and have another word to help us talk about **fork**. **Forkful** – a full fork.

EXPLORE THE PHONEMES

We just learned a new word ending, -**ful**. Say -**ful**. Say the sounds in -**ful**. (The vowel /u/ will coarticulate with /l/. Help students isolate and say the short /u/ phoneme.) -**FUL** means… full! Lots of something, filled up. What is our new word part? -**FUL**.

ORTHOGRAPHY - READING AND SPELLING

DECODE: Teach the orthography of -**ful**. Write **spoon**. Read it with the students. "We can use a **spoon** to eat ice-cream." Add -**ful** to **spoon**. "**Spoonful** is a spoon full of something." Read **spoonful**. Teach: When we spell and read the _word_ full, we spell it f-u-l-l – write it, read it. When spelling and reading words with the suffix -ful, we spell it -**FUL** – write it and read it.

Do the same with other words in the Word Bank or words from your current reading lesson. Direct students to use the words in sentences. Emphasize how the meanings change when we add -**ful**. The new words we make mean **full**.

ENCODE:

Dictate pairs of words: **spoon** and **spoonful**, **fork** and **forkful** and other words for students to spell. Use response boards and ask students to share their spellings after each word. Emphasize that -**ful** changes how we use the word in sentences and means a **full** ____. (fill in with the base word, **spoon, fork**). Use the -**ful** words in sentences – model sentences, and correct students' use of the words as needed.

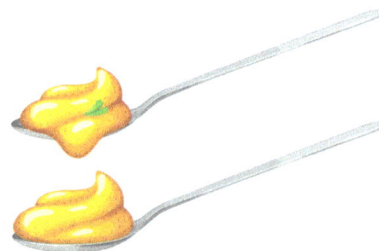

ACTIVITIES

MORPHEME GRABBER - WORD EQUATION OR DRAW AND LABEL

Direct students to create a new page in their Morpheme Grabber.

WORD + ful	= NEW WORD	MEANING
spoon + ful =	spoonful	a spoon full of something

Adjust the following exercises for your students' language and reading levels.

THE MORPHEME CARD

Display the Morpheme Cards. Instruct students to say the focus **-ful** word for each picture, explore the meanings, use the words in sentences to tell about the pictures. REVIEW: Level Three – Reteach the morpheme. Say and write the words and a sentence for each.

ORAL LANGUAGE AND WRITE

Display a list of **-ful** words provided below along with two categories into which the words can fit. Ask students to create two columns in their Morpheme Grabber for the categories and spell the words under a category. Ask students to be ready to share their thinking!

Categories: Parts of the Body and Words that Make you Happy

Word List: **earful**, **joyful**, **beautiful**, **headful**, **mouthful**, **wonderful** (ADD OTHERS)

CONNECT TO THE CLASSROOM

Ask students to think of examples of when the class might experience the following: **earful**, **headful**, **thankful**, **handful**, **hopeful**, **wasteful**. **Make sure students use the target -ful word in their responses.**

REVIEW AND PRACTICE

Display one **-ful** word each day you are on this lesson. Model how to read the word, circle the base, and then underline the suffix **-ful**. Use words from the Word Banks or from your reading program.

Use sound spelling boxes to map and spell **-ful** words. Circle the morphemes. Switch it out and display a word from previous week's lessons for review.

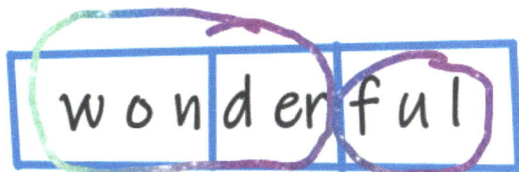

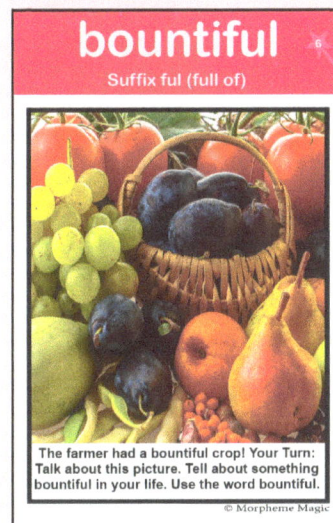

bountiful
Suffix ful (full of)

The farmer had a bountiful crop! Your Turn: Talk about this picture. Tell about something bountiful in your life. Use the word bountiful.

© Morpheme Magic

More Word Bank Words

ear – earful

eye – eyeful

head – headful

hand – handful

mouth – mouthful

thank – thankful

w o n d e r f u l

Lesson Goal:

Learn that -MENT can be added to words to make new words. It means state of or result of an action.

Teachers know:

The suffix **-ment** is an unaccented syllable, therefore the /e/ will be schwa. We hear /u/ for the vowel sound. For this reason, be explicit when teaching the spelling of -ment.

Word Bank

movement

pavement

excitement

payment

enjoyment

punishment

agreement

amazement

achievement

announcement

statement

commitment

nourishment

management

INTRODUCTION

DAY ONE: EXPLORE THE MORPHEME

Today we are going to use some familiar words and when we add our new suffix, we will use the words in sentences in a different way. (Clap the syllables as the two examples are introduced.) Say **move**. When playing freeze-tag, you cannot **move** if tagged. Say **movement**. If I see **movement**, you are out! How did we change **move** to a word meaning **result of an action**? **Movement**. Guide students to explain they added -**ment** to **move** to make **movement**. **-MENT** added to the noun **move** helps us use **move** in new way. **-MENT** means result of an action or state of, or when we see **movement,** someone has moved! Do the same with **pave**. They will **pave** the parking lot. Add -**ment** to **pave**. **Pavement**. The **pavement** was smooth and fun to ride bikes on! We add -**ment** to **pave** and have another word to help us talk about **pave**. **Pavement –** the result of paving.

EXPLORE THE PHONEMES

The suffix -**ment** will most likely be in the unaccented syllable and take on the schwa sound. Say -**ment** with a strong /e/. Ask students to segment the phonemes, /m/e/n/t/. Ask students to listen to -**ment** at the end of **movement**. Lead them to listen for the schwa vowel /u/. Explain that the vowel sound drops down to /u/ when we say -**ment** in words.

ORTHOGRAPHY - READING AND SPELLING

DECODE: Explore the orthography of words with -**ment**. Write **movement**, scoop the morphemes, **move-ment**. Decode and read the word. **Movement** is the word we use when we see something **move**. **-MENT** means a state of or result of an action.

Do the same with other words in the Word Bank or words from your current reading lesson.

ENCODE:

Dictate -**ment** words for students to spell. Ask them to scoop the parts that have meaning. Use response boards and ask students to share their spellings after each word. Emphasize -**ment** turns the verb we affix it to, into a noun.

ACTIVITIES

MORPHEME GRABBER - WORD EQUATION OR DRAW AND LABEL

Direct students to create a new page in their Morpheme Grabber.

WORD + ment	= NEW WORD	MEANING
move + ment =	movement	the result of moving

Adjust the following exercises for your students' language and reading levels.

THE MORPHEME CARD

Display the Morpheme Cards. Instruct students to say the focus **-ment** word for each picture, explore the meanings, use the words in sentences to tell about the pictures. REVIEW: Level Three – Reteach the morpheme. Say and write the words and a sentence for each.

ORAL LANGUAGE AND WRITE

Ask students to listen for the verb and respond with the **-ment** word that fits:

When we *commit* to something we make a ____. (**commitment**)

When we *argue*, we are having an ___. (**argument**)

When we *replace* a burned-out bulb, the new bulb is a ___.(**replacement**)

The people who *govern* are the ___. (**government**)

When we *arrange* the flowers, we make an ___. (**arrangement**)

CONNECT TO THE CLASSROOM

Tell the students that the principal is going to make an **announcement** tomorrow. We are going to write the script for him/her to read. It needs to have the following **-ment** words in it, and maybe others. Work with the students to write an **announcement**. Then ask the principal to read it for an **announcement**!

Commitment, **statement**, **achievement**, **amazement**, **engagement**, **enjoyment**

REVIEW AND PRACTICE

Display one **-ment** word each day you are on this lesson. Model how to read the word, circle the base, and then underline **-ment**. Use words from the Word Banks or words students and you think of.

Use syllable spelling boxes to map and spell **-ment** words. Circle the morphemes. Switch it out and display a word from previous week's lessons for review.

amazement
Suffix -ment (state of, result of an action)

I looked with amazement at the carnival rides! Your Turn: Talk about this picture. Use the word amazement.

© Morpheme Magic

More Word Bank Words

argument

commitment

government

replacement

employment

discouragement

entertainment

commandment

excitement

ex - out and cite (L) means set in motion

nourishment

Lesson Goal:

Learn UN- is a prefix. UN- means not, to undo, or opposite of.

Teachers know:

Level 1 introduced **un-** to students. Level 2 will expand the word items for reading and spelling practice. Refer to Level 1 Lesson 15 for more teaching ideas.

Word Bank

unwrap

unclean

unsafe

unlucky

uneven

uncommon

unselfish

uncover

unseat

unstrung

unbutton

untie

unlock

unlucky

INTRODUCTION

DAY ONE: EXPLORE THE MORPHEME

We have been working with suffixes, the meaningful word parts we add at the ends of words to change the meaning. Today we will begin learning about prefixes which we add before the base word. Say **wrap**. Mom will **wrap** my gift. Listen, **unwrap**. Say the new word. How did **wrap** change in our new word, **unwrap**? Lead students to identify **un-** was added to make a new word. **UN-** means reverse – the opposite. When she gives it to me, I will **unwrap** it! We added **un-** to the beginning of **wrap**, what's our new word? **Unwrap!**

UN- means opposite or reverse, but it can also mean **NOT**. **Clean** (students say it). **Unclean** (students say it). **Unclean** means **NOT** clean. Say **safe**. Change **safe** to the new word if you are **NOT** safe. Lead students to say **Unsafe** – **not safe**. **UN-** is an important word part that changes the meanings of words!

EXPLORE THE PHONEMES

Say our new prefix **un-**. What are the sounds in **un-**? Students segment **un-** and say, "**UN-** is a prefix that means **NOT** or **OPPOSITE OF.**"

ORTHOGRAPHY – READING AND SPELLING

DECODE:

Present the bases of several words. Decode each with students. Then add **un-** to one word at a time, decode, and then discuss the meanings. Use each in a sentence.

ENCODE:

Dictate **un-** words from the word bank for students to spell. Use response boards and ask students to share their spellings after each word. Emphasize **un-** and the meanings of each word. "**Un-**means _____ and so the word means _____."

ACTIVITIES

MORPHEME GRABBER - WORD EQUATION OR DRAW AND LABEL

Direct students to create a new page in their Morpheme Grabber.

UN- + WORD	= NEW WORD	MEANING
un + wrap =	unwrap	to undo the gift wrap – to open it

Adjust the following exercises for your students' language and reading levels.

THE MORPHEME CARD

Display the Morpheme Cards. Instruct students to say the prefix **un-** word for each picture, explore the meanings, use the words in sentences to tell about the pictures. REVIEW: Level Three – Reteach the morpheme. Say and write the words and a sentence for each.

ORAL LANGUAGE AND WRITE

Engage students in verbal reasoning as they work to answer the following questions. Direct them to work with partners and then share their answers. If students have difficulty, model your thinking. Ideas are provided.

How are **untie** and **unlace** the same? Different? (Think of shoes.)

How are **unable** and **unwilling** the same? Different? (running a mile)

How are **unchain** and **unlock** the same? Different? (a gate or door)

How are **unglue** and **unstick** the same? Different? (an art project)

Challenge: How are **untruthful** and **unknown** the same? Different?

CONNECT TO THE CLASSROOM

Find several **un-** words that can be used to discuss a character and plot in a read aloud this week. Ask comprehension questions using the **un-** words. for example, if reading *Charlotte's Web*, you could use **unhappy**, **unfair**, **unwise**, **uncertain** to talk about Wilbur or Charlotte.

REVIEW AND PRACTICE

Display one **un-** word each day you are on this lesson. Model how to read the word, circle the base, and then underline **un-**. Use words from the Word Banks or from your reading program. Include words with added **-ed** (**untied**, **unlocked**, **unpacked**, **unfolded**). These can be used as adjectives and/or verbs.

Use sound spelling boxes to map and spell **un-** words. Circle the morphemes. Switch it out and display a word from previous week's lessons for review, and also include word items with **-ed**.

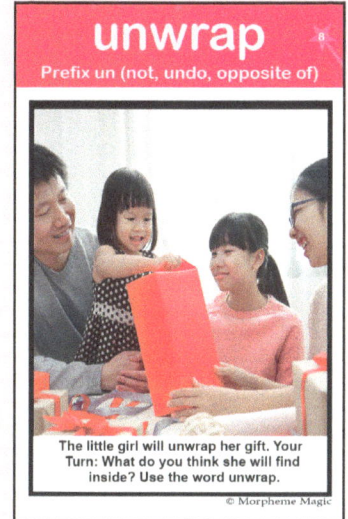

unwrap
Prefix un (not, undo, opposite of)

The little girl will unwrap her gift. Your Turn: What do you think she will find inside? Use the word unwrap.

© Morpheme Magic

More Word Bank Words

untangle

unequal

unaware

unbuckle

unjust

unkind

unknown

unwilling

unbroken

unstable

More Oral Language and Write:

Think of riding your bike: What would be **unsafe**?

How are **unbuckle, unzip**, and **unbutton** the same? How are they different?

Lesson Goal:

Learn RE- is a prefix. RE-means again or back.

Teachers know:

Level 1 introduced **re-** to students. Level 2 will expand the word items for reading and spelling practice. Refer to Level 1 Lesson 16 for more teaching ideas.

Word Bank

RE – meaning again

retell – tell again

restring – string again

recap – cap again

redo – do again

reset – set again or set back

retry – try again

rewrite – write again

reform – form again

restart – start again

INTRODUCTION

DAY ONE: EXPLORE THE MORPHEME

We have been learning about prefixes which we add in front of the base word. Today we will learn a new prefix. Say **tell**. He will **tell** us a story. Listen, **retell**. Say the new word. How did **tell** change in our new word, **retell**? Lead students to identify **re-** was added to make a new word. **RE-** means again. After he **tells** the story, I will **retell** it to my friend! I will **tell** it again. We added **re-** to the beginning of **tell**, what's our new word? **Retell!**

RE- means again, but it can also mean **back**. **Claim** (students say it). When you **claim** something, you take it as yours. That book is good! I claim it! R**eclaim** (students say it). **Reclaim** means **to take it back**. After loaning the book to a friend, you will **reclaim** it – take it back. **RE-** is an important word part that changes the meanings of words!

EXPLORE THE PHONEMES

Say our new prefix **re-**. What are the sounds in **re-?** Students segment **re-** and say, "**RE-** is a prefix that means **back or again."**

ORTHOGRAPHY - READING AND SPELLING

Present the bases of several words. Decode each with students. Then add **re-** to one word at a time, decode, and then discuss the meanings. Use each in a sentence.

ENCODE:
Dictate **re-** words from the word bank for students to spell. Use response boards and ask students to share their spellings after each word. Emphasize **re-** and the meanings of each word. "**RE-** means _____ and so the word means _____."

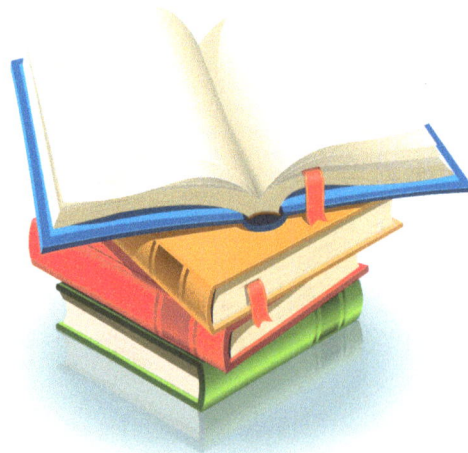

ACTIVITIES

MORPHEME GRABBER - WORD EQUATION OR DRAW AND LABEL
Direct students to create a new page in their Morpheme Grabber.

RE + WORD	= NEW WORD	MEANING
re + tell =	retell	to tell again
re + claim =	reclaim	to claim back

Adjust the following exercises for your students' language and reading levels.

THE MORPHEME CARD
Display the Morpheme Cards for Lessons 6-8 and 9. Instruct students to say the past tense for each picture, segment and explore the phonemes, use the verbs in sentences to tell about the picture. REVIEW: Review Suffix Spelling rules as needed. Level Two - say and write the words. Level Three - say and write the words and a sentence for each.

ORAL LANGUAGE AND WRITE
Ask students to supply the **re-** word to finish the sentence. Ask students to write the prefix **re-** words in their Morpheme Grabbers after they think of the words.

When I **count** something again I ___. (**recount**) What might you recount?

When I **view** something again, I ____ it. (**review**) Ask for examples of something they would **review**.

When I **call** back a memory, I ____ the memory. (**recall**) What do you recall from yesterday?

When I **start** the computer again, I ___ it. (**restart**) What else can we **restart**?

CONNECT TO THE CLASSROOM
Display the following words on the board. Tell students that you will use many of these words during the day. When they hear you say one of the words ask them to raise their hands. Let's see how many of these words we can use!

Classroom words: **rework, recount, review, rewrite, retell, restart, retry**

REVIEW AND PRACTICE
Display one **re-** word each day you are on this lesson. Model how to read the word, circle the base, and then underline the prefix. Use words from the Word Banks or from your reading program.

Use sound spelling boxes to map and spell **re-** words. Circle the morphemes. Switch it out and display a word from previous week's lessons for review.

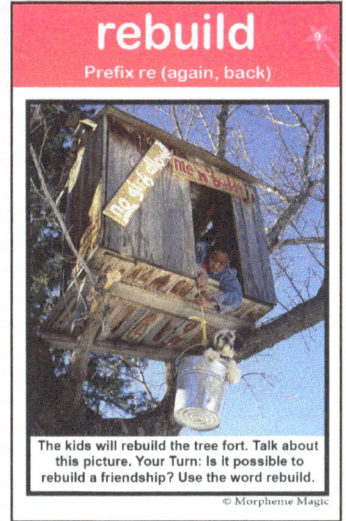

rebuild
Prefix re (again, back)
The kids will rebuild the tree fort. Talk about this picture. Your Turn: Is it possible to rebuild a friendship? Use the word rebuild.
© Morpheme Magic

More Word Bank Words

RE – meaning again

rework – work it again

review – view or look again

recount – count again

rebuild – build again

RE – meaning back

reclaim – claim back

rebound – bound back

reform – form behavior back

recall – call back

rejoin – join back or again

refresh – freshen back

Lesson Goal:

Learn PRE- is a prefix.
PRE- means before.

Teachers know:

Level 1 introduced **pre-** to students. Level 2 will expand the word items for reading and spelling practice. Refer to Level 1 Lesson 17 for more teaching ideas.

Word Bank

preheat

pretest

preview

preset

preregister

preteen

preprogram

preflight

preform

presell

prewrite

preplan

prepay

prearrange

INTRODUCTION

DAY ONE: EXPLORE THE MORPHEME

We have been learning about prefixes which we add in front of the base word. Today we will learn a new prefix. Say **heat**. We **heat** the oven to bake a cake. Listen, **preheat**. Say the new word. How did **heat** change in our new word, **preheat?** Lead students to identify **pre-** was added to make a new word. **PRE-** means before. We **preheat** the oven *before* we bake the cake. We added **pre-** to the beginning of **heat**, what's our new word? **Preheat!**

EXPLORE THE PHONEMES

Say our new prefix **PRE-.** What are the sounds in **pre-?** Students segment **pre-** and say, "PRE- is a prefix that means **before.**"

ORTHOGRAPHY - READING AND SPELLING

Present the bases of several words. Decode each with students. Then add **pre-** to one word at a time, decode, and then discuss the meanings. Use each in a sentence.

ENCODE:

Dictate **pre-** words from the word bank for students to spell. Use response boards and ask students to share their spellings after each word. Emphasize **pre-** and the meanings of each word. "**Pre**-means _____ and so the word means _____."

ACTIVITIES

MORPHEME GRABBER - WORD EQUATION OR DRAW AND LABEL

Direct students to create a new page in their Morpheme Grabber.

PRE + WORD	= NEW WORD	MEANING
pre + plan =	preplan	to plan before

Adjust the following exercises for your students' language and reading levels.

THE MORPHEME CARD

Display the Morpheme Cards. Instruct students to say the prefix **pre-** word for each picture, explore the meanings, use the words in sentences to tell about the pictures. REVIEW: Level Three – Reteach the morpheme. Say and write the words and a sentence for each.

ORAL LANGUAGE AND WRITE

Ask the following questions to stimulate discussions and provide opportunities to use words with the prefix **pre-**. Make sure kids use the **pre-** focus word in their answers.

When would you **preset** something? (TV settings, computer, clock alarm, etc.)

Are you a **preteen**? How do you know? (younger than 13 years old)

What can you **prearrange**? (a sleep over, a birthday party)

CONNECT TO THE CLASSROOM

Create an art project collage that fits the season. Direct students to determine the shapes they will need and **precut** the shapes earlier in the day before actually creating the artwork. For example if autumn – **precut** colored leaves, if winter, **precut** snow shapes, snowman, etc. use the word **precut** and ask students to share what they **precut** and use the word **precut**.

REVIEW AND PRACTICE

Display one prefix **pre-** word each day you are on this lesson. Model how to read the word, circle the base, and then underline the prefix **pre-**. Use words from the Word Banks or from your reading program.

Use sound spelling boxes to map and spell **pre-** words. Circle the morphemes. Switch it out and display a word from previous week's lessons for review.

preplan
Prefix pre (before)

It is a good idea to preplan a trip.
Your turn: Why is it helpful to preplan? Use the word preplan.

© Morpheme Magic

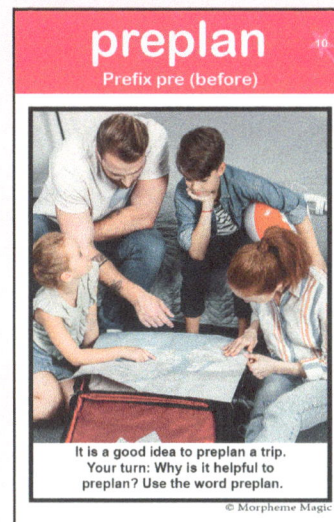

More Word Bank Words

These are Latin stems with the prefix **PRE-**:

pretend

present

predict

prefer

prevent

prepare

TIP: When teaching the prefix **PRE-**, it is always fun to use the word **PREFIX** to teach, that a **PREFIX** is the part of a word that comes **BEFORE** the base. It is **FIXED** before the base word.

p r e d i c t

dict (L) means speak

Lesson Goal:

Strengthen word knowledge with prefixes UN-, RE-, and PRE-.

Teachers know:

Students develop awareness of morphemes over time with our explicit instruction. They need to hear how words are used, modeled by you, in many contexts. They need to use words, write them, and compose sentences in which the words are used.

Word Bank

UN – NOT, UNDO

unearth

uncoil

unsnarl

RE - BACK, AGAIN

rebuild

rebound

recast

recount

replace

reflex

INTRODUCTION

DAY ONE: REVIEW THE MORPHEMES, PREFIXES UN-, RE-, PRE-

Write the review prefixes on the board. Say for each: When we add a prefix to a word, we change how the word will be used. I will say a word, you say it. Then, when I pause while saying a sentence, say the word again.

Wrap – We will ___ the gifts and hide them. **Unwrap** – To discover what is inside, I have to ___ the gift. **Rewrap** – Oh, oh. I need to ___ the presents! **Prewrapped** – When gifts are **prewrapped**, it is hard not to peek!

Wrap can become many words with the help of prefixes. **UN-** means *not wrapped,* **re-** means *wrap again* and **pre-** means *wrapped before.*

EXPLORE THE PHONEMES

Say a selection of the words in the Word Banks with **un-, re-, pre-**. Ask students to listen for the prefix on each word and whisper it to their elbow buddy. Then say the base and suffix as separate syllables.

ORTHOGRAPHY - READING AND SPELLING

DECODE: Prepare a variety of words using the review prefixes. Ensure that the words are spelled with graphemes your students have learned during your phonics lessons. Ask students to read the words together. Provide corrective feedback.

If you use words from your reading program, note them on this page for future use.

ENCODE:
Play the clue game with the words used above for decoding. Say, "Which word would I use when I want to heat up the oven *before* baking cookies? **(preheat)** Provide more information if needed: The word uses the prefix **pre-**. Direct students to share the word they are thinking of and to spell the word. Students can be asked to give clues for the class to answer and spell. Post the prefixes as a reference for students during this exercise.

ACTIVITIES

MORPHEME GRABBER - WORD EQUATION OR DRAW AND LABEL

Direct students to create a new page in their Morpheme Grabber.

PREFIX + WORD	= NEW WORD	MEANING
Choose a selection of UN-, RE-, PRE- words		

Adjust the following exercises for your students' language and reading levels.

THE MORPHEME CARD

Display the Morpheme Cards from Lessons 8-10. Instruct students to say the prefix, its meaning and key word for each picture, explore the meanings, use the words in sentences to tell about the pictures. REVIEW: Level Three – Reteach the morpheme. Say and write the words and a sentence for each.

ORAL LANGUAGE AND WRITE

Present the following words. Ask students to imagine a time when they would use the word and discuss the situation using the word. Following the oral exercise, direct students to write the word, its meaning, and a few sentences telling their story. (example situations are given)

Unlucky –at the fair when I didn't win the stuffed animal

Rebuild –when the wave destroyed my sandcastle

Prename –when I had a name ready for my new pet before I got it

CONNECT TO THE CLASSROOM

Work with the students to choose one word for each prefix that everyone could use during a school day. Write the words on the board. Challenge students and yourself to use the words.

REVIEW AND PRACTICE

Display one **un-, re-, pre-** word each day you are on this lesson. Model how to read the word, circle the base, underline the prefix and discuss meaning. Use words from the Word Banks or from your reading program.

Use sound spelling boxes to map and spell **un-, re-, pre-** words. Circle the morphemes, discuss meanings.

Use cards for Lessons 8-10 for review.

Review
un-, re-, pre-

UN-NOT	RE- BACK	PRE- BEFORE
unable	research	prewash
unaware	report	predesign
unbeaten	recent	recorrect
uncommon	reject	precook
undress	remark	predial
unemployment	repair	predessert
unfit	return	precare
unreliable	record	prebuy
untrue	require	prebuild
unpaid	release	prebutter
untie	reply	preadmit
unlikely	react	preadult
unclear	reduce	prerun
unblock	reform	preprint
untold	refuse	presale

© Morpheme Magic

More Word Bank Words

PRE- – BEFORE.

prepare

prescribe

prevent

precise – cise (L) means cut. Teachers may want to look up on etymonline.org for interesting etymology.

See Word Banks in Level 2 Lessons 8-10, Morpheme Card 11, and the Word Bank words on the previous page for more words.

Lesson Goal:

Learn that IN- can be added to the beginning of words to make new words. In these words, IN- means in, on, or toward.

Teachers know:

It is not critical that students learn the meanings of Latin roots at this Level. Building awareness that words have meaningful parts, and growing students' vocabulary are our goals. Knowing what whole words mean and using the words is our target goal until students get older and are ready for deeper study of morphemes.

Word Bank

invite

inspect

invent

indent

INTRODUCTION

DAY ONE: EXPLORE THE MORPHEME

Today we are going to work with a prefix. Prefixes come at the beginning of words to change the meaning. The part of the word we will add our prefix to, will be a word part that needs a prefix to make a word. (Clap the syllables as the two examples are introduced.) Say **in-**. Say **-vite**. **Invite**. I will **invite** my friend over after school. **IN-** is our new prefix and in this word, it is at the beginning of **-vite**. **-Vite** is not a word by itself, but it does mean something. It means *live*. **IN-** means in and **vite-** means live. When we **invite**, we ask someone in to be with us, or live with us. Let's try another one. Say **in-**. Say **-spect**. **Inspect**. **IN-** means in and **-spect** means to see. When you inspect something you **look in** very closely. We are **inspecting** these words when we look closely inside of them! What is something else you can **inspect**?

EXPLORE THE PHONEMES

We have two **IN-** words to inspect. Say **in-spect.** Segment the sounds in **in-**, meaning in. /i/n/. What are the sounds in **-spect** which means to see. Make sure students are segmenting the consonant blends in /s/p/e/c/t/. Explain that they are just starting to learn Latin roots of which many end in the /c/t/ sounds.

Do the same with **invite**.

ORTHOGRAPHY - READING AND SPELLING

DECODE: Teach the orthography and meanings of **in-** words. Teach the morphemes of each word after decoding it. Write a word, scoop the morphemes. Decode each and then blend them together to read the word. Teach and decode **invite, inspect, invent**. **-VENT** means to come – **invent** = to come *into* existence. **INDENT -Dent** means tooth – **indent** = to take a bite *in* when we start a paragraph.

ENCODE:

Dictate the **in-** words for students to spell. Ask them to draw a line for each morpheme they hear, spell each word part on the lines, and then spell the whole word. Use response boards and ask students to share their spellings after each word. Emphasize **in-** means in and this prefix is affixed to many Latin roots that need the prefix to become a word.

ACTIVITIES

MORPHEME GRABBER - WORD EQUATION OR DRAW AND LABEL

Direct students to create a new page in their Morpheme Grabber.

IN + WORD	= NEW WORD	MEANING
in + vite =	invite	ask someone in

Adjust the following exercises for your students' language and reading levels.

THE MORPHEME CARD

Display the Morpheme Cards. Instruct students to say the focus **in-** word for each picture, explore the meanings, use the words in sentences to tell about the pictures. REVIEW: Level Three – Reteach the morpheme. Say and write the words and a sentence for each.

CONNECT TO THE CLASSROOM

A few of the **in-** words lend themselves to day-to-day academic talk. Post a word a day, discuss the word with students asking them to reflect on when the word could be used during the day. Challenge students to use the terms and you will challenge yourself to use them. Set a goal with the students. Whenever someone hears the word being used, you will place a tally mark by the word. What is the goal? 10? 25? Have fun!

Post: input, infer, increase, intent

REVIEW AND PRACTICE

Display one **in-** word each day you are on this lesson. Model how to read the word, circle the root, and then underline the prefix **in-**. Use words from the Word Banks.

Use syllable spelling boxes to map and spell **in-** words. Circle the morphemes after the syllables are written. Switch it out and display a word from a previous week's lessons for review.

inhabit
Prefix in (in, on, toward)

A hermit crab will inhabit this shell. Your Turn: Name some animals and what they live in. Use the word inhabit.

© Morpheme Magic

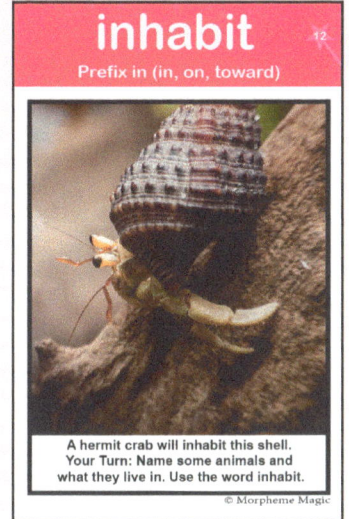

More Word Bank Words

input – to *put* in, add to the conversation

infer – to *yield* new information in your thinking

income – money that *comes* in

install – to put in place

increase – to grow in

inspire – to *breathe* new ideas in

inhabit – to *live* in

inherit – something that *stays* in the family

intent – purpose

i n h e r i t

herit (L) means to stick

Lesson Goal:

Learn that NON- can be added to the beginning of words to make new words. NON-means not.

Word Bank

nonstop

nonstick

nonsense

nonfat

nondairy

nonskid

nonreader

nonverbal

nontoxic

nonessential

nonsmoking

DAY ONE: EXPLORE THE MORPHEME

Today we are going to work with a new prefix. Remember, prefixes come at the beginning of words to change the meaning. (Clap the syllables as the two examples are introduced.) Say **non-**. Say **stop**. **Nonstop**. Our pet gerbil runs on the wheel **nonstop**. **NON-** is our new prefix at the beginning of stop. **NON-** means *not*. When we do something **nonstop,** we do **not** stop. Let's try another one. Say **non-**. Say **sense**. **Nonsense**. **NON-** means **not** and **sense** means to see. When you hear that an elephant can fly, you say, "**Nonsense**"! What is something else that is **nonsense**?

EXPLORE THE PHONEMES

Say our new prefix **non-.** What are the sounds in **non-?** Students segment **non-** and say, "**NON-** is a prefix that means **not.**"

ORTHOGRAPHY - READING AND SPELLING

DECODE: Teach the orthography and meanings of **non-** words. Teach the morphemes of each word after decoding it. Write a word, scoop the morphemes. Decode each and then blend them together to read the word. Teach and decode **nonstop, nonstick, nosense, nonfat.**

ENCODE:

Dictate the **non-** words for students to spell. Ask them to draw a line for each morpheme they hear, spell each word part on the lines, and then spell the whole word. Use response boards and ask students to share their spellings after each word. Emphasize **non-** means **not.**

ACTIVITIES

MORPHEME GRABBER - WORD EQUATION OR DRAW AND LABEL

Direct students to create a new page in their Morpheme Grabber.

NON + WORD	= NEW WORD	MEANING
non + stop =	nonstop	not stopping

Adjust the following exercises for your students' language and reading levels.

THE MORPHEME CARDS

Display the Morpheme Cards. Instruct students to say the prefix **non-** word for each picture, explore the meanings, use the words in sentences to tell about the pictures. REVIEW: Level Three – Reteach the morpheme. Say and write the words and a sentence for each.

ORAL LANGUAGE AND WRITE

Some of the **non-** words are related to food: **nonfat, nondairy, nonstick**, **nontoxic**. Pose a word and lead a discussion about how the word relates to food. Ask students to write the word and then write it in a sentence.

Don't let your students be **nonverbal** or **nonwriters**!

CONNECT TO THE CLASSROOM

Create a lesson around the words **essential** and **nonessential.** Create a two-column organizer with the two words as headings. Brainstorm a situation such as: In their classroom, in a bedroom, going on a trip (to a place you have studied, or related to a story/article you have read together). Once you pose the situation, brainstorm with students **essential** and **nonessential** items that one would need or not need. Record the ideas on the chart.

essential   nonessential

water   soda pop

REVIEW AND PRACTICE

Display one **non-** word each day you are on this lesson. Model how to read the word, circle the base, and then underline the prefix **non-**. Use words from the Word Banks or possibly from your reading program.

Use sound spelling or syllable spelling boxes to map and spell **non-** words. Circle the morphemes. Switch it out and display a word from previous week's lessons for review.

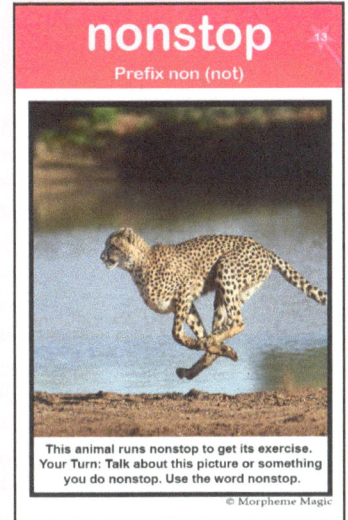

nonstop
Prefix non (not)

This animal runs nonstop to get its exercise.
Your Turn: Talk about this picture or something you do nonstop. Use the word nonstop.
© Morpheme Magic

More Word Bank Words

The prefix **NON-** can be added to almost any noun and some adjectives: **nonworker, nonplayer, nonpicky, nonbarker**. Work with students to play with words and create **NON-** words together. Ask students to define and use the *nonsense* words they create.

Lesson Goal:

Learn that MIS- can be added to the beginning of words to make new words. MIS-means wrong or bad.

Teachers know:

There are two s's in misspell because the prefix ends in S and *spell* begins with S.

Are there other **MIS-** words that we can use as examples with students?

Word Bank

mismatch

misspell

miscall

misdeal

misfire

misstep

mistake

misshape

misspend

misrule

misquote

misplace

mismanage

misconduct

INTRODUCTION

DAY ONE: EXPLORE THE MORPHEME

Today we are going to work with a new prefix. Remember, prefixes come at the beginning of words to change the meaning. (Clap the syllables as the two examples are introduced.) Say **mis-**. Say **match**. **Mismatch**. His two socks were a **mismatch**. **MIS-** is our new prefix at the beginning of **match**. **MIS-** means *wrong*. When something does not match, it could be a **mismatch,** the match is wrong. Let's try another one. Say **mis-**. Say **spell**. **Misspell**. **MIS-** means wrong and **spell** is when we write the letter sounds for a word. When I **misspell** a word, it could be hard to read and I will fix it.

EXPLORE THE PHONEMES

Say our new prefix **mis-**. What are the sounds in **mis-**? Students segment **mis-** and say, **"MIS-** is a prefix that means **wrong or bad."**

ORTHOGRAPHY - READING AND SPELLING

DECODE: Teach the orthography and meanings of **mis-** words. Teach the morphemes of each word after decoding it. Write a word, scoop the morphemes. Decode each and then blend them together to read the word. Teach and decode a selection from the word bank. Include the two introductory words **mismatch** and **misspell**.

ENCODE:
Dictate the **mis-** words for students to spell. Ask them to draw a line for each morpheme they hear, spell each word part on the lines, and then spell the whole word. Use response boards and ask students to share their spellings after each word. Emphasize **mis-** means *wrong*.

ACTIVITIES

MORPHEME GRABBER - WORD EQUATION OR DRAW AND LABEL

Direct students to create a new page in their Morpheme Grabber.

MIS + WORD	= NEW WORD	MEANING
mis + step =	misstep	wrong or bad step

Adjust the following exercises for your students' language and reading levels.

THE MORPHEME CARD

Display the Morpheme Cards. Instruct students to say the prefix **mis-** word for each picture, explore the meanings, use the words in sentences to tell about the pictures. REVIEW: Level Three – Reteach the morpheme. Say and write the words and a sentence for each.

ORAL LANGUAGE AND WRITE

Ask the following questions to stimulate verbal reasoning and initiate discussion. Follow with written responses.

What is something that you might **misplace**? (keys, toys, pencil)

What is a situation when you might have **misguided** a friend?

What is a situation you **mishandled**? (respond to something in a wrong way)

When would you use the term **misstep**?

CONNECT TO THE CLASSROOM

Seat students in a circle. Play a form of the old-fashioned game 'telephone'. Teacher creates a statement about something children are learning, whispering it in the first student's ear. That student, whispers it into the next student's ear and so forth around the circle. At the end, the last student says aloud what he heard. Did the **QUOTE** make it around the circle? Or was the statement a **MISQUOTE**?

REVIEW AND PRACTICE

Display one **mis-** word each day you are on this lesson. Model how to read the word, circle the base, and then underline the **mis-**. Use words from the Word Banks or from your reading program. Discuss the meanings.

Use sound or syllable spelling boxes to map and spell FOCUS words. Circle the morphemes. Switch it out and display a word from previous week's lessons for review.

misstep
Prefix mis (wrong, bad)

Oh, oh! She made a misstep!
Your Turn: Talk about this picture and use the word misstep.
© Morpheme Magic

More Word Bank Words

misunderstand

misfortune

misguide

misadventure

misdirect

mistook

mishandle

TIP: Teach that **miss** is a word, one whole word morpheme. "I will **miss** school when I am sick." **MIS-** is a prefix spelled with one S and cannot stand alone. It must be added to a word. Do not make a **MISTAKE** and spell the prefix MISS!.

Teachers know:

In most words, with the prefix **sub-**, it is affixed to a Latin bound root. That means, that the stem will be unfamiliar to young students. The lesson addresses the meanings of Latin roots briefly at this level. The purpose is to create awareness. Students will learn these meanings in a few years. It is more important they learn the words and can use them.

Word Bank

submarine

subtract

INTRODUCTION

DAY ONE: EXPLORE THE MORPHEME

Today we are going to work with a new prefix. Remember, prefixes come at the beginning of words to change the meaning. Say **sub-**. Say **marine**. **Submarine**. The **submarine** disappeared under the ocean surface. **SUB-** is our new prefix at the beginning of **marine**. **SUB-** means *beneath* and *marine* means sea. A special water craft that travels under the sea is a **Submarine**. Let's try another one. Say **sub-**. Say **-tract**. **Subtract**. **SUB-** means under and **tract** is a root word that needs a prefix or suffix to make it a word**. -TRACT** means pull. So **subtract** means t**o pull down.** Think about how that fits with **subtraction** we do in math. What happens to the answers we get when we **subtract?** The answer goes down. Right! When we **subtract** the answers decrease**.**

EXPLORE THE PHONEMES

Say our new prefix **sub-**. What are the sounds in **sub-?** Students segment **sub-** and say**, "SUB- is a prefix that means under or below."**

ORTHOGRAPHY - READING AND SPELLING

DECODE: Teach the orthography and meanings of **sub-** words. Teach the morphemes of each word after decoding it, but most important will be teaching the meaning of the whole word. Write a word, scoop the morphemes. Decode each and then blend them together to read the word. Teach and decode a selection from the word bank. Include the two introductory words **submarine** and **subtract**.

ENCODE: Dictate the **sub-** words for students to spell. Use response boards and ask students to share their spellings after each word. Emphasize **sub-** means under.

ACTIVITIES

MORPHEME GRABBER - WORD EQUATION OR DRAW AND LABEL

Direct students to create a new page in their Morpheme Grabber.

SUB + WORD	= NEW WORD	MEANING
sub + marine =	submarine	sub means under or beneath

Adjust the following exercises for your students' language and reading levels.

THE MORPHEME CARD

Display the Morpheme Cards. Instruct students to say the prefix **sub-** word for each picture, explore the meanings, use the words in sentences to tell about the pictures. REVIEW: Level Three – Reteach the morpheme. Say and write the words and a sentence for each.

ORAL LANGUAGE AND WRITE

Explore the meanings of a few **sub-** words that could be meaningful and have some usefulness for your students' growing vocabularies.

SUBJECT – We have a curriculum we teach and learn. The subjects, push in (ject) under the curriculum. Ask students to name the **subjects** they learn: math, reading, social studies, science, others, and of course recess! Ask them to create a web in their Morpheme Grabber to show the **subjects** they learn.

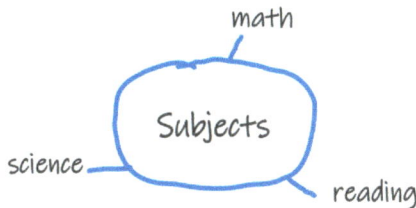

math

Subjects

science

reading

CONNECT TO THE CLASSROOM

SUBDIVIDE – to divide again below what was already divided. Demonstrate this with the class. **DIVIDE** the group into boys and girls. Then **SUBDIVIDE** each group – all girls with brown hair (now you have two groups of girls) and boys with brown hair (now you have two groups of boys). Teach **SUBGROUP**. Now we have **SUBGROUPS** of boys and girls! Groups below the whole group! Ask the students if there is another way to **SUBDIVIDE** the groups.

REVIEW AND PRACTICE

Display one **sub-** word each day you are on this lesson. Model how to read the word, circle the stem, and then underline **sub-**. Use words from the Word Banks.

Use sound spelling boxes to map and spell **sub-** words. Circle the morphemes. Switch it out and display a word from previous week's lessons for review.

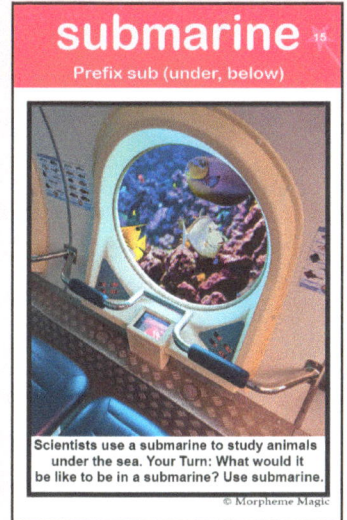

---

submarine
Prefix sub (under, below)

Scientists use a submarine to study animals under the sea. Your Turn: What would it be like to be in a submarine? Use submarine.

© Morpheme Magic

More Word Bank Words

subject – push in beneath

submit – send beneath

substitute – to stand beneath (the teacher)

submerge – move together beneath

subdivide – divide beneath

subgroup – a group beneath

subtle – beneath obvious

subtropical - beneath the tropics

subconscious – beneath conscious thought

suburb – beneath the big city

Lesson Goal:

Strengthen word knowledge with prefixes IN-, NON-, MIS-, SUB-.

Teachers know:

When we can integrate morphological awareness training with language development, vocabulary, decoding, spelling and comprehension we are enriching our students' literacy skills.

Word Bank

IN – IN

inspect

indent

install

increase

inspire

inherit

intent

inflammable

NON - NOT

nonstop

nonsense

nonstick

nonfat

nondairy

nonverbal

INTRODUCTION

DAY ONE: REVIEW THE MORPHEMES, IN-, NON-, MIS-, SUB

Write the review prefixes on the board. When we add a prefix to a word, we change the meaning of that word, and we have a new word! Create and display the chart below. Review each prefix, its meaning and a sample word. Discuss each, work with the class to use each word in a sentence.

PREFIX	in	non	mis	sub
MEANS	in	not	bad, wrong	under, beneath
EXAMPLE WORD	inspect	nonsense	mistake	subtract

EXPLORE THE PHONEMES

Say a selection of the words in the Word Banks with **in-, non-, mis-, sub-**. Ask students to listen for the prefix on each word and whisper it to their elbow buddy. Then say the base and suffix as separate word parts.

ORTHOGRAPHY - READING AND SPELLING

DECODE: Prepare a variety of words using the review prefixes. Ensure that the words are spelled with graphemes your students have learned during your phonics lessons. Ask students to read the words together. Provide corrective feedback.

If you use words from your reading program, note them on this page for future use.

ENCODE: Leave the words students decoded on the board. Play the clue game with the words. For example - "Which word means to pull *under*, down or lower?" (**subtract**) Provide more information if needed: "The word uses the prefix **sub-**." Direct students to share the word they are thinking of and to spell the word. Students can be asked to give clues for the class to answer and spell. Post the prefixes as a reference for students during this exercise.

ACTIVITIES

MORPHEME GRABBER - WORD EQUATION OR DRAW AND LABEL

Direct students to create a new page in their Morpheme Grabber.

PREFIX + WORD	= NEW WORD	MEANING
Choose a selection - IN-, NON-, MIS-, SUB- words		

Adjust the following exercises for your students' language and reading levels.

THE MORPHEME CARD

Display the Morpheme Cards from Lessons 12-15. Instruct students to say the prefix, its meaning and key word for each picture, explore the meanings, use the words in sentences to tell about the pictures. REVIEW: Level Three – Reteach the morpheme. Say and write the words and a sentence for each.

ORAL LANGUAGE AND WRITE -

Work with students to create a PREFIX Book – **in-, non-, mis-, sub-**. Instruct students to choose a word item for each prefix from the groups of words that were displayed for decoding and spelling or from the Morpheme Card. Have available colored paper that is cut in half lengthwise. Instruct them to set up their pages as illustrated below. When they are ready to write their sentences, ask them to share orally with a partner first. They proceed to create each page.

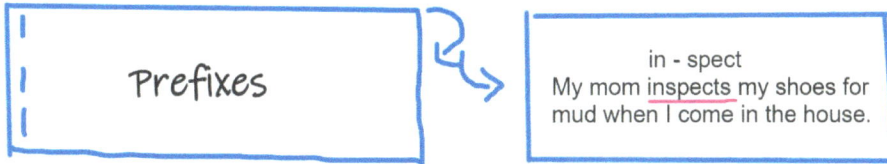

Prefixes →

in - spect
My mom inspects my shoes for mud when I come in the house.

CONNECT TO THE CLASSROOM

Work with the students to choose one word for each prefix that everyone could use during a school day. Write the words on the board. Challenge students and yourself to use the words. Ask students to raise a hand and indicate they heard the word being used. Tally the numbers by each word and see which word wins!

REVIEW AND PRACTICE

Display one review word each day you are on this lesson. Model how to read the word, circle the base, and then underline the prefix. Use words from the Word Banks or from the Morpheme Cards.

Use sound or syllable spelling boxes to map and spell the review words. Circle the morphemes.

Use cards for Lessons 12-15 for review.

Review
in-, non-, mis-, sub-

IN - IN	MIS - WRONG, BAD
inspect, invite, indent, install, increase, inspire, inherit, intent inflammable	misquote, misconduct, mismatch, misdial, mistake, misdirect, mishandle, misunderstand

NON - NOT	SUB - UNDER, BENEATH
nonstop, nonessential, nonverbal, nonsense, nonflammable nonmarine nonlocal nonacid	subtract, submarine, subsoil, subject, substitute

© Morpheme Magic

TIP: Post the Morpheme Cards on a permanent room display. Create a Morpheme Wall!

More Word Bank Words

MIS – WRONG, BAD
misquote
misconduct
mismatch
mistake
misdial
misdirect
mishandle
misunderstand

SUB – UNDER, BENEATH
subtract
subway
subconscious
submarine
suburb
subject
substitute
submerge

Lesson Goal:

Learn that -ION can be added to bases to make nouns. It means act of or state of.

Teachers know:

Teachers know that -**tion,** -**sion** are voiced syllables in words and -**ion** is the morpheme. The t and s are part of the stem to which the morpheme -**ion** is affixed.

Word Bank

/shun/

adopt – adoption

reflect – reflection

instruct – instruction

direct – direction

celebrate – celebration

vibrate – vibration

inspire – inspiration

express – expression

confess – confession

expanse – expansion

INTRODUCTION

DAY ONE: EXPLORE THE MORPHEME

Say the word **adoption**. **Adoption** of a stray animal is one way to get a new pet. The word **adoption** is made up of **adopt** plus **ion**. **Adopt** is a verb, I will **adopt** a pet. When we affix -**ion** on the end, we create a noun! **Adoption**. The **adoption** was successful! -**ION means act of or state of**. **Adoption** literally means, the act of **adopting**.

EXPLORE THE PHONEMES

For ease of delivery, pronounce the suffix -**ion** */shun/. In reality,* -**ion** *needs the t or s on the base,* -**tion**, -**sion**, *to spell /shun/. Say the letter names* **i-o-n** *when referring to the suffix when decoding or encoding*

Say /**shun**/. The suffix we are learning is /**shun**/. Ask students to say it. The suffix /**shun**/is on the ends of many words. When you hear /**shun**/ on the end of a word, it is most likely a naming word, a noun. What is our new suffix and what does it mean? /**shun**/ and it means **act of or state of**.

ORTHOGRAPHY - READING AND SPELLING

DECODE: Teach the orthography and meanings of -**ion** words. Write **adopt** on the board. Decode it. I will **adopt** a pet. Add the suffix -**ion**. Scoop the syllables and say **adoption**. Explain that **TION** (or **SION**) is the last syllable in the word, but the suffix is -**ion**. Circle -**ion**. -**ION** means **act of or state of**. Teach the morphemes of each word after decoding, but most importantly teach the meaning of the whole word. Write a word, scoop the syllables and then circle -**ion**. Decode each part and then blend them together to read the word. Teach and decode a selection from the word bank.

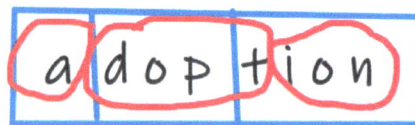

a = to, dopt = to choose

ENCODE:

Dictate the -**ion** words for students to spell. Direct students to scoop syllables (**tion** and **sion**) and circle the new suffix -**ion**. Use response boards and ask students to share their spellings after each word. Emphasize -**ion** means act or state of.

Do the same with other words in the Word Bank or words from your current reading lesson.

ACTIVITIES

MORPHEME GRABBER - WORD EQUATION OR DRAW AND LABEL

Direct students to create a new page in their Morpheme Grabber.

WORD + ION	= NEW WORD	MEANING
adopt + ion =	adoption	ion means act of doing

Adjust the following exercises for your students' language and reading levels.

THE MORPHEME CARD

Display the Morpheme Cards. Instruct students to say the focus -**ion** word for each picture, explore the meanings, use the words in sentences to tell about the pictures. Write the words. Compose and write sentences. REVIEW: Level Three – Reteach the morpheme. Say and write the words and a sentence for each.

ORAL LANGUAGE AND WRITE -

Ask the following questions to get some verbal reasoning going! Model your own answers to get the thinking started. Ask students to repeat the -**ion** word. Follow the oral language lesson with a writing lesson.

When can **organization** be helpful?

What are some examples of **instruction**?

When would you have a **celebration**?

Give an example of a **confession**.

What would cause **confusion** in our classroom?

Are your friends' ideas **inspiration** for yours? When?

CONNECT TO THE CLASSROOM

Display the words **expand** and **expansion**. Introduce your lessons with this phrase: Today we are going to **expand** our brains. We are going to have a brain **expansion**! Let's learn about _____. Do the same with **instruct – instruction, confuse – confusion, direct-direction** and vary the phrases you use.

REVIEW AND PRACTICE

Display one -**ion** word each day you are on this lesson. Model how to read the word, circle the base, and then underline the -**ion**. Use words from the Word Banks or from your reading program.

Use sound spelling boxes to map and spell -**ion** words. Circle the syllables and then morphemes. Display a sword from previous week's lessons for review.

adoption
Suffix ion (act of, state of)

This animal's adoption will happen soon. Your Turn: What is adoption? Did you adopt any of your pets? Use the words adopt and adoption.

© Morpheme Magic

More Word Bank Words

/zhun/

equate – equation

vis (to see) – vision

confuse – confusion

invade – invasion

abrade – abrasion

TIP: When students are composing sentences, provide a framework: _What or who + did what + when, how, and/or why._

Model how to use the framework. Provide oral language practice with the activity before writing.

Lesson Goal:

Maintain a focus on developing morphological awareness. Develop curiosity about words and their meaningful parts.

Teachers know:

When developing morphological awareness with little ones, affix prefixes and suffixes to known words. Always discuss how the base word changed and the new meaning!

TIP: It is always a good idea to reinforce morphology when spelling. Use sound boxes at least 2-3 times per week. Segment phonemes, spell with graphemes, circle the morphemes!

Congratulations! You have completed Level 2 with your students. Your students' development of morphological awareness has deepened significantly. Keep up the focus on morphology through lots of P&R – Practice and Review.

1) Keep your Morpheme Wall dynamic. This means you change out the Morpheme Cards occasionally; refer your students to the wall when they are searching for a word to use in their writing, or need a refresher about the meanings of morphemes.

2) Guide students to use their Morpheme Grabbers as a reference, and to continue to collect words they find under the headings they created in Level 2.

3) See Review Tips and Additional Activities in the Introduction Section for ideas to keep you and your students focused on building morphological awareness.

4) Engage students in multiple daily oral language opportunities to express themselves. Is your classroom a Language Rich Classroom?

5) Keep in mind the lexical qualities of words (Perfetti, 2007). Include in your lesson: pronunciations (phonological form), and spellings. These aspects of a word require PRECISION. When working with meaning, present words in multiple contexts over time to build FLEXIBILITY with understanding words. See the visual below:

Words have Lexical Qualities that extend beyond 'definitions'.

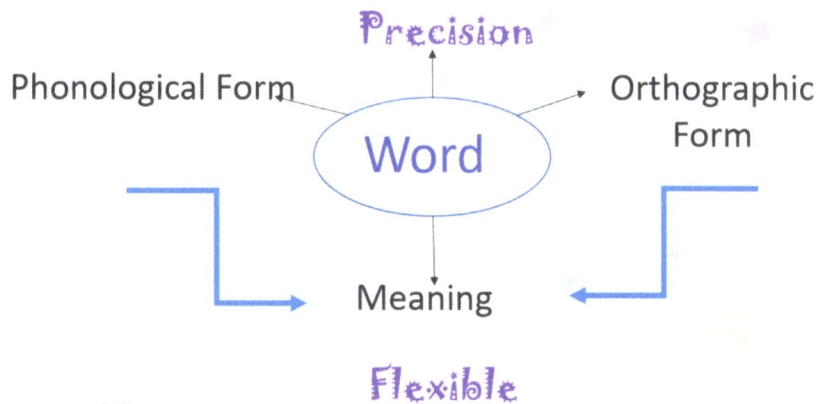

Precision

Phonological Form → **Word** ← Orthographic Form

Meaning

Flexible

LEVEL 3 LESSONS
– The Magic of Language

THE FIRST THREE LESSONS IN LEVEL 3 ARE REVIEW LESSONS:

1) If students have completed Levels 1 and 2, the first three Lessons will refresh and reteach the earliest morphemes students learned.

2) Use the Lessons in Levels 1 and 2 as indicated on the following few pages to guide your planning for the first several weeks of word study and review. The assessments in the Appendix can provide information about students' current morphological awareness.

3) If students are just beginning the program at Level 3, these first three Review Lessons will establish the awareness of morphemes before advancing to more advanced study of prefixes, suffixes, and the roots to which they are affixed.

TIPS FOR TEACHING THE REVIEW LESSONS 1-3

- Determine how familiar students are with the morphemes in the Review Lessons using the **Informal Criterion Assessments** found in the Appendix of this book.

- Plan a schedule: For some, one week per Review Lesson, three weeks total, is enough to establish morphological awareness before continuing with Lesson 4. For others, 1-2 months will be dedicated to this review.

- Plan your lessons: Use Levels 1 and 2 lessons to plan your approach. The Level 1 and 2 Lesson numbers are provided for each morpheme in each table.

REMINDERS:

Use all language learning processes in your **Morphemes for Little Ones** lessons:

★ Model how the morphemes and words **sound** and how they are used.

★ Direct student to **say** the focus morphemes and words aloud.

★ Share **meanings** using student accessible definitions and examples.

★ Ask students to **read** the focus morphemes and words.

★ Provide opportunities for students to **practice** using the words they learn in meaningful sentences. It is best to apply the words to topics they are studying.

★ **Write!** Direct students to put into words what they are learning using the words in the lessons.

★ **Model** how to use words in sentences when students struggle to use the words correctly.

★ **Provide sentence frames** when students are not sure how to use a word.

Lesson Goal:

Learn that suffixes can be added to words to change meaning. Suffixes in this lesson include plurals, past tense, comparatives, superlatives, and verb suffixes.

Teachers know:

The base spelling often changes when suffixes are added. Review of the Spelling Rules is frequently necessary for many students.

TIP: Draw attention to how phonemes and stress change: When we add **-al to nature**, the A in **nature** sounds like /ae/ but in **natural**, the A sounds like /a/. Be explicit, compare and contrast phonemes when morphemes are added or changed in words.

LEVEL 3 REVIEW CONTENT

Compound Words and Suffixes: PLURALS, PAST TENSE, COMPARATIVES, SUPERLATIVES, VERB SUFFIXES

Note: Read through Prepare for Level 3 Lessons at the beginning of this Level to help you plan how to best use the first three Review and Learn Lessons for your students.

Begin use of the Morpheme Grabber with these first sets of review lessons. Lessons in Levels 1 and 2 provide guidance to help set students up for success with creating their Morpheme Grabbers.

COMPOUND WORDS

DAY/WEEK 1 Compound Words	TEACH: A compound word is one word with two morphemes.	REVIEW: Level 1 Lesson 1.
Word Items: aircraft babysit birthday bellbottom blackbird buttermilk clockwise	Present and read with students: **backpack**. Explain: **Backpack** is one word. Circle **back** and **pack**. Say: **Back** has meaning and **pack** has meaning. **Backpack** has two meaningful parts called morphemes, but this is one word. It means a **pack** that you wear on your **back**.	**Word Items:** baseball football basketball classmate grasshopper sunflower teamwork

PLURALS

DAY/WEEK 2 Plurals	TEACH: The morphemes -s and -es can sound like /s/, /z/, /ez/, and /eez/.	REVIEW: Level 1 Lessons 2-5.

Teach The Drop It, Change It and Double It Spelling Rules As Needed.

Word Items: /s/ **No Spelling Change**	Word Items: /z/	Word Items: /eez/ **Change y to i. Add -es.**	Word Items: /eez/ **Don't change y to i. Add -s.**
exploits	storms	candy	monkey
projects	waves	copy	valley
suspects	potatoes	duty	kidney
robots	salads	balcony	chimney
benefits	pencils	agency	trolley
tastes	papers	vacancy	jersey
suits	fires	factory	journey
	clowns		
	mirrors		

PAST TENSE VERBS

DAY/WEEK 3	TEACH:	REVIEW:
Past Tense -ed and Irregular	We affix -ed to verbs to indicate something finished and done. Irregular verbs do not add -ed, and these are one morpheme.	Level 1 Lessons 6-8. Level 1 Lessons will help teach the other past tense sounds for -ed.

Teach The Drop It, Change It and Double It Spelling Rules As Needed.

/d/ Change y to i	Irregular Verbs:	Irregular Verbs:	Irregular Verbs
carry – carried	drink – drank	come – came	lead – led
bury – buried	eat – ate	build – built	pay – paid
try – tried	fall – fell	fight – fought	rise – rose
study – studied	feel – felt	light – lit	run – ran
cry – cried	buy – bought	fly – flew	sell – sold
supply – supplied	catch – caught	forgive – forgave	send – sent
reply – replied	choose – chose	freeze – froze	swim – swam
apply – applied	drive – drove	lay – laid	teach – taught
rely – relied	wake – woke	write – wrote	win – won

Present simple sentences to teach irregular verbs: Today we **DRINK** yesterday we (**DRANK**). Students fill in the irregular past tense verb. Write class sentences to practice.

COMPARATIVES AND SUPERLATIVES

DAY/WEEK 4	TEACH:	REVIEW:
	We add -er and -est to adjectives to indicate comparison.	Level 1 Lessons 10-12

Teach The Drop It, Change It and Double It Spelling Rules As Needed.

Comparative:	Superlative:	Comparative:	Superlative:
deep – deeper	deepest	bad – worse	worst
great – greater	greatest	far – farther*	farthest*
hot – hotter	hottest	far – further*	furthest*
brave – braver	bravest	good – better	best
noisy – noisier	noisiest	old – older/elder	oldest/eldest

*Use **farther** when the distance can be measured. It's farther to the next town. Use **further** when the distance cannot be measured. That is **further** from the truth.

PRESENT TENSE VERBS -ING, -S, -ES

DAY/WEEK 5	TEACH:	REVIEW:
	We affix the morphemes -ing, -s, -es to verbs. They are present tense.	Level 1 Lessons 13 - 14

Teach The Drop It Change It and Double It Spelling Rules As Needed.

No Spelling Change	Drop It	Double It	HF Words
pair – pairing	handle – handling	knit – knitting	coming
listen – listening	mine – mining	plan – planning	taking
fly – flying	come – coming	stop – stopping	having
paint – painting	leave – leaving	travel – travelling	making

Review and Learn Compound Words, Plurals, Past Tense, Comparatives, Verb Suffixes

Compounds – two free bases make one word — schoolyard

Plurals – -s, -es more than one — houses

Past Tense Verbs – -ed and Irregular — cleaned

Comparatives -er Superlatives -est — happy, happier, happiest

Verb Suffixes – Present Tense -s, -es, -ing — roll, rolls, rolling – wish, wishes, wishing

© Morpheme Magic

Use Morpheme Cards from Levels 1 and 2 Lessons as needed.

More Comparatives:

modern – more
modern – most
modern
difficult – more
difficult – most
difficult

More Change y to i
dirty – dirtier, dirtiest
crunchy – crunchier, crunchiest
friendly – friendlier, friendliest

Lesson Goal:

Learn that suffixes can be added to words to change meaning. Suffixes in this lesson include: -LY, -LESS, -NESS, -FUL, -MENT.

Teachers Know:

All of the suffixes in this lesson begin with a consonant. There will be no spelling changes needed when affixing these suffixes to the base.

LEVEL 3 REVIEW CONTENT

Suffixes: -LY, LESS, NESS, FUL, MENT

Note: Read through Prepare for Level 3 Lessons at the beginning of this Level to help you plan for the first three Review and Learn lessons.

SUFFIX -LY, *LIKE OR MANNER OF*

DAY/WEEK 1 Suffix -ly	TEACH: The suffix -ly is added to adjectives to make adverbs telling how. -LY means like or manner of.		REVIEW: Level 2 Lesson 2.
Word Items: blindly broadly candidly	Word Items: delightedly foolishly forcefully	Word Items: lonely pleasantly longingly	Word Items: rudely shakily wisely

SUFFIX -LESS, *WITHOUT*

DAY/WEEK 2 Suffix -less	TEACH: The suffix -less is added to mostly Anglo Saxon base words and these words become adjectives. -LESS means without		REVIEW: Level 2 Lesson 3.
Word Items: ageless blameless breezeless	Word Items: cheerless pointless shameless	Word Items: senseless nameless formless	Word Items: timeless* priceless* thoughtless

*The meanings of these words require subtle understanding of how to use them. Model the use of these words: The **timeless** beauty of the night sky delights us (eternal, no beginning or end). The **priceless** ruby necklace was worn by the queen (value beyond any price).

SUFFIX -NESS, *STATE OF BEING LIKE THE BASE*

DAY/WEEK 2 Suffix -ness	TEACH: The suffix -ness is added to mostly Anglo Saxon bases to make nouns. -NESS means a state of being like the base.		REVIEW: Level 2 Lesson 4.
Word Items: alertness bluntness cautiousness	Word Items: exactness expertness shyness	Word Items: quietness promptness lightness	Word Items: heaviness strictness softness

NOTE: You may also use the Lesson 2 Review Lesson #5 to teach the suffixes -ly, -less, and -ness.

SUFFIX -FUL, *FULL OF*

DAY/WEEK 3 Suffix -ful	TEACH: The suffix -ful is mostly added to Anglo Saxon bases to make adjectives. -FUL means full of.		REVIEW: Level 2 Lesson 6.
Word Items: eventful stressful remindful sorrowful	Word Items: skillful painful trustful lawful	-FUL Nouns: The suffix -ful can also make nouns: armful bellyful	-FUL Nouns: sackful mouthful bagful roomful

Can students think of other nouns formed from adding **-ful** to a base? **Pocketful**?

SUFFIX -MENT, *STATE OF OR RESULT OF AN ACTION*

DAY/WEEK 4 SUFFIX -MENT	TEACH: The suffix -ment is noun forming. -MENT means act of, state of, result of an action.		REVIEW: Level 2 Lesson 7.
Word Items: retirement disappointment confinement basement	Word Items: engagement enchantment ornament advertisement	Word Items: embarrassment compliment enforcement development	Word Items: adjustment placement assessment refreshment

Review and Learn
Suffixes -ly, -less, -ness, -ful, -ment

Suffix -ly – like or manner of — longingly
Suffix -less – without — cheerless
Suffix -ness – state of being like the base — exactness
Suffix -ful – full of — painful
Suffix -ment – state of or result of an action — refreshment

© Morpheme Magic

Use Morpheme Cards from Level 2 Lessons as needed.

ACTIVITIES:

Concentration:

Most of the suffixes in these review lists are added to bases that can stand alone. Work with students to create sets of cards from these lists with the base written on one card, and the suffix written on another. Place the base cards in one column upside down, and the suffixes in another column upside down. Then, taking turns with a partner, direct students to choose a base and choose a suffix, combine them. If a real word is made when the two are combined, then the student keeps the set. If not, the cards are returned to the table. After all sets are chosen, students read back through their sets and say the suffix and whole word meanings.

Post a **-ment** word such as **disappointment**. Ask students to find words with other suffixes that could fit under the category **disappointment** and be ready to share their thinking. **Stressful, sorrowful, quietness,** and **foolishly** might be words that students would choose.

Lesson Goal:

Learn that prefixes can be added to words to change meaning. Prefixes in this lesson include: un-, re-, pre-, in-, and suffix -ion.

Teachers Know:

Our students' reading and spelling levels, and oral language levels, will determine how long we spend on these review lessons.

LEVEL 3 REVIEW CONTENT

Prefixes: UN-, RE-, PRE-, IN, and Suffix -ION

Note: Read through Prepare for Level 3 Lessons at the beginning of this Level to help you plan for the first three Review and Learn lessons.

PREFIX UN-, *NOT, TO UNDO, OR OPPOSITE OF*

DAY/WEEK 1 Prefix un-	TEACH: The prefix un- PRE- means before, not, to undo, or opposite of.		REVIEW: Level 2 Lesson 8.
Word Items: unfed uncap uncut	Word Items: unclip uncork untuck	Word Items: unfixable unchecked unjudged	Word Items: unblinking unadjusted unexamined

PREFIX RE-, *BACK OR AGAIN*

DAY/WEEK 2 Prefix re-	TEACH: The prefix re- means before.		REVIEW: Level 2 Lesson 9.
Word Items: recheck refreeze remind	Word Items: refixed recharge reaction	Word Items: reclaim recall recover	Word Items: recycle redirect redeliver

PREFIX PRE-, *BEFORE*

DAY/WEEK 2 SUF- FIX -NESS	TEACH: THE PREFIX PRE-. PRE- MEANS BEFORE.		REVIEW: LEVEL 2 LESSON 10.
Word Items: prefer premix present	Word Items: prepare prearrange prevent	Word Items: prehistorical prejudice (pre-judge) preregister	Word Items: prewrap premade preload

SYLLABLE SPELLING PLUS MORPHEMES

un ex am ined
not + out + perform + past tense

pre fer
before + to carry

re ac tion
back+ do+ state of

PREFIX IN-, *IN*

DAY/WEEK 3 Suffix in-	TEACH: The prefix in- means in, on, toward. Other forms include -il, -im, -ir.		REVIEW: Level 2 Lesson 12.
Word Items: inject injure	**Word Items:** index induce	**Word Items:** infill illustrate	**Word Items:** immigrant irrigate

SUFFIX -ION, ACT OF, *STATE OF, OR RESULT OF*

DAY/WEEK 4 Suffix -ion*	TEACH: The suffix -ion is noun forming. -ION means act of, state, of, or result of.		REVIEW: Level 2 Lesson 17.
Word Items: abbreviation affirmation	**Word Items:** emotion application	**Word Items:** ambition absorption	**Word Items:** subtraction addition

*Words ending in **-ion** (**sion, tion**) are numerous. Your students will find multiple examples of this suffix in their daily reading activities.

ACTIVITIES DURING EVERY LESSON:

Syllable Spelling – Provide a Syllable Spelling form for each student.

1) Dictate a word. Students segment the syllables by saying each and placing a dot at the bottom of each grid section.
2) Guide students to then return to each syllable and spell the syllables.
3) Work with students to circle the morphemes in the word.
4) Discuss meaning and use the word in a familiar context.
5) Write the word at the end of the column for future practice review.

CONNECT VOCABULARY TO CLASSROOM LEARNING:

Daily Oral Language and Write.

1) Select 3-5 words that you think your students can use to reflect on their learning in content areas.
2) Display the word selection. Discuss the word meanings as they relate to the morphemes and a general meaning for the words. Model how you would use one of the words to talk about the selected content (a classroom novel, science, social studies, current events, etc.).
3) Engage students in the same use of the terms through oral language.
4) Students write their learning in their Morpheme Grabber under the current lesson heading.

Review and Learn
Prefixes un-, re-, pre-, in-,
Suffix -ion

Prefix un- not, to undo, or opposite
untangle

Prefix re- back or again
reject

Prefix pre- before or earlier
prehistory

Prefix in- in, on, towards
intense

Suffix -ion act of, state of, result of
navigation

© Morpheme Magic

Use Morpheme Cards from Level 2 Lessons as needed.

NOTE: You may also review the prefixes **non-**, **mis-**, and **sub.**- Lessons for these prefixes and suffix are found in Level 2 Lessons 13 -16.

Lesson Goal:

Learn that -AL can be added to words to make adjectives. It means related to, or characterized by.

Teachers know:

Provide sentence frames to assist with development of word knowledge.

Word Bank

seasonal – related to a season

skeletal – related to a skeleton

spinal – related to the spine

personal – related to a person

regional – related to a region

universal – related to everywhere

professional – related to a profession

INTRODUCTION

DAY ONE: EXPLORE THE MORPHEME

Today we are going to learn a new suffix. Write **-al** on the board. Ask students to read it with you. **-AL** means **related to**. Write **seasonal** on the board. Students read it with you. Underline **-al,** circle **season.** When I see the word **seasonal**, I know that the -al means **related to** so this word means **related to a season**. The **seasonal** colors of autumn are orange, red, and yellow.

ORTHOGRAPHY - READING AND SPELLING

DECODE: Teach the orthography for **-al**. Create a list of 5-10 words from the Word Bank. Display the words one at a time creating a column of words for reading and spelling instruction. Model decoding, word meaning, and word use.

TEACHER	STUDENTS
Write and read -al. -AL means **related to**.	Read -al and turn and say the meaning to a partner.
Write **seasonal**. Circle and say **season**. Underline **-al,** say "**-al means related to**." Read the parts. Say **seasonal – related to a season. What are some seasonal clothing for winter?**	Read **-al**, blend the parts to read **seasonal**. Use **seasonal** in a sentence (assisted by the teacher).
Follow the same process with 5-10 words. After reading the words, direct students to read them again with you. Prompt students to say -al and word meanings each time.	Read through the word list as directed by the teacher. Say -al and word meanings as directed. Use the words in sentences. Teacher provides sentence frames as needed.

Leave the words displayed. Read them again prior to the encoding lesson.
ENCODE:
Dictate **-al** words for students to spell. Use response boards or the Morpheme Grabber and ask students to share their spellings after each word, provide corrective feedback. Ask students for **-al** meaning and word meanings after each spelling. Work with students to generate oral/written sentences with **-al** words.

ACTIVITIES

MORPHEME GRABBER - WORD EQUATION OR DRAW AND LABEL

Direct students to create a new page in their Morpheme Grabber.

WORD + AL	= NEW WORD	AL MEANS
season + al =	seasonal	characterized by

Adjust the following exercises for your students' language and reading levels.

THE MORPHEME CARD

Display the Morpheme Cards. Instruct students to say the **-al** word for each picture, explore the meanings, and use the words in sentences to tell about the pictures. Add the cards to your Morpheme Wall for frequent review.

ORAL LANGUAGE AND WRITE

Display, read, discuss meaning for each of the following **-al** words, then say the sentence frame. Direct students to say and then write the sentences as they provide the missing information.

(**skeletal**) The _____ remains of the dinosaur were found (where), (how).

(**medical**) My big sister went to _____ school and learned (what).

(**regional**) One of our _____ foods is (what) and I eat it (when).

(**personal**) I keep my _____ things (where) because (why).

CONNECT TO THE CLASSROOM

Use the following questions to engage discussion about your school. Highlight **-al** and the word meanings: What are some **custodial** duties we have in our classroom? In what ways is the **principal** our leader? What activities are **optional** in our classroom and which are not **optional**? What is a **universal** belief and/or positive **universal** behavior in our school?

REVIEW AND PRACTICE

Daily Morpheme Problem to Solve: Display one **-al** word each day while on this lesson. Model how to read the word, circle the base, and then underline **-al**. Use words from the Word Banks or from your reading program.

universal

one + transform + state of

Use sound spelling boxes to map and spell **-al** words. Circle the morphemes. Switch it out and display a word from previous week's lessons for review.

BASE ENDS IN C = CIAL		BASE ENDS IN T = TIAL
artificial	facial	initial
beneficial	glacial	potential
commercial		substantial

industrial

Suffix -al (related to, adj)

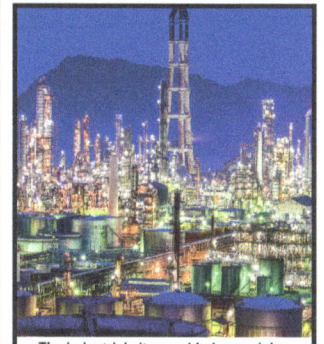

The industrial city provided many jobs. Your Turn: What do you see and hear in industrial settings? Use the word industrial.

© Morpheme Magic

More Word Bank Words

industrial – related to industry

optional – characterized by option, choice

medical – related to medicine

formal – characterized by a known form

gradual – characterized by step by step

dental – related to teeth

national -related to the nation

original – related to origin

NOTE: -IAL is the **-al** suffix used after bases ending in **c** as in **facial (cial)** and **t initial (tial)**.

Teach the **-al** spelling first. See words in the table.

Lesson Goal:

Learn that -Y can be added to words to make adjectives. It means inclined to or being like the base.

Teachers know:

Point to **-y** say letter name and then explain that when we see this suffix **-y** on the end of a word this week, a new syllable is added and we say **/ee/**.

Word Bank

windy

jumpy

cloudy

earthy

floppy

fishy

creepy

skinny

foggy

spooky

snappy

hairy

lengthy

jerky

healthy

rainy

INTRODUCTION

DAY ONE: EXPLORE THE MORPHEME

Today we are going to learn a new suffix. Write **-y** on the board. Ask students to say /ee/ with you -y. **-Y** means **inclined to or like the word it is affixed to**. Write **windy** on the board. Students read it with you. Underline **-y,** circle **wind**. When I see the word **windy**, I know that the **-y** says /ee/ and means **being like wind** so this word means **being like wind**. I use it to describe a certain kind of day. **When it is windy, the trees thrash around!**

ORTHOGRAPHY – READING AND SPELLING

DECODE: Teach the orthography for **-y**. Create a list of 5-10 words from the Word Bank. Display the words one at a time creating a column of words for reading spelling instruction. Model decoding, word meaning, and word use.

TEACHER	STUDENTS
Write and read **-y** /ee/. **-Y** means **inclined to or being like the base**.	Read **-y** and turn and say the meaning to a partner.
Write **windy**. Circle and say **wind**. Underline **-y**. Read the parts. Say **windy**. **-Y means being like the wind. What do you do on a windy day?**	Read **-y**, blend the parts to read **windy**. Use **windy** in a sentence (assisted by teacher).
Follow the same process with 5-10 words. After reading the words, direct students to read them again with you. Prompt students to say **-y** and word meanings each time.	Read through the word list as directed by the teacher. Say **-y** and word meanings as directed. Use the words in sentences. Teacher provides sentence frames as needed.

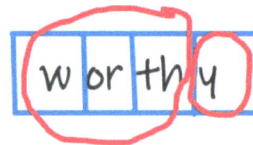

Leave the words displayed. Read them again prior to the encoding lesson.

ENCODE:

Dictate **-y** words for students to spell. Use response boards or the Morpheme Grabber and ask students to share their spellings after each word, provide corrective feedback. Ask students for **-y** meaning and word meaning after each spelling. Work with students to generate oral/written sentences with **-y** words.

ACTIVITIES

MORPHEME GRABBER - WORD EQUATION

Direct students to create a new page in their Morpheme Grabber.

WORD + -Y	= NEW WORD	-Y MEANS
wind + y =	windy	inclined to or being like the base

Adjust the following exercises for your students' language and reading levels.

THE MORPHEME CARDS

Display the Morpheme Cards. Instruct students to say the **-y** word for each picture, explore the meanings, and use the words in sentences to tell about the pictures. Add the cards to your Morpheme Wall for frequent review.

ORAL LANGUAGE AND WRITE - AN EXTRAORDINARY DAY

Brainstorm and list **-y** words that we can use to describe weather. Several are in the Word Bank already. Work with the class to create a story about a field trip and use as many weather words as you can. Post the story, *An Extraordinary Day*, and ask students to create pictures (label with **-y** words) to illustrate their story.

CONNECT TO THE CLASSROOM

Work with students to determine **-y** words that can describe a character, or a character's experiences in a story the class is reading. List a few, and model the task, to get students started. Provide a list for them to choose from. Engage students in oral discussion and then writing their sentences using **-y** words.

REVIEW AND PRACTICE

Daily Morpheme Problem to Solve: Display one **-y** word each day while on this lesson. Model how to read the word, circle the base, and then underline **-y,** and say the meaning. Use words from the Word Banks or from your reading program.

healthy

Use sound spelling boxes to map and spell **-y** words. Circle the morphemes. Switch it out and display a word from previous week's lessons for review.

---

windy
Suffix -y (inclined to, be like, adj)

How can you tell it is windy? Your Turn: Talk about this picture. Use the word windy.

© Morpheme Magic

More Word Bank Words

funny

worthy

noisy

steady

handy

silky

fuzzy

fluffy

dreary

leafy

messy

oily

TIP: Explore different meanings for **-y** words. **Fishy** can mean a smell like a fish, or something suspicious. **Snappy** can describe something that **snaps** or a quick brief answer. Others?

Lesson Goal:

Learn that -ITY, or -TY can be added to words to make nouns. It means state of, quality of.

Teachers know:

-ITY is the most common of the two suffixes -ity and -ty.

Word Bank

There are limited -ity, -ty words appropriate for 3rd grade vocabulary levels. Use the words best suited for your students for reading and language activities.

reality

legality

frailty

liberty

quality

nationality

quantity

capacity

impulsivity

INTRODUCTION

DAY ONE: EXPLORE THE MORPHEME

Today we are going to learn a new suffix. Write **-ity** on the board. Ask students to say **/i/tee/** with you. **-ITY** means **state of or quality of**. Write **reality** on the board. Students read it with you. Underline **-ity**, circle **real**. When I see the word **reality**, I know that the **-ity** means **state of** so this word means **the state of being real. Watching the reality TV show was like being there in person!**

ORTHOGRAPHY - READING AND SPELLING

DECODE: Teach the orthography for **-ity and -ty**. Create a list of 5-10 words from the Word Bank. Display the words one at a time creating a column of words for reading and spelling instruction. Model decoding, word meaning, and word use.

TEACHER	STUDENTS
Write and read **-ity. -ITY** means **having the quality or being like the base word**.	Read **-ity** and turn and say the meaning to a partner.
Write **reality**. Circle and say **real**. Underline **-ity**. Read the parts. Say **reality means being real. Is it a reality to have cake for lunch?** Teach how real changes to two syllables in re-al-it-y.	Read **-ity**, blend the parts to read **reality**. Use **reality** in a sentence (assisted by teacher – see **Tip** on next page).
Follow the same process with 5-10 words. After reading the words, direct students to read them again with you. Prompt students to say **-ity (-ty)** and word meanings each time	Read through the word list as directed by the teacher. Say **-ity** and word meanings as directed. Use the words in sentences. Teacher provides sentence frames as needed.

reality

Leave the words displayed. Read them again prior to the encoding lesson.

ENCODE:

Dictate **-ity, -ty** words for students to spell. Use response boards or the Morpheme Grabber and ask students to share their spellings after each word, provide corrective feedback. Ask students for **-ity, -ty** meaning and word meaning after each spelling. Work with students to generate sentences with **-ity** words.

ACTIVITIES

MORPHEME GRABBER - WORD EQUATION

Direct students to create a new page in their Morpheme Grabber.

WORD + -ITY (OR -TY)	= NEW WORD	-ITY AND -TY MEAN
real + ity =	reality	state of or quality of
frail + ty =	frailty	

Adjust the following exercises for your students' language and reading levels.

THE MORPHEME CARDS

Display the Morpheme Cards. Instruct students to say the **-ity, -ty** word for each picture, explore the meanings, and use the words in sentences to tell about the pictures. Add the cards to your Morpheme Wall for frequent review.

ORAL LANGUAGE AND WRITE

Say the **-ity** bolded word, explore its meaning. Ask students to respond and use the key word in their responses.

responsibility – What is your **responsibility** to your classroom? Friends? Family?

nationality – What is your family's **nationality**?

flexibility – When is it good to have **flexibility**?

predictability – What **predictability** is there when you go to a friend's house?

CONNECT TO THE CLASSROOM -ITY GEOMETRY

Some shapes can take on the suffix **-ity**: Display, read, and discuss the meanings of these words with students: **triangularity, rectangularity, circularity, hexagonality**, (What would the *made up word* be for square? *Squarity*?) Then use these shape words to talk about the classroom: The **rectangularity** of our desks helps us organize them into rows (pods) in the room.

REVIEW AND PRACTICE

Daily Morpheme Problem to Solve: Display one **-ity, -ty** word each day while on this lesson. Model how to read the word, circle the base, and then underline **-ity, -ty**. Use words from the Word Banks or from your reading program.

Use sound spelling boxes to map and spell **-ity, -ty** words. Circle the morphemes. Switch it out and display a word from previous week's lessons for review.

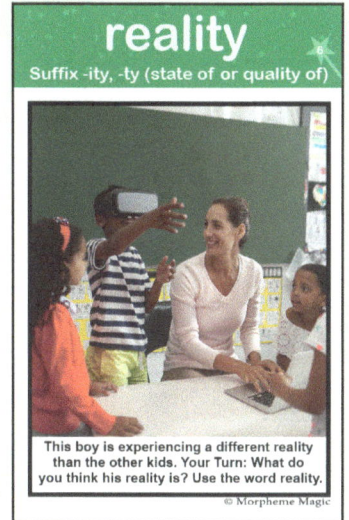

flex | i | bili | i | ty

---

reality

Suffix -ity, -ty (state of or quality of)

This boy is experiencing a different reality than the other kids. Your Turn: What do you think his reality is? Use the word reality.

© Morpheme Magic

More Word Bank Words

responsibility

musicality

flexibility

predictability

accountability

absurdity

oddity

profanity

TIP: Words with the suffix **-ity** and **-ty** are nouns. Set students up to use these words as the *naming* part of a sentence. "The (*what - **reality***) of his day was very pleasant." "Her (*what – **frailty***) kept her indoors when she wanted to play."

Lesson Goal:

Learn that -IC can be added to words to make adjectives. It means having the qualities of the *base*, or pertaining to.

Word Bank

elastic – elast means flexible

historic – history means story

poetic – poet means creative

public – publ means people

Nouns or Adj:

music – mus means song (music box -adj)

magic – mag means power (magic wand -adj)

plastic – plasma means molded

(plastic fork -adj)

NOTE: Elastic is also an adjective, though we often use it as a noun. I need to buy some **elastic**. Teach students the noun form using **-ITY**. **Elasticity** is the noun! **Elasticity** makes my clothes comfortable!

INTRODUCTION

DAY ONE: EXPLORE THE MORPHEME

Today we are going to learn a new adjective suffix. Write **-ic** on the board. Ask students to read it with you. **-IC** means **having qualities of the base**. Write **elastic** on the board. Students read it with you. Underline **-ic,** circle **elast. Elast means flexible.** When I see the word **elastic**, I know that the **-ic** means **having the qualities of** so this word means **having flexible qualities. The elastic band helped my clothing stay in place!**

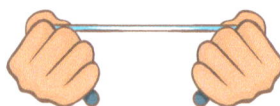

ORTHOGRAPHY - READING AND SPELLING

DECODE: Teach the orthography for **-ic**. Create a list of 5-10 words from the Word Bank. Display the words one at a time creating a column of words for reading spelling instruction. Model decoding, word meaning, and word use.

TEACHER	STUDENTS
Write and read **-ic.** **-IC** means **having the qualities of the base**.	Read **-ic** and turn and say the meaning to a partner.
Write **elastic**. Circle and say **elast**. Underline **-ic**. Read the parts. Say **elastic – having a flexible quality. The elastic hat was tight on my head.** Scoop the syllables in e-las-tic, then circle morphemes	Read **-ic**, blend the syllables and morphemes to read **elastic**. Use **elastic** in a sentence (assisted by teacher).
Follow the same process with 5-10 words. After reading the words, direct students to read them again with you. Prompt students to say **-ic** and word meanings each time.	Read through the word list as directed by the teacher. Say **-ic** and word meanings as directed. Use the words in sentences. Teacher provides sentence frames as needed.

elast ic

Leave the words displayed. Read them again prior to the encoding lesson.

ENCODE:

Dictate **-ic** words for students to spell. Use response boards or the Morpheme Grabber and ask students to share their spellings after each word, provide corrective feedback. Ask students for **-ic** meaning and word meaning after each spelling. Work with students to generate sentences with **-ic** words.

ACTIVITIES

MORPHEME GRABBER - WORD EQUATION

Direct students to create a new page in their Morpheme Grabber.

BASE + IC	= NEW WORD	IC MEANS
elast + ic =	elastic	qualities of or pertaining to

Adjust the following exercises for your students' language and reading levels.

THE MORPHEME CARDS

Display the Morpheme Cards. Instruct students to say the **-ic** word for each picture, explore the meanings, and use the words in sentences to tell about the pictures. Add the cards to your Morpheme Wall for frequent review.

ORAL LANGUAGE AND WRITE

Present the following questions. Ask students to write their answers using the **-ic** words and be ready to share their thinking.

What would seem **gigantic** to an ant, but **microscopic** to a giant?

Is a **music hall** a **public** place? Why or why not?

How are **elastic** and **automatic** the same? Different?

The class was jumping up and down when they heard they won the contest. Which word best describes this reaction: **hectic** or **enthusiastic**? Why?

Project: Teach the term **comic** (**L. comicus = funny**). Share a **comic** strip with students, discuss, then work with them to create a 4-panel **comic** strip that tells a story related to the classroom. Students may want to create their own!

CONNECT TO THE CLASSROOM

Teach the term **academic**. Provide a list of words and ask students to determine which words would fit the category **academic**. Students write the heading **Academic** in their Morpheme Grabber and write their word choices underneath. Ask students to justify their choices. Some words to use include: **realistic, mathematic, automatic, historic, poetic, strategic, analytic.** Include distractors that could be justified through creative thinking: **hectic, magic, energetic, comic.**

REVIEW AND PRACTICE

Daily Morpheme Problem to Solve: Display one **-ic** word each day while on this lesson. Model how to read the word, circle the base, and then underline **-ic**. Use words from the Word Banks or from your reading program.

Use sound spelling boxes to map and spell **-ic** words. Circle the morphemes. Switch it out and display a word from previous week's lessons for review.

c o m i c

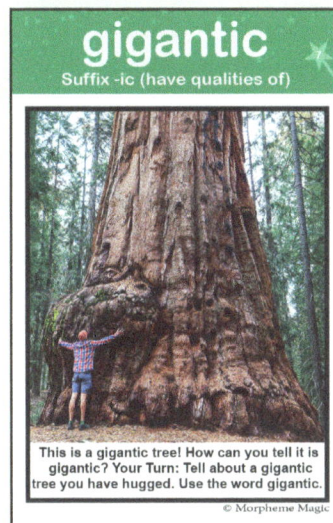

gigantic
Suffix -ic (have qualities of)

This is a gigantic tree! How can you tell it is gigantic? Your Turn: Tell about a gigantic tree you have hugged. Use the word gigantic.

© Morpheme Magic

More Word Bank Words

gigantic
hectic
microscopic
academic
mathematic(s)
automatic
comic
strategic
specific
terrific
electric

Other Words:
enthusiastic
sympathetic
realistic
energetic
analytic

NOTE: See Level 3 Word Origin and Root Meanings at the end of Level 3 for more information about **-ous** words in this lesson.

Lesson Goal:

Learn that -OUS is added to mostly Latin roots to make adjectives. It means full of or having.

Teachers know:

-OUS is pronounced /us/ or /is/. Variants are -**cious**, -**ious**, and -**tious** depending on the root spelling.

Word Bank

prefixes & roots are *italicized*

famous

adventurous

jealous

dangerous

delicious

enormous

fabulous

generous

hazardous

humorous

joyous

meticulous

nervous

tremendous

INTRODUCTION

DAY ONE: EXPLORE THE MORPHEME

Today we are going to learn a new suffix. Write **-ous** on the board. Ask students to read it with you /us/. -**OUS** means **full of**. Write **famous** on the board. Students read it with you. Underline **-ous**, circle **fam(e)**. When I see the word **famous**, I know that the **-ous** means **full of** so this word means **full of fame** and **fame means popular**. **We were all thrilled when the famous author came to our school!**

ORTHOGRAPHY - READING AND SPELLING

DECODE: Teach the orthography for **-ous**. Create a list of 5-10 words from the Word Bank. Display the words one at a time creating a column of words for reading spelling instruction. Model decoding, word meaning, and word use.

TEACHER	STUDENTS
Write and read **-ous.** -**OUS** means **full of**.	Read **-ous** and turn and say the meaning to a partner.
Write **famous**. Circle and say **fam(e)**. Underline **-ous**. Read the parts. Say **Famous means full of fame. Famous people are not always popular to everyone.** Scoop the syllables in fa-mous then circle and say the morphemes. Write fame + ous and go through the Drop It checklist for spelling.	Read **-ous**, blend the parts to read **famous**. Use **famous** in a sentence (assisted by teacher).
Follow the same process with 5-10 words. After reading the words, direct students to read them again with you. Prompt students to say **-ous** and word meanings each time.	Read through the word list as directed by the teacher. Say **-ous** and word meanings as directed. Use the words in sentences. Teacher provides sentence frames as needed.

humor)ous

whim, state of mind + full of

Leave the words displayed. Read them again prior to the encoding lesson.

ENCODE:

Dictate **-ous** words for students to spell. Use response boards or the Morpheme Grabber and ask students to share their spellings after each word, provide corrective feedback. Ask students for **-ous** meaning and word meaning after each spelling. Work with students to generate sentences with **-ous** words.

ACTIVITIES

MORPHEME GRABBER - WORD EQUATION

Direct students to create a new page in their Morpheme Grabber.

WORD + OUS	= NEW WORD	OUS MEANS
fame + ous =	famous	full of or having

Adjust the following exercises for your students' language and reading levels.

THE MORPHEME CARDS

Display the Morpheme Cards. Instruct students to say the **-ous** word for each picture, explore the meanings, and use the words in sentences to tell about the pictures. Add the cards to your Morpheme Wall for frequent review.

ORAL LANGUAGE AND WRITE

Display the two words for each example below. Ask students to work in pairs to develop a response. Share with the class and include the meaning of **-ous**, full of.

(**hazardous, dangerous**) How are these two words alike? What are some examples of something that we would describe with these words?

(**tremendous**, **enormous**) How are these words the same? How are they different? What might we describe with these words?

(**joyous**, **humorous**) How are these words the same? How are they different? What might we describe with each of these words?

CONNECT TO THE CLASSROOM

Post a list of **-ous** words from the Word Bank and other sources. Give the students a category and ask them to find all of the **-ous** words that would help to describe that category. Example categories: *Lunch Today, Inside your Desk, Character Descriptors* (from a class novel), *Going Out to Recess*. Expand your categories to outside of school and/or ask students to come up with categories for the class to work with.

REVIEW AND PRACTICE

Daily Morpheme Problem to Solve: Display one **-ous** word each day while on this lesson. Model how to read the word, circle the base, and then underline **-ous, or its variants**. Use words from the Word Banks or from your reading program.

naz | ard | ous

Use sound spelling boxes to map and spell **-ous** words. Assist students to circle the morphemes. Display a word from previous week's lessons for review.

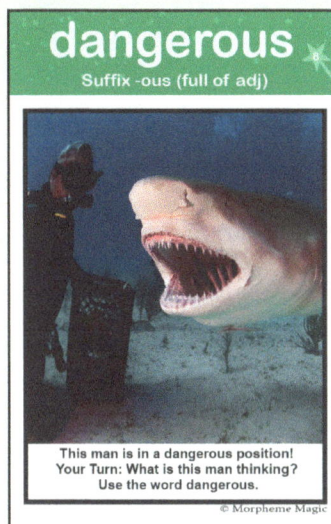

dangerous
Suffix -ous (full of adj)

This man is in a dangerous position!
Your Turn: What is this man thinking?
Use the word dangerous.

© Morpheme Magic

More Word Bank Words

Latin prefix & root are *italicized*

-cious

*suspi*cious

*loqua*cious

-ious

*cur*ious

previous

*hilar*ious

-tious

*nutri*tious

scrumptious

*infec*tious

(L *fecere* does not end in -ct, therefore t is part of the suffix -tious).

NOTE: See Appendix, Level 3 Word Origin and Root Meanings at the end of Level 3 for more information about **-ous** words in this lesson.

Lesson Goal:

Learn that -EN can be added to words to make verbs or adjectives. It means to make or made of.

Teachers know:

Most words to which **-en** is affixed are familiar Anglo Saxon bases. **-EN** means **made of** when an adjective is formed, e.g., **oaken.**

Word Bank

-EN = to make

tighten

loosen

darken

lighten

harden

soften

weaken

strengthen

widen

hasten

roughen

waken

blacken

freshen

spoken

mistaken

broken

INTRODUCTION

DAY ONE: EXPLORE THE MORPHEME

Today we are going to learn a new suffix. Write **-en** on the board. Ask students to read it with you. **-EN** means **to make**. Write **tighten** on the board. Students read it with you. Underline **-en,** circle **tight.** When I see the word **tighten**, I know that the **-en** means **to make** so this word means **to make tight. I will tighten my shoe laces so I won't trip over them.**

ORTHOGRAPHY - READING AND SPELLING

DECODE: Teach the orthography for **-en**. Create a list of 5-10 words from the Word Bank. Display the words one at a time creating a column of words for reading/spelling instruction. Model decoding, word meaning, and word use.

TEACHER	STUDENTS
Write and read **-en.** **-EN** means **to make**.	Read **-en** and turn and say the meaning to a partner.
Write **tighten**. Circle and say **tight**. Underline **-en.** Read the parts. Say **tighten means to make tight. Tighten your bracelet so it doesn't slip off.** Other -igh words include, lighten, brighten, frighten.	Read **-en**, blend the parts to read **tighten**. Use **tighten** in a sentence (suggest items that can be **tightened** if needed).
Follow the same process with 5-10 words. After reading the words, direct students to read them again with you. Prompt students to say **-en** and word meanings each time.	Read through the word list as directed by the teacher. Say **-en** and word meanings as directed. Use the words in sentences. Teacher provides sentence frames as needed.

tight en

Leave the words displayed. Read them again prior to the encoding lesson.

ENCODE:

Dictate **-en** words for students to spell. Use response boards or the Morpheme Grabber and ask students to share their spellings after each word, provide corrective feedback. Ask students for **-en** meaning and word meaning after each spelling. Work with students to generate sentences with **-en** words.

ACTIVITIES

MORPHEME GRABBER - WORD EQUATION OR DRAW AND LABEL

Direct students to create a new page in their Morpheme Grabber.

WORD + -EN	= NEW WORD	-EN MEANS
broke+ en =	broken	make or made of

Adjust the following exercises for your students' language and reading levels.

THE MORPHEME CARDS

Display the Morpheme Cards. Instruct students to say the **-en** word for each picture, explore the meanings, and use the words in sentences to tell about the pictures. Add the cards to your Morpheme Wall for frequent review.

ORAL LANGUAGE AND WRITE

We put foods in the freezer to **harden** them. Where do we **soften** foods?

What is something we could use **silken** to describe?

If we **hasten** to finish our work, how are we moving?

If your feet feel **leaden**, how will you walk?

Would you wear **woolen** clothes in summer? Why or why not?

Share something you have learned from your family about the **olden** days.

CONNECT TO THE CLASSROOM

Post a list of **-en** words for students to read and study. Ask them to work in small groups to find 5 words they can use to talk about the classroom, the work and learning they do, and their lives in school. Ask them to write down their thinking and share with the class.

REVIEW AND PRACTICE

Daily Morpheme Problem to Solve: Display one **-en** word each day while on this lesson. Model how to read the word, circle the base, and then underline **-en.** Use words from the Word Banks or from your reading program.

straight + en

Use sound spelling boxes to map and spell **-en** words. Circle the morphemes. Switch it out and display a word from previous week's lessons for review.

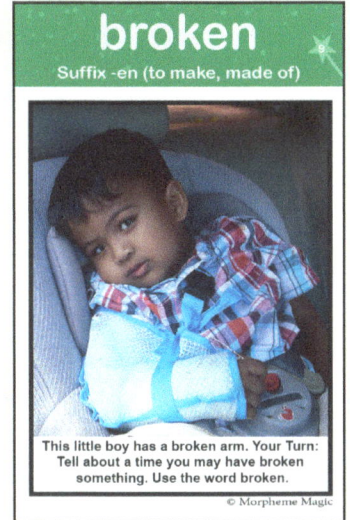

broken
Suffix -en (to make, made of)

This little boy has a broken arm. Your Turn: Tell about a time you may have broken something. Use the word broken.

© Morpheme Magic

More Word Bank Words

-EN = to make

slacken

olden

ashen

straighten

lessen

flatten

moisten

thicken

-EN = made of

oaken

earthen

leaden

silken

wooden

woolen

golden

Lesson Goal:

Learn that -IVE can be added to words to make adjectives. It means causing or making.

Teachers know:

Sometimes **a** or **i** comes before **ive**, which adds another syllable: **transformative, appreciative, preventative competitive, punitive sensitive**

Word Bank

active

reactive

adaptive

supportive

constructive

cooperative

decisive

destructive

expensive

creative

massive

negative

positive

impressive

expansive

predictive

appreciative

erosive

INTRODUCTION

DAY ONE: EXPLORE THE MORPHEME

Today we are going to learn a new suffix. Write **-ive** on the board. Ask students to read it with you. **-IVE** means **causing or making**. Write **active** on the board. Students read it with you. Underline **-ive,** circle **act.** When I see the word **active**, I know that the **-ive** means **making** so this word means **making movement or acting. An active lifestyle is good for our health.**

ORTHOGRAPHY - READING AND SPELLING

DECODE: Teach the orthography for **-ive**. Create a list of 5-10 words from the Word Bank. Display the words one at a time creating a column of words for reading/spelling instruction. Model decoding, word meaning, and word use.

TEACHER	STUDENTS
Write and read **-ive. -IVE** means **causing or making**.	Read **-ive** and turn and say the meaning to a partner.
Write **active**. Circle and say **act**. Underline **-ive**. Read the parts. Say **active means to act or move. Some say a full moon makes children more active.** Review the Drop It spelling rule for bases that end in e; creative, expensive, offensive.	Read **-ive**, blend the parts to read **active**. Use **active** in a sentence (assisted by teacher).
Follow the same process with 5-10 words. After reading the words, direct students to read them again with you. Prompt students to say **-ive** and word meanings each time.	Read through the word list as directed by the teacher. Say **-ive** and word meanings as directed. Use the words in sentences. Teacher provides sentence frames as needed.

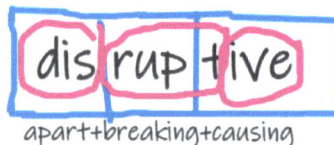
dis rup tive
apart+breaking+causing

Leave the words displayed. Read them again prior to the encoding lesson.

ENCODE:

Dictate **-ive** words for students to spell. Use response boards or the Morpheme Grabber and ask students to share their spellings after each word, provide corrective feedback. Ask students for **-ive** meaning and word meaning after each spelling. Work with students to generate sentences with **-ive** words.

ACTIVITIES

MORPHEME GRABBER - WORD EQUATION

Direct students to create a new page in their Morpheme Grabber.

WORD + IVE	= NEW WORD	IVE MEANS
act + ive =	active	causing or making

Adjust the following exercises for your students' language and reading levels.

THE MORPHEME CARDS

Display the Morpheme Cards. Instruct students to say the **-ive** word for each picture, explore the meanings, and use the words in sentences to tell about the pictures. Add the cards to your Morpheme Wall for frequent review.

ORAL LANGUAGE AND WRITE - CONNECT TO THE CLASSROOM

Display and read with students the list of **-ive** words on the previous page. Read the prompts below and decide as a class which word to use to answer each prompt. Record the word choices in a column list. Then, read the **Crazy Story** below inserting the words the class picked.

Prompts: Choose a word that means: *something big*; *causing to move*; *it costs a lot*; *a good way to be with a friend*; *building something*; *feeling good about it*.

When we walked into (your name)'s room today, we saw a ____ pinata! We became very ____ as our enthusiasm and curiosity grew. The pinata was made of gold and must have been very ____. (your name) said, "Today we are going to ____ and decide how to play the pinata game to celebrate Cinco de Mayo. Once we break it, we will also be ____ and decide how to put it back together! Your work will be ____."

Discuss how the story turned out with the word choices they made. Would they change any of the words? You can also project the story and ask students to decide what **-ive** words they want to use, write, then read their stories aloud.

REVIEW AND PRACTICE

Daily Morpheme Problem to Solve: Display one **-ive** word each day while on this lesson. Model how to read the word, circle the base, and then underline **-ive**. Use words from the Word Banks or from your reading program.

im press ive

in+ make a permanent + to cause
image

Use sound spelling boxes to map and spell **-ive** words. Circle the morphemes. Switch it out and display a word from previous week's lessons for review.

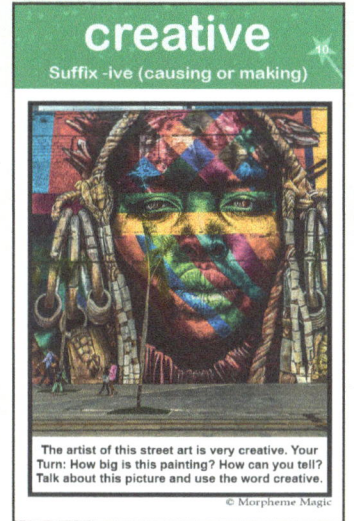

creative
Suffix -ive (causing or making)

The artist of this street art is very creative. Your Turn: How big is this painting? How can you tell? Talk about this picture and use the word creative.

© Morpheme Magic

More Word Bank Words

relative

sensitive

receptive

disruptive

eruptive

explosive

primitive

progressive

native

effective

competitive

consecutive

instinctive

Lesson Goal:

Learn that -ABLE can be added to words to make adjectives. It means can do or be.

Teachers know:

-IBLE is a variant of -able. It is mostly used with Latin roots. See Word Bank on next page for word examples.

Word Bank

believable

fixable

eatable

kissable

drinkable

floatable

trainable

likeable

lovable

payable

answerable

excitable

enjoyable

comfortable

allowable

forgivable

respectable

supportable

suitable

notable

INTRODUCTION

DAY ONE: EXPLORE THE MORPHEME

Today we are going to learn a new suffix. Write **-able** on the board. Ask students to read it with you. **–ABLE** means **can do**. Write **believable** on the board. Students read it with you. Underline **-able,** circle **believe.** When I see the word **believable**, I know that the **-able** means **can do or be** so this word means **can be believed**. **Is it believable that it will snow today?**

ORTHOGRAPHY - READING AND SPELLING

DECODE: Teach the orthography for **-able**. Create a list of 5-10 words from the Word Bank. Display the words one at a time creating a column of words for reading and spelling instruction. Model decoding, word meaning, and word use.

TEACHER	STUDENTS
Write and read **-able.** **ABLE** means **can do or be.**	Read **-able** and turn and say the meaning to a partner.
Write and read **believe**. Erase e and add **able**. **believable**. Circle and say **believe**. Underline **-able**. Read the parts. Say **believable – can be believed. The story we are reading is believable.** Reteach the Drop It rule for bases ending in e.	Read **-able**, blend the parts to read **believable**. Use **believable** in a sentence (assisted by teacher).
Follow the same process with 5-10 words. After reading the words, direct students to read them again with you. Prompt students to say **-able** and word meanings each time.	Read through the word list as directed by the teacher. Say **-able** and word meanings as directed. Use the words in sentences. Teacher provides sentence frames as needed.

be liev able

Leave the words displayed. Read them again prior to the encoding lesson.

ENCODE:

Dictate **-able** words for students to spell. Use response boards or the Morpheme Grabber and ask students to share their spellings after each word, provide corrective feedback. Ask students for **-able** meaning and word meaning after each spelling. Work with students to generate sentences with **-able** words.

ACTIVITIES

MORPHEME GRABBER - WORD EQUATION

Direct students to create a new page in their Morpheme Grabber.

WORD + -ABLE	= NEW WORD	-ABLE MEANS
believe + able =	believable	can do or be

Adjust the following exercises for your students' language and reading levels.

THE MORPHEME CARDS

Display the Morpheme Cards. Instruct students to say the **-able** word for each picture, explore the meanings, and use the words in sentences to tell about the pictures. Add the cards to your Morpheme Wall for frequent review.

ORAL LANGUAGE AND WRITE

Post a set of **-able** words for students to read and refer to. Direct students to write the heading **Pet ___** in their Grabbers and fill in the blank with a pet of their choice (dog, cat, hamster, etc). Then choose **-able** - words that could describe the pet they chose. Ask students to share their answers with a partner with reasons and examples for their word choices.

Dog
trainable
kissable
likeable
excitable

CONNECT TO THE CLASSROOM

Over the course of the week, see how many **-able** words students can use to discuss and write about what they are learning. Pose a brief list of words that you think may apply. Add to the list each day. Consider all content areas including aspects of the social classroom. Model your use of the **-able** words. Tally the number of times words are used. Ask for a classroom helper to assist with this.

REVIEW AND PRACTICE

Daily Morpheme Problem to Solve: Display one **-able** word each day while on this lesson. Model how to read the word, circle the base, and then underline **-able**. Use words from the Word Banks or from your reading program.

ex press i ble
out + make a + can do
permanent image

Use sound spelling boxes to map and spell **-able** words. Circle the morphemes. Switch it out and display a word from previous week's lessons for review.

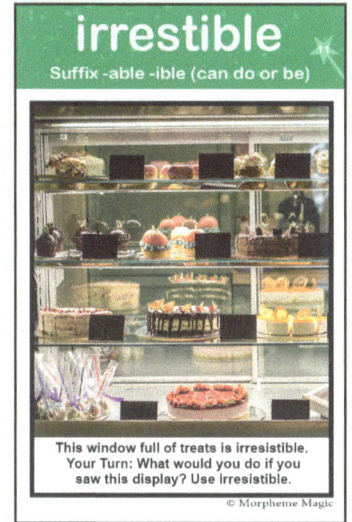

irrestible
Suffix -able -ible (can do or be)

This window full of treats is irresistible.
Your Turn: What would you do if you saw this display? Use irresistible.
© Morpheme Magic

More Word Bank Words

-IBLE Words

edible

flexible

legible

resistible

irresistible

responsible

sensible

terrible

accessible

compatible

comprehensible

eligible

expressible

possible

NOTE: See Appendix, Level 3 Word Origin and Root Meanings at the end of Level 3, for more information about **-able** words in this lesson.

Lesson Goal:

Learn that -ER and -OR can be added to words to make nouns or adjectives. It means one who or that which.

Teachers know:

-**ER** is mostly used with Anglo Saxon bases. -**OR** is used with mostly Latin roots.

Word Bank

-ER Words

sprinkler

baker

teacher

banker

hanger

heater

keeper

manager

miner

performer

runner

shipper

skater

tracker

walker

talker

splasher

watcher

pitcher

prowler

INTRODUCTION

DAY ONE: EXPLORE THE MORPHEME

Today we are going to learn a new suffix. Write **-er** on the board. Ask students to read it with you. **-ER** means **one who or that which**. Write **sprinkler** on the board. Students read it with you. Underline **-er,** circle **sprinkl(e).** When I see the word **sprinkler**, I know that the **-er** means **that which** so this word means **that which sprinkles. We turn on the sprinkler and run through it to cool off on a hot day.**

ORTHOGRAPHY - READING AND SPELLING

DECODE: Teach the orthography for **-er, -or**. Create a list of 5-10 words from the Word Bank. Display the words one at a time creating a column of words for reading and spelling instruction. Model decoding, word meaning, and word use.

TEACHER	STUDENTS
Write and read **-er and -or.** **-ER, -OR** mean **one who or that which**.	Read **-er, -or** and turn and say the meaning to a partner.
Write and read **sprinkle**. Erase **e** and add **er**. Read it. Circle and say **sprinkl(e)** Underline **-er**. Read the parts. Say **sprinkler – that which sprinkles. The sprinkler helps us water the grass.** Review spelling rules as needed. Also see Note on next page.	Read **-er**, blend the parts to read **sprinkler**. Use **sprinkler** in a sentence (assisted by teacher).
Follow the same process with 5-10 words. After reading the words, direct students to read them again with you. Prompt students to say **-er, -or** and word meanings.	Read through the word list as directed by the teacher. Say **-er, -or** and word meanings as directed. Use the words in sentences. Teacher provides sentence frames as needed.

sprinkl er

Leave the words displayed. Read them again prior to the encoding lesson.

ENCODE:

Dictate **-er, -or** words for students to spell. Use response boards or the Morpheme Grabber and ask students to share their spellings after each word, provide corrective feedback. Ask students for **-er, -or** meaning and word meaning after each spelling. Work with students to generate sentences with **-er, -or** words.

ACTIVITIES

MORPHEME GRABBER - WORD EQUATION OR DRAW AND LABEL

Direct students to create a new page in their Morpheme Grabber.

WORD + -ER, -OR	= NEW WORD	-ER, -OR MEANS
sprinkle + er = invent + or =	sprinkler inventor	that which one who

Adjust the following exercises for your students' language and reading levels.

THE MORPHEME CARDS

Display the Morpheme Cards. Instruct students to say the -**er, -or** word for each picture, explore the meanings, and use the words in sentences to tell about the pictures. Add the cards to your Morpheme Wall for frequent review.

ORAL LANGUAGE AND WRITE

Post these words in random order: **actor, performer, manager, educator, teacher, instructor, competitor, runner, pitcher, spectator (others?)**. Ask the following questions. Students write their answers and share in small groups.

Words that go with theater.

Words that go with school.

Words that go with sports.

Post additional words and create your own categories. Encourage verbal reasoning to support answers.

CONNECT TO THE CLASSROOM

Divide the class into teams and provide a clicker or buzzer for each. Project an **-er-,** or **-or** word. Teams decide which meaning best fits – **one who ___** or **that which ___**. The first team to ring the buzzer and give the right answer wins. **Pitcher = one who pitches!**

REVIEW AND PRACTICE

Daily Morpheme Problem to Solve: Display one **-er, -or** word each day while on this lesson. Model how to read the word, circle the base, and then underline **-er, -or**. Use words from the Word Banks or from your reading program.

educator

Use sound spelling boxes to map and spell **-er, -or** words. Circle the morphemes. Switch it out and display a word from previous week's lessons for review.

---

performer 12

Suffix -er, -or (one how or that which)

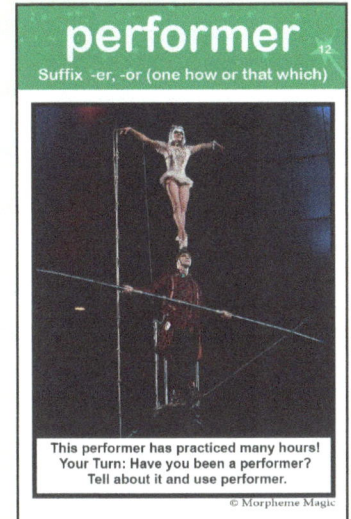

This performer has practiced many hours!
Your Turn: Have you been a performer?
Tell about it and use performer.

© Morpheme Magic

More Word Bank Words

-OR Words

inventor

actor

advisor

calculator

collector

confessor

creator

competitor

educator

instructor

juror

narrator

protector

spectator

translator

visor

NOTE: Teach students that **one who** is the meaning when **-er, -or** are affixed to people words. We use **that which**, when **-er, -or** are affixed to objects or other inanimate base words.

Lesson Goal:

Learn that -AGE can be added to words to make nouns. It means a collection of, related to.

Teachers know:

-**AGE** is an unaccented syllable. It will have the schwa vowel sound and be pronounced /uge/or /ige/. Be explicit with students about what they hear and how -**age** is spelled.

Word Bank

mileage

wreckage

storage

village

voyage

package

luggage

baggage

passage

leakage

drainage

courage

beverage

bandage

acreage

INTRODUCTION

DAY ONE: EXPLORE THE MORPHEME

Today we are going to learn a new suffix. Write -**age** on the board. Ask students to read it with you. -**AGE** means **a collection of, related to**. Write **mileage** on the board. Students read it with you. Point out how -**age** sounds when it is in a word /uge/. Underline -**age,** circle **mile.** When I see the word **mileage**, I know that the -**age** means **collection of** so this word means **a collection of miles**. **The mileage I walk to school is two miles and my friend's driving mileage is 10 miles.**

ORTHOGRAPHY - READING AND SPELLING

DECODE: Teach the orthography for -**age**. Create a list of 5-10 words from the Word Bank. Display the words one at a time creating a column of words for reading and spelling instruction. Model decoding, word meaning, and word use.

TEACHER	STUDENTS
Write and read -**age.** -**AGE** means **a collection of or related to.**	Read -**age** and turn and say the meaning to a partner.
Write **mileage**. Circle and say **mile**. Underline -**age**. Read the parts. Say **mileage -a collection of miles. His milage for the trip was high.** Say, even though we hear /uge/ we always spell it -**age.** Mileage is a great word to go through the checkpoints for Drop It.	Read -**age**, blend the parts to read **mileage**. Use **milage** in a sentence (assisted by teacher).
Follow the same process with 5-10 words. After reading the words, direct students to read them again with you. Prompt students to say -**age** and word meanings each time.	Read through the word list as directed by the teacher. Say -**age** and word meanings as directed. Use the words in sentences. Teacher provides sentence frames as needed.

Leave the words displayed. Read them again prior to the encoding lesson.

ENCODE:

Dictate -**age** words for students to spell. Use response boards or the Morpheme Grabber and ask students to share their spellings after each word, provide corrective feedback. Ask students for -**age** meaning and word meaning after each spelling. Work with students to generate sentences with -**age** words.

ACTIVITIES

MORPHEME GRABBER - WORD EQUATION

Direct students to create a new page in their Morpheme Grabber.

WORD + AGE	= NEW WORD	AGE MEANS
mile + age =	mileage	collection of or related to

Adjust the following exercises for your students' language and reading levels.

THE MORPHEME CARDS

Display the Morpheme Cards. Instruct students to say the **-age** word for each picture, explore the meanings, and use the words in sentences to tell about the pictures. Add the cards to your Morpheme Wall for frequent review.

ORAL LANGUAGE AND WRITE

Pose this scenario to the class: we are going on a trip to (relate the destination to someplace you are learning about or a location in a story the class is reading). List the **-age** words you could use to discuss the trip. Then ask students to create a Beginning – Middle with a problem – and Ending with a problem solution for the story. Share resulting adventures with the class.

CONNECT TO THE CLASSROOM

Ask these questions using **-age** words to stimulate conversation.

What is something you need **courage** to do at school?

If a **package** were delivered to our classroom, what could be in it?

What is something we might have a **shortage** of in our classroom?

What **percentage** of students are present today?

Why don't you need **postage** to send an email?

REVIEW AND PRACTICE

Daily Morpheme Problem to Solve: Display one **-age** word each day while on this lesson. Model how to read the word, circle the base, and then underline **-age**. Use words from the Word Banks or from your reading program.

an chor age

Use sound spelling boxes to map and spell **-age** words. Circle the morphemes. Switch it out and display a word from previous week's lessons for review.

voyage

Suffix -age (collection of, related to)

A voyage over the ocean would be thrilling! Your Turn: What would you see on an ocean voyage? Use the word voyage.

© Morpheme Magic

More Word Bank Words

blockage

slippage

shortage

percentage

spillage

anchorage

coverage

postage (n, adj)

NOTE: Village is a fun word to explore. **Vill+age** (French) literally means a *collection* of cottages, houses, and other buildings.

Lesson Goal:

Learn that DE- can be added to words to make verbs and nouns. It means down, away from

Teachers know:

Most **de-** words are added to bound bases, Latin roots.

Word Bank

defog

deice

defrost

decay

decrease

decode

deduct

deflect

defeat

deform

deplane

defer

debug

delight

degrease

dethrone

INTRODUCTION

DAY ONE: EXPLORE THE MORPHEME

Today we are going to learn a new prefix. Prefixes come at the beginnings of words to change meaning. Write **de-** on the board. Ask students to read it with you. **DE-** means **down, away from**. Write **defog** on the board. Students read it with you. Underline **de-,** circle **fog.** When I see the word **defog,** I know that the **de-** means **away from** so this word means **do away with the fog. She will defog and deice the windshield before driving so she can see where she is going! What does deice mean? Do away with the ice!**

ORTHOGRAPHY - READING AND SPELLING

DECODE: Teach the orthography for **de-**. Create a list of 5-10 words from the Word Bank. Display the words one at a time creating a column of words for reading and spelling instruction. Model decoding, word meaning, and word use.

TEACHER	STUDENTS
Write and read **-de. DE-** means **down, away from**.	Read **de-** and turn and say the meaning to a partner.
Write **defog**. Circle and say **fog**. Underline **de-**. Read the parts. Say **defog – means away with the fog. Can we defog the air?**	Read **de-**, blend the parts to read **defog**. Use **defog** in a sentence (assisted by teacher).
Follow the same process with 5-10 words. After reading the words, direct students to read them again with you. Prompt students to say **-de** and word meanings each time.	Read through the word list as directed by the teacher. Say **-de** and word meanings as directed. Use the words in sentences. Teacher provides sentence frames as needed.

de fog

Leave the words displayed. Read them again prior to the encoding lesson.

ENCODE:

Dictate **-de** words for students to spell. Use response boards or the Morpheme Grabber and ask students to share their spellings after each word, provide corrective feedback. Ask students for **-de** meaning and word meaning after each spelling. Work with students to generate sentences with **-de** words.

ACTIVITIES

dethrone
Prefix de- (down, away from)

When playing chess, the goal is to dethrone the king. Your Turn: What does dethrone mean? Use the word dethrone.

© Morpheme Magic

MORPHEME GRABBER - WORD EQUATION

Direct students to create a new page in their Morpheme Grabber.

DE + WORD	= NEW WORD	DE MEANS
de + throne =	dethrone	down, away from

Adjust the following exercises for your students' language and reading levels.

THE MORPHEME CARDS

Display the Morpheme Cards. Instruct students to say the **de-** word for each picture, explore the meanings, and use the words in sentences to tell about the pictures. Add the cards to your Morpheme Wall for frequent review.

ORAL LANGUAGE AND WRITE

Read the first sentence and highlight the italicized base. Then, students supply the **de-**form of the base to finish the second in the pair of sentences. Ask students to write their answers, then a sentence using the **de-** word they formed.

I will *activate* the app. My mom will (**deactivate**) it.

I get on the *plane* to go somewhere. When I get there, I (**deplane**).

I *compress* the pillow to put it in this bag. When I take it out, I (**decompress**) it.

There is *frost* on the window. The sun will (**defrost**) the window.

There is a *bug* in my computer. The repair person will (**debug**) it for me.

CONNECT TO THE CLASSROOM

Post the word **decrease**. Students read it and discuss meaning (**de-***away from* + **crease-***growing* = away from growing). Ask students to brainstorm things that **decrease** in your classroom. Examples: numbers when we subtract; kids when there is sickness or somebody moves; books when we take them home to read; water in our water bottles.

REVIEW AND PRACTICE

Daily Morpheme Problem to Solve: Display one **de-** word each day while on this lesson. Model how to read the word, circle the base, and then underline **de-**. Use words from the Word Banks or from your reading program.

de (crease)

Use sound spelling boxes to map and spell **de-** words. Circle the morphemes. Switch it out and display a word from previous week's lessons for review.

More Word Bank Words

decompose

detergent

decompress

deactivate

deport *This might be a sensitive word for some of our students.* **Examples** might be: When I find a spider in my house, I **deport** it! **de-away + port - carry = to carry away. I put it outside.**

TIP: Create word equations to teach the meanings of the prefix **de-** and the roots to which it is affixed. **De-** + crease = **decrease** - away from growing.

143

Lesson Goal:

Learn that TRANS- can be added to words to make nouns. It means across or beyond.

Teachers know:

TRANS- is affixed to mostly Latin roots.

Word Bank

transport

transform

transfer

transfix

translate

translator

transcribe

transaction

transparent

transit

transmit

INTRODUCTION

DAY ONE: EXPLORE THE MORPHEME

Today we are going to learn a new prefix. Write **trans-** on the board. Ask students to read it with you. **TRANS-** means **across or beyond**. Write **transport** on the board. Students read it with you. Underline **trans-,** circle **port and say, "Port** means **to carry.** When I see the word **transport**, I know that the **trans-** means **beyond** so this word means **to carry beyond. The trucks will transport the fresh food from the farm to the market. The trucks will carry the food beyond the farm.**

ORTHOGRAPHY - READING AND SPELLING

DECODE: Teach the orthography for **trans-**. Create a list of 5-10 words from the Word Bank. Display the words one at a time creating a column of words for reading and spelling instruction. Model decoding, word meaning, and word use.

TEACHER	STUDENTS
Write and read **trans-**. **TRANS-** means **across or beyond**.	Read **trans** and turn and say the meaning to a partner.
Write **transport**. Circle and say **port**. Underline **trans-**. Read the parts. Say **transport – to carry beyond. Mother cat will transport her kittens to a new hiding place.**	Read **trans**-, blend the parts to read **transport**. Use **transport** in a sentence (assisted by teacher).
Follow the same process with 5-10 words. After reading the words, direct students to read them again with you. Prompt students to say **trans-** and word meanings each time.	Read through the word list as directed by the teacher. Say **trans-** and word meanings as directed. Use the words in sentences. Teacher provides sentence frames as needed.

trans port

Leave the words displayed. Read them again prior to the encoding lesson.

ENCODE:

Dictate **trans-** words for students to spell. Use response boards or the Morpheme Grabber and ask students to share their spellings after each word, provide corrective feedback. Ask students for **trans-** meaning and word meaning after each spelling. Work with students to generate sentences with **trans-** words.

ACTIVITIES

MORPHEME GRABBER - WORD EQUATION

Direct students to create a new page in their Morpheme Grabber.

TRANS + WORD	= NEW WORD	TRANS MEANS
trans + form =	transform	across or beyond

Adjust the following exercises for your students' language and reading levels.

THE MORPHEME CARDS

Display the Morpheme Cards. Instruct students to say the **trans-** word for each picture, explore the meanings, and use the words in sentences to tell about the pictures. Add the cards to your Morpheme Wall for frequent review.

ORAL LANGUAGE AND WRITE

Pose the following questions and ask students to research any possible answers. Give them the paragraph frame to write a brief paragraph about what they learn. Provide opportunities to share.

When was the first heart **transplant**?

What does it mean to **transplant** a plant?

Can people be **transplanted**? What are some examples?

> Today I learned about ___. The first interesting detail I learned is ___. Another is _____. The most intriguing information is _____. Transplanting ___ is a topic I _____.

CONNECT TO THE CLASSROOM

Transfix means you are fixed beyond reality. Your attention is focused and you cannot break away! What is a story we have read, or a movie you have seen that **transfixed** you? Discuss.

Transcribe means to write beyond. If you break your arm and cannot write, someone can **transcribe** your thoughts for you. They can write your thoughts. Take turns with a partner. One of you **transcribe** a thought for the other and then switch! Read the **transcriptions** to the class!

REVIEW AND PRACTICE

Daily Morpheme Problem to Solve: Display one **trans-** word each day while on this lesson. Model how to read the word, circle the base, and then underline **trans-**. Use words from the Word Banks or from your reading program.

Use sound spelling boxes to map and spell **trans-** words. Circle the morphemes. Switch it out and display a word from previous week's lessons for review.

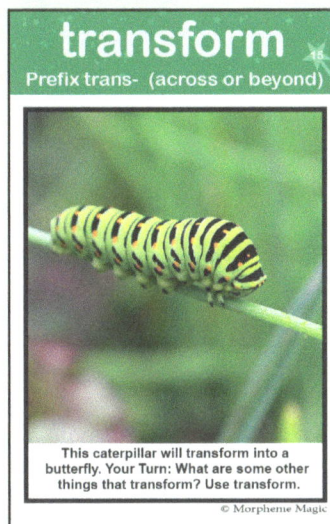

transform
Prefix trans- (across or beyond)

This caterpillar will transform into a butterfly. Your Turn: What are some other things that transform? Use transform.

© Morpheme Magic

More Word Bank Words

translucent

transplant

transcend

transgress

transact

transaction

transfusion

Lesson Goal:

Learn that DIS- can be added to words to make verbs and nouns. It means not, absence of, or apart.

Teachers know:

Words to teach the alternate meanings of **dis**: Disable *a machine*. DIS- means take it **apart** (*most common meaning*).

Disinterest *in a game*. DIS- means **absence of**.

Word Bank

DIS- means apart, separated from:

disable

dissolve

displace

discharge

disclose

discuss

disgrace

dispose

disrupt

disjoint

INTRODUCTION

DAY ONE: EXPLORE THE MORPHEME

Today we are going to learn a new prefix. Write **dis-** on the board. Ask students to read it with you. **DIS-** means **not.**. Write **dishonest** on the board. Students read it with you. Underline **dis-,** circle **honest.** When I see the word **dishonest**, I know that the **dis-** means **not** so this word means **not honest**. Being dishonest can create distrust. What does distrust mean? It means not able to trust that person.

ORTHOGRAPHY - READING AND SPELLING

DECODE: Teach the orthography for **dis-**. Create a list of 5-10 words from the Word Bank. Display the words one at a time creating a column of words for reading and spelling instruction. Model decoding, word meaning, and word use.

TEACHER	STUDENTS
Write and read **dis-**. **DIS-**means **not, but can also mean absence of or apart**.	Read **dis-** and turn and say the meaning to a partner.
Write **dishonest**. Circle and say **honest**. Underline **dis-**. Read the parts. Say **dishonest – not honest. It is best to apologize if we are dishonest.**	Read **dis**, blend the parts to read **dishonest**. Use **dishonest** in a sentence (assisted by teacher).
Follow the same process with 5-10 words. After reading the words, direct students to read them again with you. Prompt students to say **dis-** and word meanings each time.	Read through the word list as directed by the teacher. Say **dis-** and word meanings as directed. Use the words in sentences. Teacher provides sentence frames as needed.

dis honest

Leave the words displayed. Read them again prior to the encoding lesson.

ENCODE:

Dictate **-dis** words for students to spell. Use response boards or the Morpheme Grabber and ask students to share their spellings after each word, provide corrective feedback. Ask students for **-dis** meaning and word meaning after each spelling. Work with students to generate sentences with **-dis** words.

ACTIVITIES

MORPHEME GRABBER – WORD EQUATION

Direct students to create a new page in their Morpheme Grabber.

DIS- + WORD	= NEW WORD	DIS- MEANS
dis + honest =	dishonest	not honest
dis + charge =	discharge	apart from something
dis + interest =	disinterest	absence of interest

Adjust the following exercises for your students' language and reading levels.

THE MORPHEME CARDS

Display the Morpheme Cards. Instruct students to say the **-dis** word for each picture, explore the meanings, and use the words in sentences to tell about the pictures. Add the cards to your Morpheme Wall for frequent review.

ORAL LANGUAGE AND WRITE

Build in a review of suffixes **-ion**, **-ive**, **-al**, others? Give students the first word and then work with them to build another word from it using the target suffix.

-ion (state of)	-al (relating to)	-ive (inclined to)
discuss (discussion)	dispose (disposal)	disrupt (disruptive)
distract (distraction)	**-ment (act or state of)**	distract (distractive)
disrupt (disruption)	disfigure (disfigurement)	
	displace (displacement)	

CONNECT TO THE CLASSROOM

Choose words that could be used to discuss classroom expectations. Post one per day and ask students to define and provide examples of how the word relates to the classroom rules/expectations: **displace** – when we **displace** our pencil, this is what we do… **discuss** – when partner sharing, we take turns **discussing** the topic.

REVIEW AND PRACTICE

Daily Morpheme Problem to Solve: Display one **dis-** word each day while on this lesson. Model how to read the word, circle the base, and then underline **dis-**. Use words from the Word Banks or from your reading program.

dis | a | bili | ty
not + able + state of

Use sound spelling boxes to map and spell **-dis** words. Circle the morphemes. Switch it out and display a word from previous week's lessons for review.

discharge
Prefix dis- (not, absence of, apart)

Sparks discharge from these fireworks.
Your Turn: Talk about your experience with sparks discharging. Use discharge.

© Morpheme Magic

More Word Bank Words

DIS- means not:

dishonest

distrust

dislike

discount

distract

disorder

DIS- means absence of:

disappear

disability

disfavor

disfigure

NOTE: Sometimes it is hard to tell which meaning of **dis-** fits best with the word meaning. Try them all and see what fits best! Have a class vote!

Lesson Goal:

Learn that EX- can be added to words to make verbs, nouns, and adjectives. It means out.

Teachers know:

A variant of **ex-** is **e-** as in eject = to push out. Also in erase = to scrape out.

Word Bank

EX-

exit

exact

example

exceed

excel

excellent

except

excite

excitement

exclude

excuse

exercise

exist

expand

expect

expedition

expel

INTRODUCTION

DAY ONE: EXPLORE THE MORPHEME

Today we are going to learn a new prefix. Write **ex-** on the board. Ask students to read it with you. **Ex-** means **out**. Write **exit** on the board. Students read it with you. Underline **ex-**, circle **it**. When I see the word **exit**, I know that the **ex-** means **out** and **it** is from Latin (*ire*) meaning **to go** so this word means **to go out, a way out, or departure**. We will exit the room in an orderly manner. Where is the exit sign?

ORTHOGRAPHY – READING AND SPELLING

DECODE: Teach the orthography for **ex- and e-**. Create a list of 5-10 words from the Word Banks. Display the words one at a time creating a column of words for reading and spelling and instruction. Model decoding, word meaning, and word use.

TEACHER	STUDENTS
Write and read **ex-**. **EX-** means **out**. You might see the prefix **e-**. It means **out.**	Read **ex- and e-** and turn and say the meaning to a partner.
Write **exit**. Circle and say **it**. Underline **ex-**. Read the parts. Say **exit – exit means to go out. A door can be an exit. Do the same with erase.** Erase – e- = out, rase = to scrape. Erase – = to scrape out. Erase the error.	Read **ex-**, blend the parts to read **exit**. Use **exit** in a sentence (assisted by teacher). Do the same with **erase**.
Follow the same process with 5-10 words. After reading the words, direct students to read them again with you. Prompt students to say **ex-** or **e-** and word meanings each time.	Read through the word list as directed by the teacher. Say **ex-** or **e-** and word meanings as directed. Use the words in sentences. Teacher provides sentence frames as needed.

Leave the words displayed. Read them again prior to the encoding lesson.

ENCODE:

Dictate **ex-** words for students to spell. Use response boards or the Morpheme Grabber and ask students to share their spellings after each word, provide corrective feedback. Ask students for **ex-** meaning and word meaning after each spelling. Work with students to generate sentences with **ex-** words.

ACTIVITIES

MORPHEME GRABBER - WORD EQUATION

Direct students to create a new page in their Morpheme Grabber.

EX- + WORD	= NEW WORD	EX- AND E- MEAN
ex + it =	exit	to go out
e + rase =	erase	to scrape out

Adjust the following exercises for your students' language and reading levels.

THE MORPHEME CARDS

Display the Morpheme Cards. Instruct students to say the **ex-** and **e-** word for each picture, explore the meanings, and use the words in sentences to tell about the pictures. Add the cards to your Morpheme Wall for frequent review.

ORAL LANGUAGE AND WRITE - GIVE EXAMPLES!

What is an **example** of something that can **emit (e-out, mit-send = send out)**?

What is an **example** of something that can **expand (ex-out, pand-spread=spread out)**?

What is an **example** of an **event (e-out, vent-to come=to come out together)**?

Other ideas to present: Give **examples** for: when it is important to be **exact**; types of **exercise**; when to **evaluate** something.

CONNECT TO THE CLASSROOM

Expedition is a fun word. **Ex-out**, **ped-foot**, **ion – state of** = **a state of going out on foot.** Present a couple of famous **expeditions** for students to research. Ask them to use the word **expedition** in their "reports" that they will share with the class. Four ideas online: *The Arctic Has a Trail of Frozen Bodies*; *Marie Dorion's Expedition Westward; Weird Facts about Lewis and Clark, First Man on the Moon*.

REVIEW AND PRACTICE

Daily Morpheme Problem to Solve: Display one **ex-** or **e-** word each day while on this lesson. Model how to read the word, circle the base, and then underline **ex-** and **e- affixes**. Use words from the Word Banks or from your reading program.

ex pe di tion

Use sound spelling boxes to map and spell **ex-** and **-e** words. Circle the morphemes. Switch it out and display a word from previous week's lessons for review.

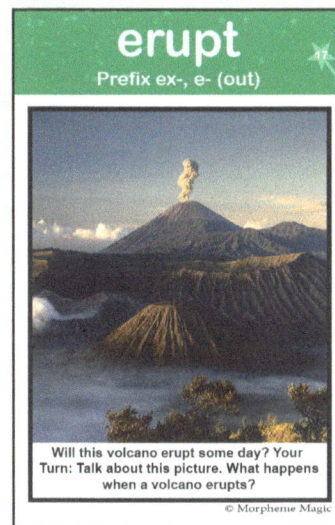

erupt
Prefix ex-, e- (out)

Will this volcano erupt some day? Your Turn: Talk about this picture. What happens when a volcano erupts?

© Morpheme Magic

More Word Bank Words

E- is a variant of EX-

erase

eject

elect

emit

erect

erupt

evacuate

evaluate

event

NOTE: EX- is usually pronounced /egz/ when followed by a vowel. When followed by a consonant, /eks/.

Lesson Goal:

Continue to develop morphological awareness. Develop curiosity about words and their meaningful parts.

Teachers know:

When developing morphological awareness with little ones, know that many of the affixes you teach will be affixed to Latin roots. You can begin to prepare students for **Morpheme Magic** lessons by attending to the Latin roots when opportunities arise. See the following Appendix for Latin root meanings in many of the words presented in Level 3 lessons. Most important outcome is that students know the meanings of and can use the words.

Congratulations! You have completed Level 3 with your students. Your students' development of morphological awareness has deepened significantly as they have now been exposed to Latin roots during your affix lessons. Keep up the focus on morphology through lots of P&R – Practice and Review.

KEYS TO SUCCESSFUL MORPHOLOGICAL AWARENESS INSTRUCTION:

- Continue to teach awareness of morphemes during your reading block as part of your vocabulary instruction. Then, be aware of how the morphemes and words you teach can transfer to discussion about the reading materials in your reading lesson.

- Slowly step back, over time, with modeling your inquiry about words, encouraging students to voice their own inquiry. Initially you will be the lead, asking questions about words in student reading material. "I wonder what the root in this word means." "What other words fit into the family of words with this root?" "Is de- a prefix in this word?"

- Apply the R & P - Review and Practice. Be consistent. Review previously learned morphemes during a Daily Word Problem to Solve. Draw attention to your Morpheme Wall multiple times throughout the day. Observe for your students' voluntary reference to the display as an indicator that the Morpheme Wall is doing its work!

- Model the use of the vocabulary that was presented in the Lessons. Determine which words are academic and apply them regularly during class discussions and when giving directions.

- Include a spelling/dictation element in your vocabulary lessons. Make sure students say the words aloud, discuss meanings and use the words within meaningful contexts, and write the words.

There are about 87,000 word families based on shared morphemes. Teach morphology productively, so learning one word leads to learning many! How many words can be created from these combinations?

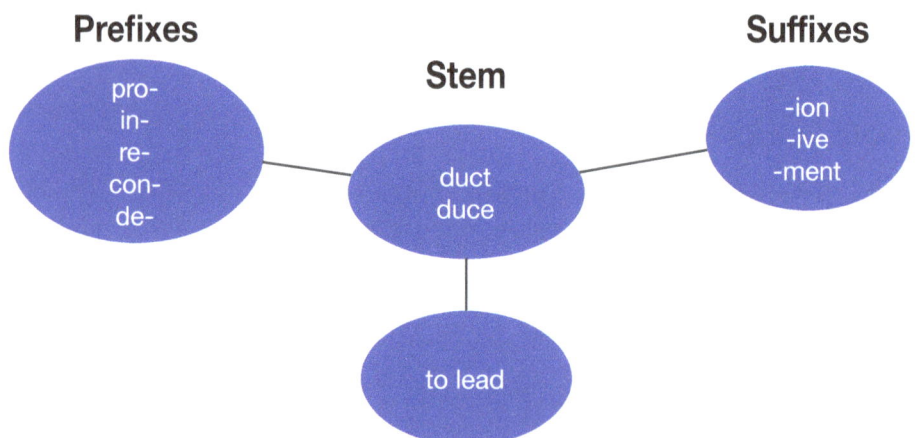

Prefixes

pro-
in-
re-
con-
de-

Stem

duct
duce

Suffixes

-ion
-ive
-ment

to lead

LEVEL 3 – ADDITIONAL MORPHEME MEANINGS FOR MANY WORDS IN THE LEVEL 3 LESSONS

LESSON 7 SUFFIX -IC , HAVING QUALITIES OF	
gigantic – gigant - giants + ic	**strategic** – strategy - art of a general + ic
hectic – hect - fever + ic	**energetic** – en - at + ergon work + ic
microscopic – micro - very small + scope - to look at + ic	**specific** —species - particular kind, sort + ficus - making, doing + ic
academic – academ(y) - school + ic	**electric** – electron - resembling amber + ic So called because amber was the first substance to attract other substances when rubbed
mathematic(s) – math - learning + ic	**terrific** – terrificus - frightening + ic
automatic – auto - self + ic	**analytic** — ana -up, back, throughout + lysis - loosening
comic – comos – revelry + oidos - singer, poet + ic	**enthusiastic** – en - in + theos - god + ic; inspired by a god; intensely eager
sympathetic – syn - together + pathos - to suffer + ic	**realistic** – real - actually existing + ist - one who does or makes + ic

LESSON 8 SUFFIX -OUS , FULL OF	
adventurous – ad - to + venereto - come + ous	**joyous** – gaudia- expressions of delight, gladness + ous
jealous – *jeal* - zeal, full of zeal + ous	**meticulous** – met - fussy about details (F –1840's) + ous
dangerous – danger - power to harm + ous	**nervous** – nerv - full of nerves + ous
delicious – de - away + lic - lure or entice away + ous	**tremendous** – tremend – tremble, full of trembling + ous
enormous – e(ex) - out + norma - outside of the norm + ous	**loquacious** – loqui - to talk, full of talking + ous
fabulous – fab - full of fable (story or tale) + ous	**suspicious** – sub- beneath + spec - look at + ous
generous – genus - birth, plentiful, unselfish + ous	**curious** – cur - care + ous
hazardous – originally an unfortunate throw of dice in a game of chance + ous	**previous** – pre - before + via - road + ous
hilarious – hilarus - cheerful and merry + ous	**nutritious** – nutria - nourish, suckle, feed + ous
scrumptious – American English from **sumptuous** - sumere - spend, consume, take + ous	**infectious** – in - in + facere - to make or do + ous
humorous – humor-mood, state of mind, indulge + ous	

adaptive – ad - to + apt - join or fit + ive

supportive – sup - form of sub meaning up from under + portare - to carry + ive

decisive – de - off + caedere - cut, strike + ive marked by prompt determination

expensive – ex - out + pendere - weigh, pay + ive

constructive – con - with, together + struere-to pile up + ive

negative -- negat - deny, say no + ive

destructive -- de - reverse + struere - pile up + ive

positive – posit - put, placed + ive meaning concentrating on what is constructive and good

cooperative – com - together + operari - work + ive

impressive – im - in + press - exert force + ive meaning affecting forcefully or deeply

expansive -- expans-to spread out + ive

appreciative – ad-to + pretium - price+ ive

erosive – eros - gnaw away + ive

extinctive – ex - out + stinguere - put out + ive

native – nat - from birth, born + ive

consecutive – com - with, together + sequi - to follow + ive

competitive – com - with + petere - to strive + ive meaning eager to compete

disruptive – dis - apart + rupt - break + ive

instinctive – in - on + stinct - prick, goad + ive

effective – ef - out + facere - make do + ive

detergent – de - off, away + tergere to rub, polish, wipe

decrease – de - away from + crease-growing

transform – trans - beyond + form - shape

transfer – trans – across + ferre - to carry

transfix – trans - beyond + figere to fix, fasten meaning to make motionless or helpless

translate – trans - across + latus - carried - carried across from one language to another

translator – trans - across + latus - born or carried + or - one who

transcribe – trans - across + scriber-to write

transit – trans - across + it-to go

transmit – trans - across + mit - to release, let go; send, throw

transaction – trans - across + act - do perform + ion - noun

transparent – trans - across + parere show, appear

example – ex - out + emere - take meaning something taken out so it can be considered separately	**exceed** – ex - out + cedere - to go, yield
excel – ex - out + cellere - rise, be high, tower	**except** – ex - out + capere - to take
excite – ex - out + ciere - set in motion, call	**exclude** – ex - out + claudere-to close, shut
expel – ex - out + pellere - to drive	**expand** – ex - out + pandere - to spread, stretch
exist – ex - out + sister - stand forth	**eject** – e - out + icere - to throw
erect -- e - out + regere - to direct, keep straight	**erupt** e - out + rumpere - to break, rupture
evacuate – e - out + vacuus - empty	**evaluate** – e - out + valuer - be strong, be of value

KEY FEATURES OF AFRICAN AMERICAN ENGLISH

VERB MORPHOLOGY	DESCRIPTION	EXAMPLES
Variable past tense	The -ed marker is variably attached to verb forms in past tense contexts.	The cow jump_ over the moon. He fix_ the broken car.
Variable plural	The -s marker is variably attached to nouns.	She saw three cat_ in the window. A girl puttin' some glass_ on the table to drink.
Variable third person -s	The -s marker is variably included on the verb in third-person singular contexts.	My friend want_ to buy some candy when we get to the store.
Variable possessive	The -s marker is variably included to mark possession, and possessive pronouns are variably marked.	I rode in my uncle_ car. They waitin' for they car.
SYNTAX		
Variable subject-verb agreement	Subject and verb do not agree in tense and number.	My friends was runnin' fast to catch the bus.
Variable inclusion of to be in copula (linking) and auxiliary forms	Main and auxiliary forms of the verb to be are variably included.	This __ my red car. They __ watchin' the girls jump rope.*
PHONOLOGY		
Consonant cluster reduction	Consonant clusters in the final position of words are reduced to one final consonant.	col_/cold fiel_/field cas_/cast
Dropped "g"	Variable inclusion of g in the final position of a word ending in -ing.	jumpin_/jumping waitin_/waiting goin_/going
Intervocalic and postvocalic positions for f/θ, v/ð, and t/θ	Following a vowel, voiceless (θ) and voiced (ð) th sounds in medial and final positions of words are replaced by /f/, /t/, or /v/.	wif/with wit/with bave/bathe
Prevocalic positions for d/ð	Preceding a vowel, the voiced (ð) th sound in initial position of words is replaced with /d/.	dis/this dem/them dat/that
Consonant cluster movement	The /sk/ consonant cluster is transposed, becoming /ks/.	aks/ask ekscape/escape

*These examples were taken from the transcripts of child speakers of African American English. Some examples include another AAE feature in addition to the feature being highlighted. In this sentence, for example, the child deletes the auxiliary form are and also drops the final g. Production of multiple AAE features in a single sentence is common.

Reprinted with permission from Julie A. Washington. Originally published in American Educator. Washington, J. A. & Seidenberg, M. S. (2021). Teaching Reading to African American Children: When Home and School Language Differ. American Federation of Teachers: American Educator. https://www.aft.org/ae

MORPHOLOGY RESOURCES

LEARNING RESOURCES FOR TEACHERS

Speech to Print: Language Essentials for Teachers, 3rd Edition. Louisa C. Moats. Brookes Publishing.

Dr. Moats created a beloved tutorial for teachers in this book. In its third edition, she continues to remove the mystery of English morphology but informing and building teachers' understanding. Through multiple practice exercises, teachers grow in their knowledge and pedagogy. A great section on Morphology will delight *Morpheme Magic* and *Morphemes for Little Ones* fans!

Teaching How the Written Word Works, Peter Bowers. Kendore Publishing.

This reference manual takes teachers through how English spelling uses morphology to represent the meaning of words. It contains a series of ready to use lessons, and it targets reading, spelling, and vocabulary.

Unlocking Literacy: Effective Decoding and Spelling Instruction, 2nd Edition, Marcia K. Henry. Brookes Publishing.

A rich resource for teachers. This text presents a history of language and orthography. It explains a lot of the mystery of spelling, and explains how to teach spelling. Teachers will appreciate the attention to morphology and great lists of morphemes and associated words.

Beneath the Surface of Words: What English Spelling Reveals & Why It Matters, Sue Scibetta Hegland. Published by Learning About Spelling, Sioux Falls, SD.

A compelling explanation of English Spelling can help us reconstruct many spellings rather than memorizing them. This book explains the basic morphological framework that is present in everyword.

MORPHOLOGY, VOCABULARY, AND SPELLING PROGRAMS

Let's Know! Language and Reading Research Consortium (LARRC)
https://larrc.ehe.osu.edu/

As part of a study, the LARRC team developed a 25-week curriculum supplement for children in grades pre-kindergarten to third grade designed to improve children's language skills as a means to improving their reading comprehension: **Let's Know! Pre-Kindergarten to Grade 3**, English language, and Vamos a Aprender! (Pre-Kindergarten only, Bilingual Spanish-English). *These supplements are available to download for free.*

Nuffield Early Language Intervention (NELI), Snowling, Bowyer-Crane, Hulme.
www.Nuffieldfoundation.org
The Nuffield Early Language Intervention (NELI) is an evidence-based oral language intervention for children in nursery and reception who show weakness in their oral language skills and who are therefore at risk of experiencing difficulty with reading. It is delivered over 30 weeks by teaching assistants in groups of three to four children.

Talk 2 Learn, Dahlgren, Aufil, & Schenk. Tools 4 Reading. Tools4Reading.com.
Engaging and fun, Talk 2 Learn asks students to use sentence stems and starter questions to demonstrate their understanding of the theme while building background knowledge and vocabulary.

Improving Morphemic Awareness: Using Basewords and Affixes, Donah.
www.wvced.com
Series of morphological awareness lessons used for oral language drill each scripted lesson helps students practice manipulating morphemes in words based on a specific morpheme; this level focuses on compound words and basic morphemes.

Spellography, Moats and Rosow. Tools 4 Reading.
Grades 4 and up. This classroom-tested program teaches spelling concepts explicitly, systematically, cumulatively, and enjoyably! A perfect complement to your current reading and language arts program, Spellography was designed to help all students make sense of the English spelling system, and thus become better at understanding, reading, and writing words.

Neuhaus Academy Online Literacy Lessons for Adolescents & Adults. Neuhaus Education Center.
Three volumes support this training through Neuhaus. Excellent resource for developing morphological lessons.

PS- Prefixes, Suffixes, Roots: Resource of Lists, Phrases, Sentences, Poems and Stories, by Hickey Gold, et.al. Jeld Ed Materials.
This resource provides an experience with morphology through lessons that engage students and teachers. They provide lots of context in which students engage with morphemes in meaningful ways.

Vocabulary Surge – Books A (grades 2-3) and B (grades 3-6), Susan Hall - 95% Group
This program provides a series of 15-minute explicit daily lessons to show students how to break words into parts, hypothesize the meanings of unknown parts, and check meaning in context.

ASSESSMENTS

OxEd and Assessment – A Language Screener https://oxedandassessment.com/
Accurately identify preschool and kindergarten children who would benefit from additional support using this fast, fun and intuitive app for teachers and TAs.

RESOURCES WITH WORD LISTS

Online:
A dictionary of affix meanings – Affixes.org

An online resource of word origins – Etymonline.com

An online resource that will clarify how to divide your words into syllables – HowManySyllables.com

The Reading Teacher's Book of Lists, J. Kress & E. Fry. Wiley Publishers.

The Vocabulary Teacher's Book of Lists, E. Fry. Wiley Publishers.

Unlocking Literacy: Effective Decoding and Spelling Instruction, 2nd Edition, Marcia K. Henry. Brookes Publishing.

APPENDIX A - ASSESSMENTS

MORPHEMES FOR LITTLE ONES ASSESSMENTS - ADMINISTRATION GUIDELINES

The criterion assessments included in this book are informal. Their purpose is to help teachers gain a basic understanding of their students' morphological knowledge. Teachers use their best judgement when scoring students' answers.

LEVEL ONE ADMINISTRATION DIRECTIONS

ASSESSMENT	RECOMMENDED GRADE	SCORING
Level 1 Assessment	(Kindergarten) Grade 1 Administer One-on-One.	Stop assessment when 3 consecutive errors occur. Each question is worth 1 point if correct, and 0 points if incorrect. The assessment is worth 16 points.

Materials:

- Level 1 Scoring Sheet

- If the student is decoding, use a whiteboard or paper upon which the stimulus words **backpack**, **wanted**, and **playing** are written. If students are not yet decoding, these words will be presented orally to assess awareness.

Questions:

- Give the following Assessment Example to prepare students for the assessment items 1-10.

- Say the base word, "Book. Listen carefully and say a word like book when I pause." Say the sentence, "I have one *book*. My friend has two _____." Pause for student to say the word BOOKS.

- If student does not reply, ask, "How can you change ***book*** to finish the sentence?"

- If there is still no response, say, "Listen to how I would change ***book*** to finish the sentence: I have one **book**. My friend has two **books**." I changed **book** to **books** because my friend has two **books**."

- Your turn, let's try some more. Start with question 1.

- If student does not provide a correct answer, move on to the next question.

- Stop administering the assessment if student misses 3 consecutive questions.

LEVEL TWO ADMINISTRATION DIRECTIONS

ASSESSMENT	RECOMMENDED GRADE	SCORING
Level 2 Assessment	Grade 2 Administer one-on-one for questions 1-15. Spelling Words can be administered to a group or one-on-one.	Stop administering Part 1 of the assessment if students miss 3 consecutive questions. Move to **Reading Words** and **Spelling Words**. If students miss the first 3 questions, give the Level 1 Assessment. The assessment is worth 34 points.

Materials:

- Level 2 Scoring Sheet

- Whiteboard or paper upon which the stimulus suffixes are written: -es, -ed, -er

- List of word items 8-15 printed for students to read and identify the morphemes. See Master Copy - **Level 2 Reading Words Identifying Morphemes - Student Page**

- Paper and pencil for spelling the words in part 16

- Follow the directions on the assessment sheet for the first two questions. Use your best judgement to determine if students understand the concepts of prefix and suffix and if they understand the basic suffixes -es, -ed, -er.

Give the following Assessment Example to prepare students for the assessment items 3-7.

- Say the base word, "Book. Listen carefully and say a word like book when I pause." Say the sentence, "I have one *book*. My friend has two _____." Pause for student to say the word BOOKS.

- If student does not reply, ask, "How can you change *book* to finish the sentence?"

- If there is still no response, say, "Listen to how I would change *book* to finish the sentence: I have one **book**. My friend has two **books**." I changed **book** to **books** because my friend has two **books**."

- Your turn, let's try some more. Start with question 1.

- If student does not provide a correct answer, move on to the next question.

Follow scoring recommendations in the chart above for remaining assessment items.

LEVEL THREE ADMINISTRATION DIRECTIONS

ASSESSMENT	RECOMMENDED GRADE	SCORING
Level 3 Assessment	Grade 3 Administer one-on-one or as a group assessment with students providing written responses. The **Reading Words** section will need to be administered individually.	If students are unable to answer any of the first 5 questions correctly, move to the **Reading Words** and **Spelling Words** portions of the assessment. Teachers may also discontinue Level 3 assessment and choose to administer Level 2. Level 3 Assessment is worth 53 points.

Materials:

- Level 3 Scoring sheet

- Whiteboard or paper upon which the stimulus suffixes are written: -es, -ed, -er.

- List of word items 14-21 printed for students to read and identify the morphemes. See Master Copy - **Level 3 Reading Words Identifying Morphemes - Student Page**

- Paper and pencil for spelling the words in part 16.

- Follow the directions on the assessment sheet for the first two questions. Use your best judgement to determine if students understand the concepts of prefix and suffix and if they understand the basic suffixes -es, -ed, -er.

Give the following Assessment Example to prepare students for the assessment items 3-7.

- Say the base word, "Book. Listen carefully and say a word like book when I pause." Say the sentence, "I have one *book*. My friend has two _____." Pause for student to say the word BOOKS.

- If student does not reply, ask, "How can you change ***book*** to finish the sentence?"

- If there is still no response, say, "Listen to how I would change ***book*** to finish the sentence: I have one **book**. My friend has two **books**." I changed **book** to **books** because my friend has two **books**."

- Your turn, let's try some more. Start with question 1.

- If student does not provide a correct answer, move on to the next question.

Follow scoring recommendations in the chart above for remaining assessment items.

LEVEL 1 MORPHEMES FOR LITTLE ONES CRITERION ASSESSMENT

Directions: This sheet can be used to score individuals or use Class Scoring Sheet to record scores.

Name: _____ Date: _____

TARGET MORPHEME	BASE WORD	QUESTION WITH ANSWER Give Assessment Example found in Administration Guidelines to prepare students for the first 10 questions.	CIRCLE SCORE 16 total
1.Plurals /s/	park	Our town has one **park**. Some towns have many **PARKS.**	0 1
2.Plurals /z/	bird	The **bird** does not like to **fly** alone. She wishes she knew other **BIRDS**.	0 1
3.Plurals /ez/	wish	I made one **wish** now. When it is my birthday, I will make seven **WISHES**.	0 1
4.Past tense -ed / ed	want	Today my brother **wants** a new bike. Yesterday , a scooter is what he **WANTED.**	0 1
5.Past tense ed /d/	fan	On a hot day I **fan** myself. Yesterday was hot so I **FANNED** (myself).	0 1
6.Past tense ed /t/	clap	I feel happy when my friends **clap** for me. Last week when I was in the play, they **CLAPPED**!	0 1
7.Comparative -er	small	I am pretty **small** next to my dad. My little brother is even **SMALLER** (than him)	0 1
8.Superlatives -est	strong	A cat is **strong**. A dog is **stronger**. A lion is the **STRONGEST**.	0 1
9.Present tense verb /z/	sing	I **sing**. My brother can **sing**. My parents like to **sing**. My whole family **SINGS**.	0 1
10.Present tense verb -ing	climb	The hikers **climb** all day. What do the hikers do all day? They are **CLIMBING**.	0 1
MORPHEME KNOWLEDGE ORAL AND WRITTEN *When reading: 1-point for chunking morpheme word parts; 0 points for sound-by-sound decoding.*			
11.**Write backpack**. Ask student to read it. 0 points for nonreader			0 1
All students. Say backpack. Ask: What two words make up this word? (**BACK** & **PACK**) 1 point for correct answer			0 1
12.**Write wanted**. Ask student to read it. 0 points for nonreader			0 1
All students. Say wanted. Ask: What is the main part of this word? (**WANT**) 1 point for correct answer			0 1
13.**Write playing**. Ask student to read it. 0 points for nonreader			0 1
All students. Say playing. Ask: What is the main part of this word? (**PLAY**) 1 point for correct answer			0 1
		TOTAL SCORE	

LEVEL 2 MORPHEMES FOR LITTLE ONES CRITERION ASSESSMENT

Directions: This sheet can be used to score individuals or use Class Scoring Sheet to record scores.

Name: _____ Date: _____

TARGET MORPHEME	BASE WORD	QUESTIONS: Give Assessment Example found in Administration Guidelines to prepare students for the first 10 questions.	CIRCLE SCORE 34 possible
1.Define prefix and suffix		What is a prefix? **(A prefix is a part of a word that comes at the beginning.)** 1 point What is a suffix? **(A suffix is a part of a word that comes at the end.)** 1 point	0 2
2.Suffixes -es, -ed, -er	Write -es, -ed, -er for student to see	Point to each suffix. **Ask: What does this mean on the end of a word? -es** (plural or present tense verb) **-ed** (past tense verb) **-er** (comparative or one who or that which) 1 point/question	0 3
3.Suffix -ly	quiet	I was very **quiet** when I hummed the song. How did I hum? **QUIETLY**.	0 1
4.Suffix -less	sleeve	There were no **sleeves** on his shirt. His shirt was **SLEEVELESS.**	0 1
5.Suffix -ness	sad	The class was **sad** that the game was cancelled. The class was filled with **SADNESS.**	0 1
6.Suffix -ful	rest	I had a lot of **rest** last weekend. My weekend was **RESTFUL.**	0 1
7.Suffix -ment	excite-excited	The kids were **excited** to go on a field trip. They were filled with **EXCITEMENT**!	0 1

READING WORDS
1-point for chunking; 0 points for sound-by-sound decoding.

Display and ask students to read the following words. Do students read the affixes and bases as units or do they attempt to decode the words sound-by-sound?				
8. unsafe	9. pretend	10. nonstick	11. subdivide	0- 8 # correct
12. reflect	13. inside	14. mismatch	15. nation	

Ask students to circle the bases and underline the affixes in the words they just read. (0 – incorrect answer, 1 – correct answer) un-safe, re-flect, pre-tend, in-side, non-stick, mis-match, sub-divide, nat-ion	0 -8 # correct

16. Spelling Words - Check for understanding of the Double It – Drop It – Change It spelling rules.			
wishes	hotter (Double It)	plugged (Double It)	driving (Drop It)	0-8 # correct
jumped	copies (Change It)	coming (Drop It)	greeted	

TOTAL SCORE

LEVEL 3 MORPHEMES FOR LITTLE ONES CRITERION ASSESSMENT

Directions: This sheet can be used to score individuals or use Class Scoring Sheet to record scores.

Name: _____ Date: _____

TARGET MORPHEME	KEY WORD	QUESTIONS: Give Assessment Example found in Administration Guidelines to prepare students for questions 3-13.	CIRCLE SCORE 53 possible
1.Define prefix, suffix, base		What is a prefix? **(A prefix is a part of a word that comes at the beginning.)** 1 point What is a suffix? **(A suffix is a part of a word that comes at the end.)** 1 point What is a base or root? **(the main part of a word that has suffixes or prefixed added to it.)**	0 3
2.Suffixes -es, -ed, -er	Write -es, -ed, -er for student to see	Point to each suffix. **Ask: What does this mean on the end of a word? -es (plural or present tense verb) -ed (past tense verb) -er (comparative or one who or that which)** 1 point/question	0 3
3.Suffix -ly	quiet quietly	I was very **quiet** when I hummed the song. How did I hum? **QUIETLY**.	0 1
4.Suffix -less	sleeve sleeveless	There were no **sleeves** on his shirt. His shirt was **SLEEVELESS.**	0 1
5.Suffix -ness	sad sadness	The class was **sad** that the game was cancelled. The class was filled with **SADNESS.**	0 1
6.Suffix -ful	rest restful	I had a lot of **rest** last weekend. My weekend was **RESTFUL.**	0 1
7.Suffix -ment	excite-excited excitement	The kids were **excited** to go on a field trip. They were filled with **EXCITEMENT**!	0 1
8.Suffix -al	person personal	A desk belongs to a **person.** The desk is her **PERSONAL** area.	0 1
9.Suffix -y	cloud cloudy	There were many **clouds** in the sky. The sky was **CLOUDY.**	0 1
10.Suffix -ic	history historic	When an event is important it becomes **history.** The event is **HISTORIC.**	0 1
11.Prefix de-	frost defrost	What is it called when you remove the **frost** from a car window? **DEFROST**	0 1
12.Suffix -ous	danger dangerous	The sign by the cliff said **'danger'.** The boys knew that the cliff was **DANGEROUS.**	0 1

TARGET MORPHEME	KEY WORD	LEVEL 3 ASSESSMENT · CONTINUED Give Assessment Example found in Administration Guidelines to prepare students for questions 3-13.	CIRCLE SCORE 53 possible
13.Prefix dis-	pose dispose	The city will pose a new recycling option. People will **DISPOSE** their cardboard and plastics n blue bins.	0 1
Reading Words - Read the words in columns. If student attempts to decode words sound by sound, their word recognition is not yet consolidated. Discontinue the assessment. Begin morphological awareness training with Level 1 or 2 and continue phonics instruction.			
14. act actor inactive reaction	15. tend extend distend retention	16. form 17. claim deform proclaim conformed reclaiming information disclaimer	0 16 # correct:
Ask students to circle the bases and underline the affixes in the words they just read. Do not score first base in each group. 0 – incorrect answer, 1 – correct answer = 12			
18. act act-<u>or</u> in-act-<u>ive</u> <u>re</u>-act-<u>ion</u>	19. tend <u>ex</u>-tend <u>dis</u>-tend <u>re</u>-tent-<u>ion</u>	20. form 21. claim <u>de</u>-form <u>pro</u>-claim <u>con</u>-form-<u>ed</u> <u>re</u>-claim-<u>ing</u> <u>in</u>-format-<u>ion</u> <u>dis</u>-claim-<u>er</u>	12
22. Spelling Words - Check for understanding of the Double It – Drop It – Change It spelling rules.			
flashes crashed	hotter (Double It) copies (Change It)	unplugged (Double It) driving (Drop It) ashamed (Drop It) floated	0-8 # correct
		TOTAL SCORE	

NOTES FOR INSTRUCTION:

LEVEL 1 - INFORMAL ASSESSMENT OF BASIC MORPHOLOGICAL KNOWLEDGE CLASS SCORING SHEET

Student																
1. Plural /s/ (1)																
2. Plural /z/ (1)																
3. Plural /ez/ (1)																
4. Past tense /ed/ (1)																
5. Past tense /d/ (1)																
6. Past tense /t/ (1)																
7. Comparative -er (1)																
8. Superlative -est (1)																
9. Present tense /z/ (1)																
10. Present tense -ing (1)																
11. Compound backpack (2)																
12. Past tense wanted (2)																
13. Present tense playing (2)																
SCORE Correct #/16																

NOTES:

LEVEL 2 – INFORMAL ASSESSMENT OF BASIC MORPHOLOGICAL KNOWLEDGE CLASS SCORING SHEET

Student															
1. Prefix Suffix (2)															
2. -es, -ed, -er (3)															
3. Suffix -ly (1)															
4. Suffix -less (1)															
5. Suffix -ness (1)															
6. Suffix -ful (1)															
7. Suffix -ment (1)															
8. unsafe (2)															
9. pretend (2)															
10. non-stick (2)															
11. sub-divide (2)															
12. re-flect (2)															
13. inside (2)															
14. mis-match (2)															
15. nation (2)															
16. Spelling note errors(8)															
SCORE Correct #/34															

NOTES:

unsafe
pretend
nonstick
subdivide
reflect
inside
mismatch
nation

Student																	
1. Prefix Suffix Base (3)																	
2. -es, -ed, -er (3)																	
3. Suffix -ly (1)																	
4. Suffix -less (1)																	
5. Suffix -ness (1)																	
6. Suffix -ful (1)																	
7. Suffix -ment (1)																	
8. Suffix -al (1)																	
9. Suffix –y (1)																	
10. Suffix –ic (1)																	
11. Suffix de- (1)																	
12. Suffix –ous (1)																	
13. Prefix dis- (1)																	
14. act family (4)																	
15. tend family (4)																	
16. form family (4)																	
17. claim family (4)																	
18. Identify morphemes act (3)																	
19. Identify morphemes tend (3)																	
20. Identify morphemes form (3)																	
21. Identify morphemes claim (3)																	
22. Spelling note errors (8)																	
SCORE Correct #/53																	

NOTES:

act
actor
inactive
reaction

tend
extend
distend
retention

form
deform
conformed
information

claim
proclaim
reclaiming
disclaimer

APPENDIX B -
MORPHEME GRABBER BLACKLINE MASTERS

name:

© Kindergarten Morpheme Grabber

WORD + NEW MORPHEME	= NEW WORD	PICTURE OR SENTENCE

WORD + NEW MORPHEME	= NEW WORD	PICTURE OR SENTENCE

name: _____

WORD + NEW MORPHEME	= NEW WORD	PICTURE OR SENTENCE

_____

_____

_____

_____

_____

_____

_____

_____

_____

_____

_____

MORPHEME COMBO	= NEW WORD	MEANING

_____

_____

_____

_____

_____

_____

_____

_____

_____

_____

Here is an assortment of Morpheme Grabber Headings. If students use their own notebooks, choose which heading will work best for your students. Students copy and paste the heading you choose at the top of each new morpheme page.

Use these headings with Level 1

WORD + NEW MORPHEME	= NEW WORD	PICTURE OR SENTENCE

WORD + NEW MORPHEME	= NEW WORD	PICTURE OR SENTENCE

Use these headings with Levels 2 and 3.

MORPHEME COMBO	= NEW WORD	MEANING

MORPHEME COMBO	= NEW WORD	MEANING

Name: _____

Date: _____

<table>
<tr><td></td><td></td><td></td><td></td><td></td><td></td><td></td><td></td></tr>
<tr><td></td><td></td><td></td><td></td><td></td><td></td><td></td><td></td></tr>
<tr><td></td><td></td><td></td><td></td><td></td><td></td><td></td><td></td></tr>
<tr><td></td><td></td><td></td><td></td><td></td><td></td><td></td><td></td></tr>
<tr><td></td><td></td><td></td><td></td><td></td><td></td><td></td><td></td></tr>
<tr><td></td><td></td><td></td><td></td><td></td><td></td><td></td><td></td></tr>
</table>

Name: _____ Date: _____

Syllable Spelling
